CHAPTER 14

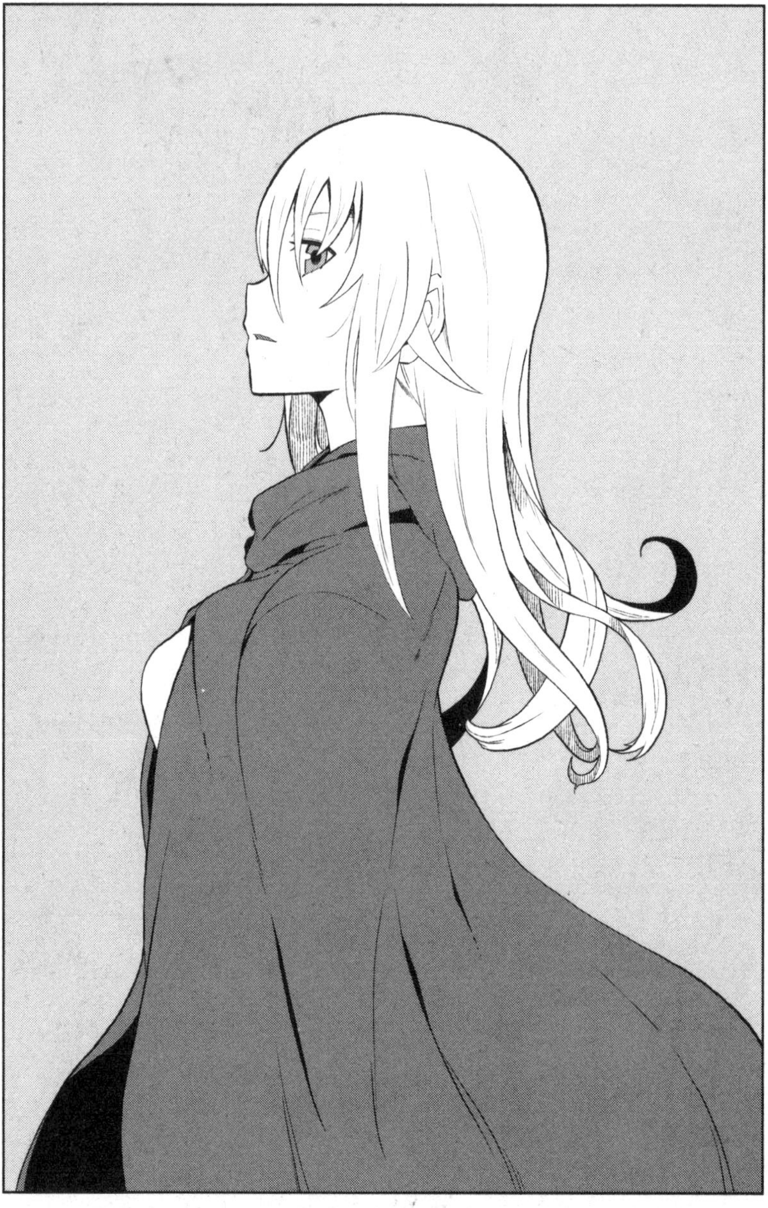

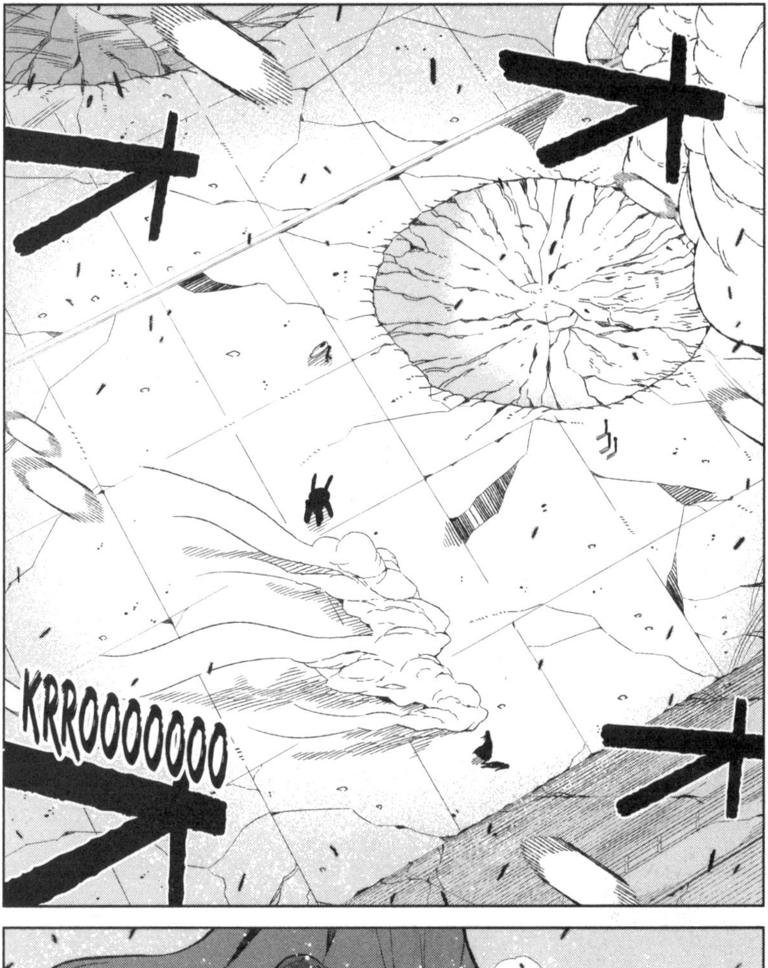
KRROOOOOOO
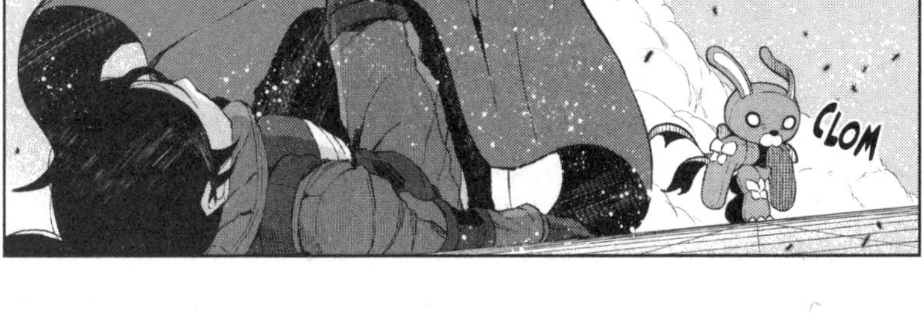
CLOM

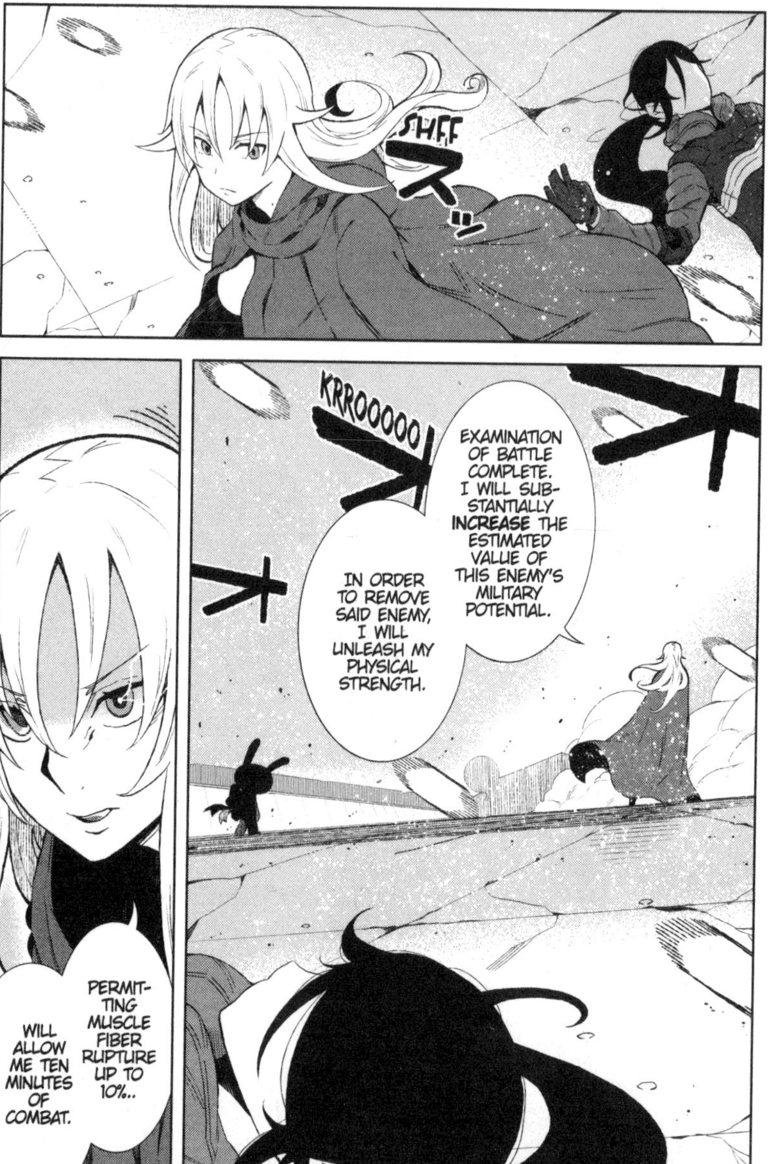
SHFF
KRROOOOOO
EXAMINATION OF BATTLE COMPLETE. I WILL SUB-STANTIALLY **INCREASE** THE ESTIMATED VALUE OF THIS ENEMY'S MILITARY POTENTIAL.
IN ORDER TO REMOVE SAID ENEMY, I WILL UNLEASH MY PHYSICAL STRENGTH.
PERMIT-TING MUSCLE FIBER RUPTURE UP TO 10%..
WILL ALLOW ME TEN MINUTES OF COMBAT.

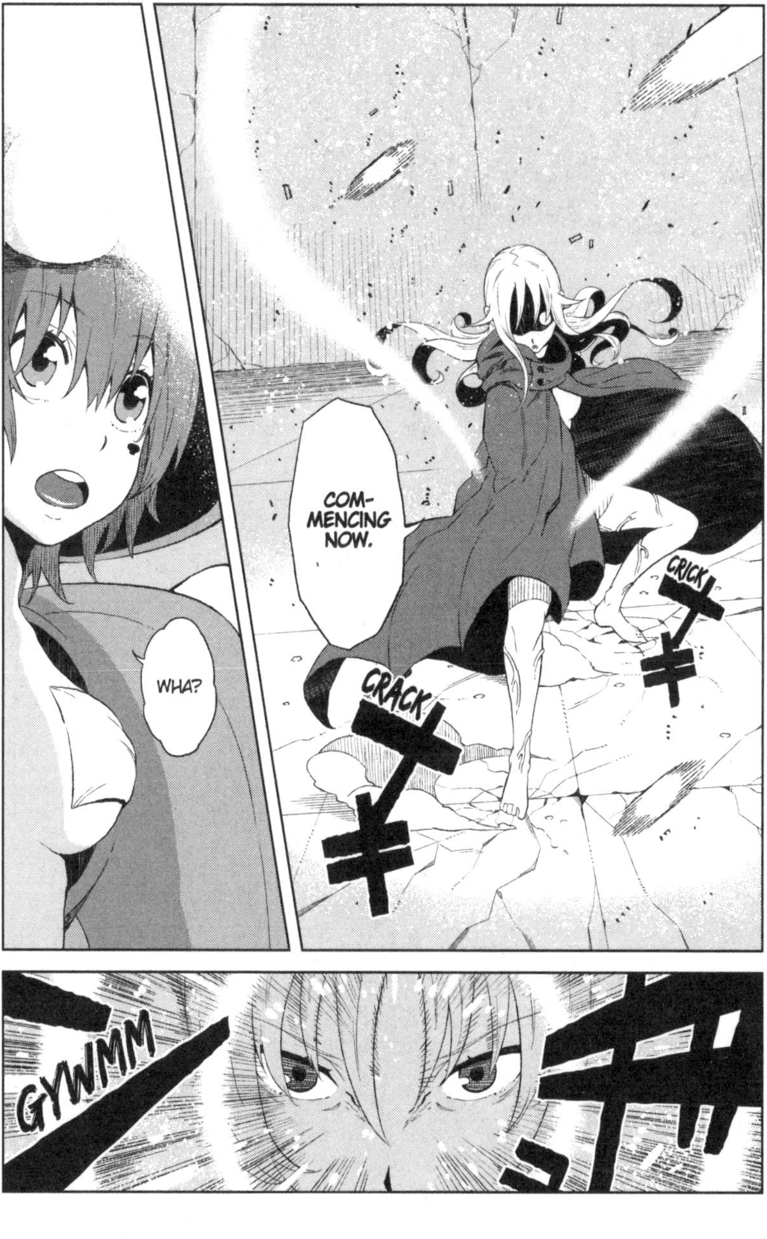
COM-MENCING NOW.
CRICK
CRACK
WHA?
ギュ
GYWMM

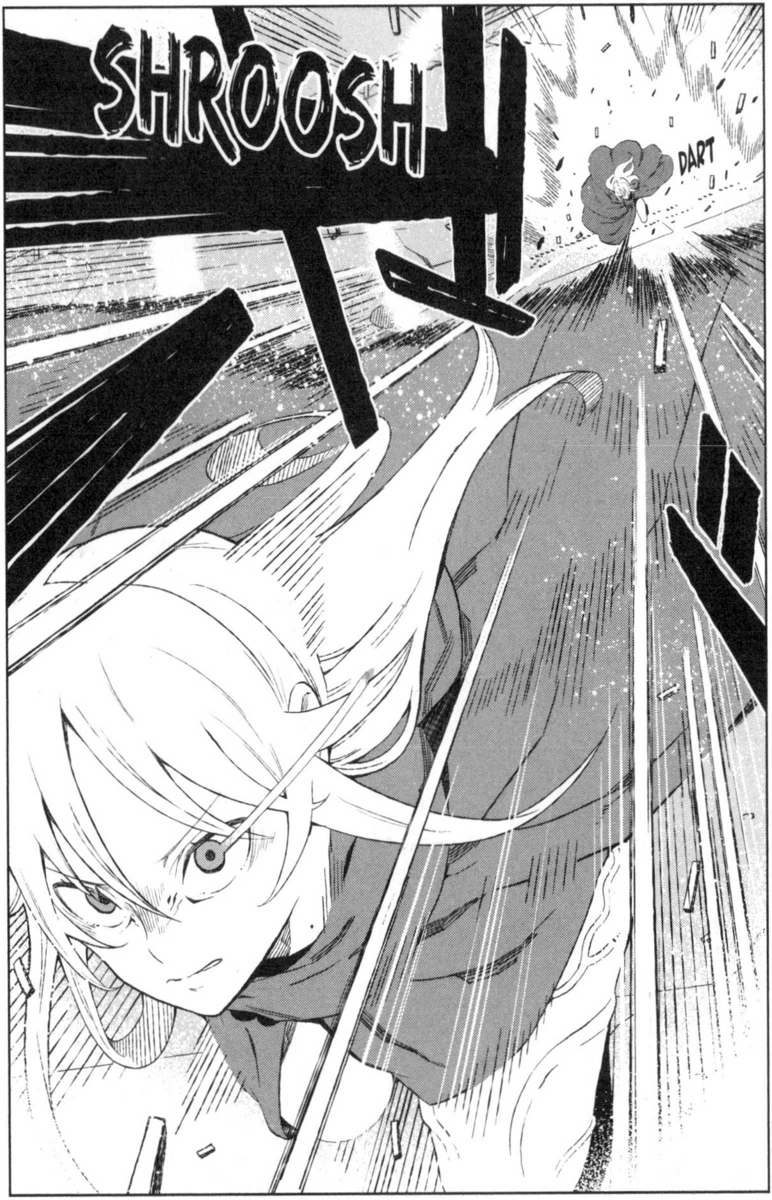
SHROOSH
DART

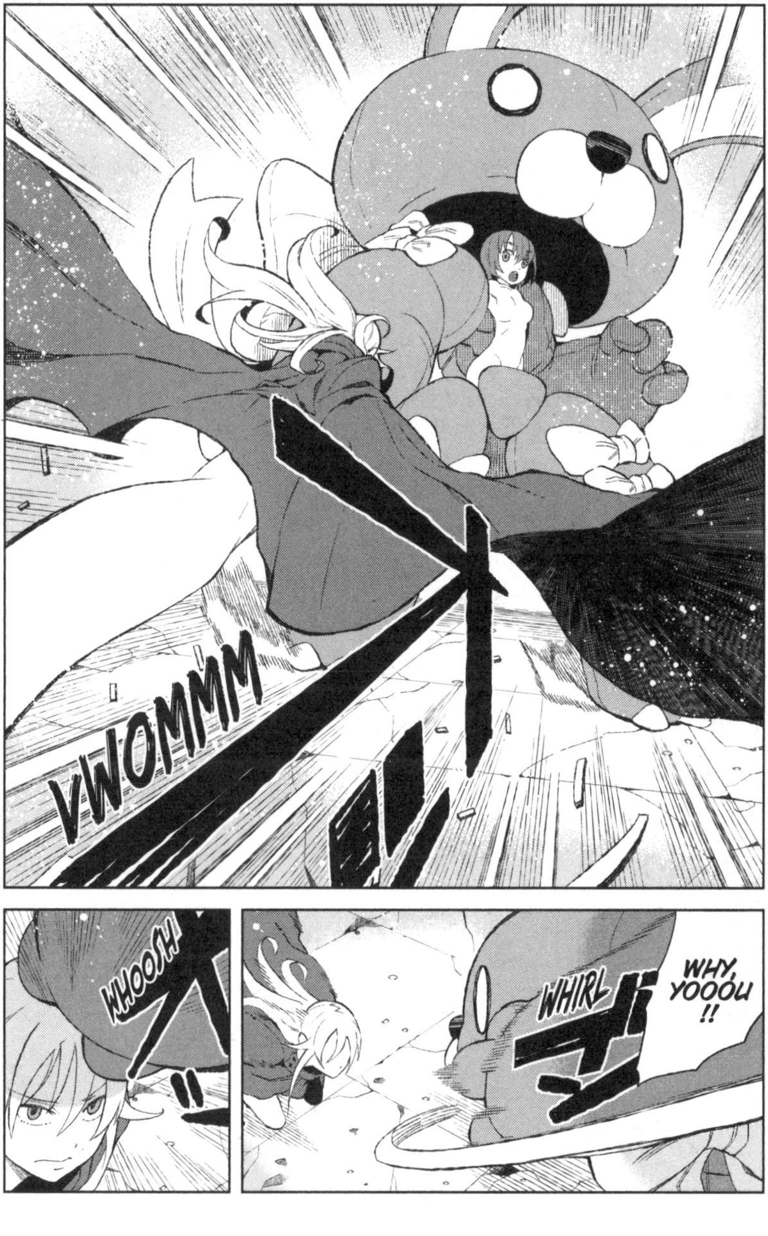
VWOMMM
WHY, YOOOU !!
WHIRL
WHOOSH

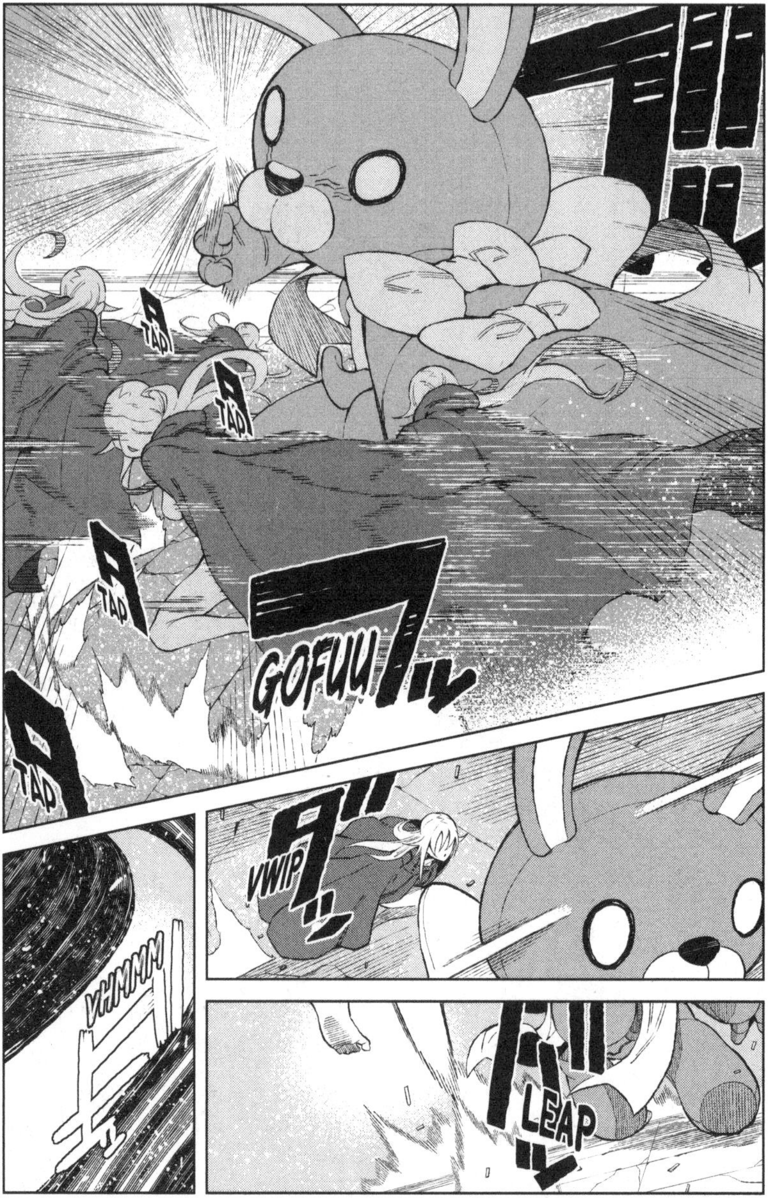
TAP!
TAP!
GOFUU
TAP
TAP
VWIP
LEAP
VHMMM

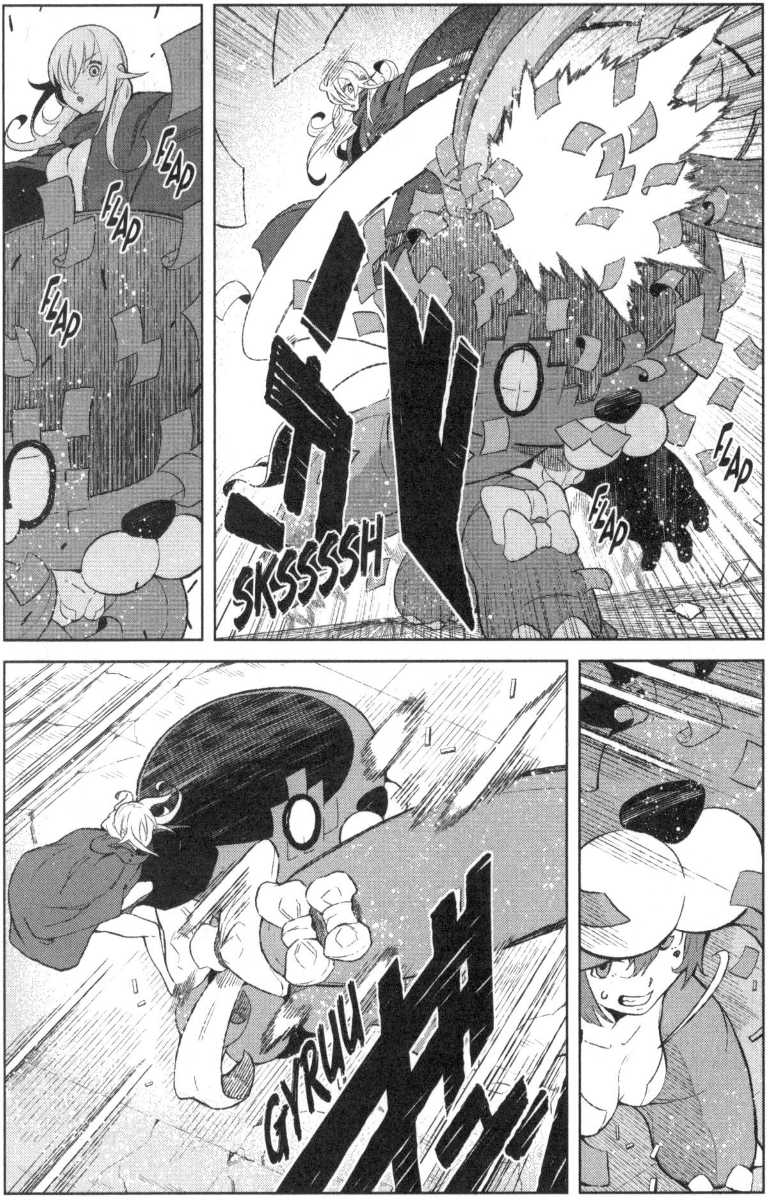
FLAP
FLAP
SKSSSSSH
FLAP
FLAP
FLAP
GYRUU

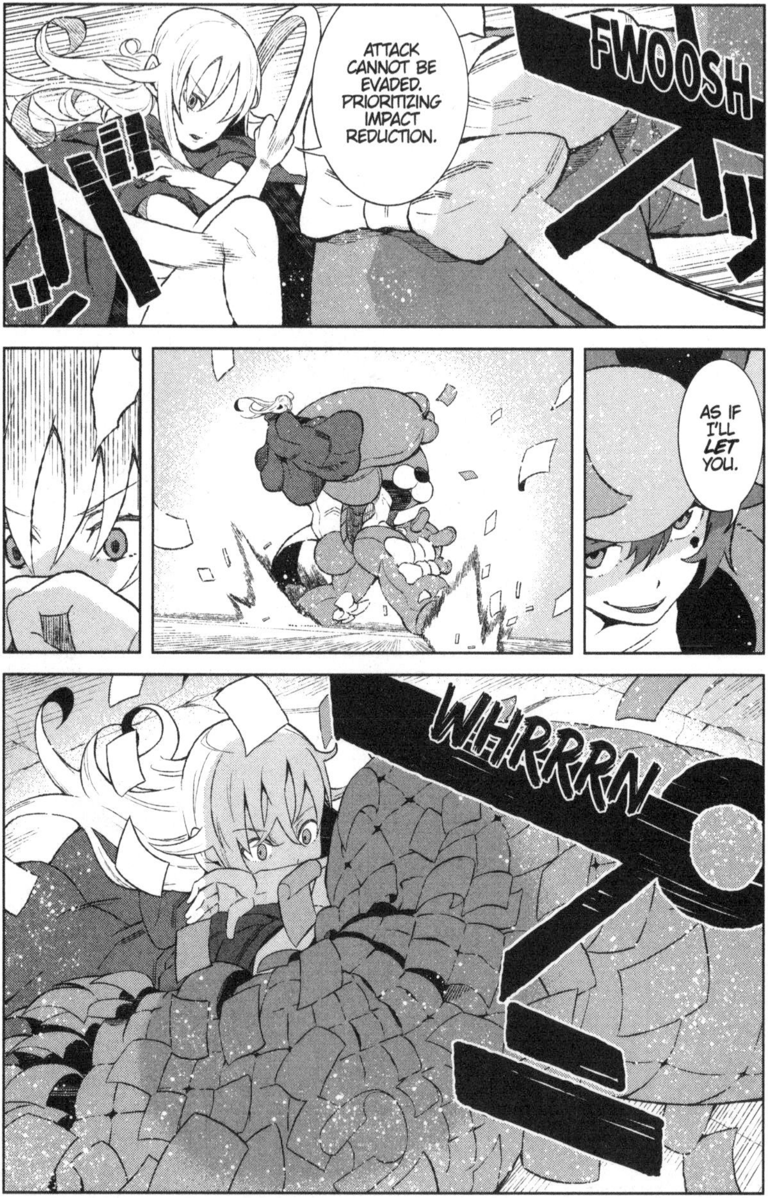
FWOOSH
ATTACK CANNOT BE EVADED. PRIORITIZING IMPACT REDUCTION.
AS IF I'LL LET YOU.
WHRRRN

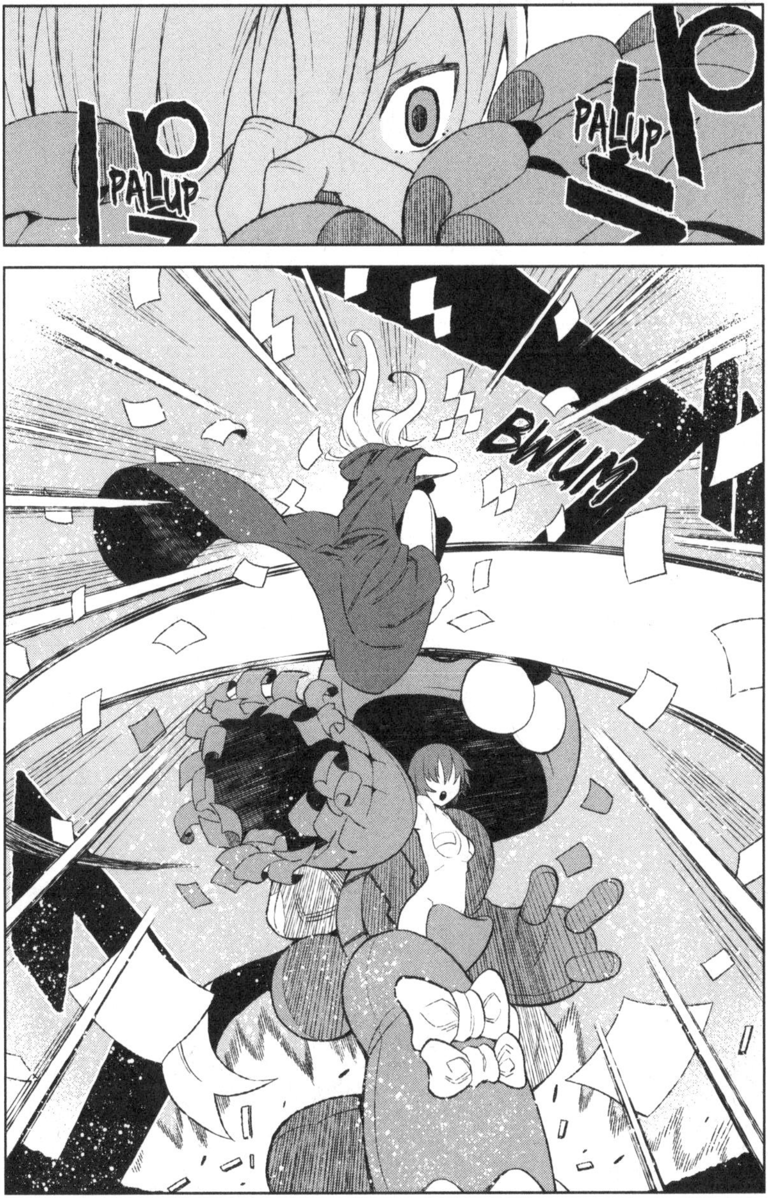
PALUP
PALUP
BWUM

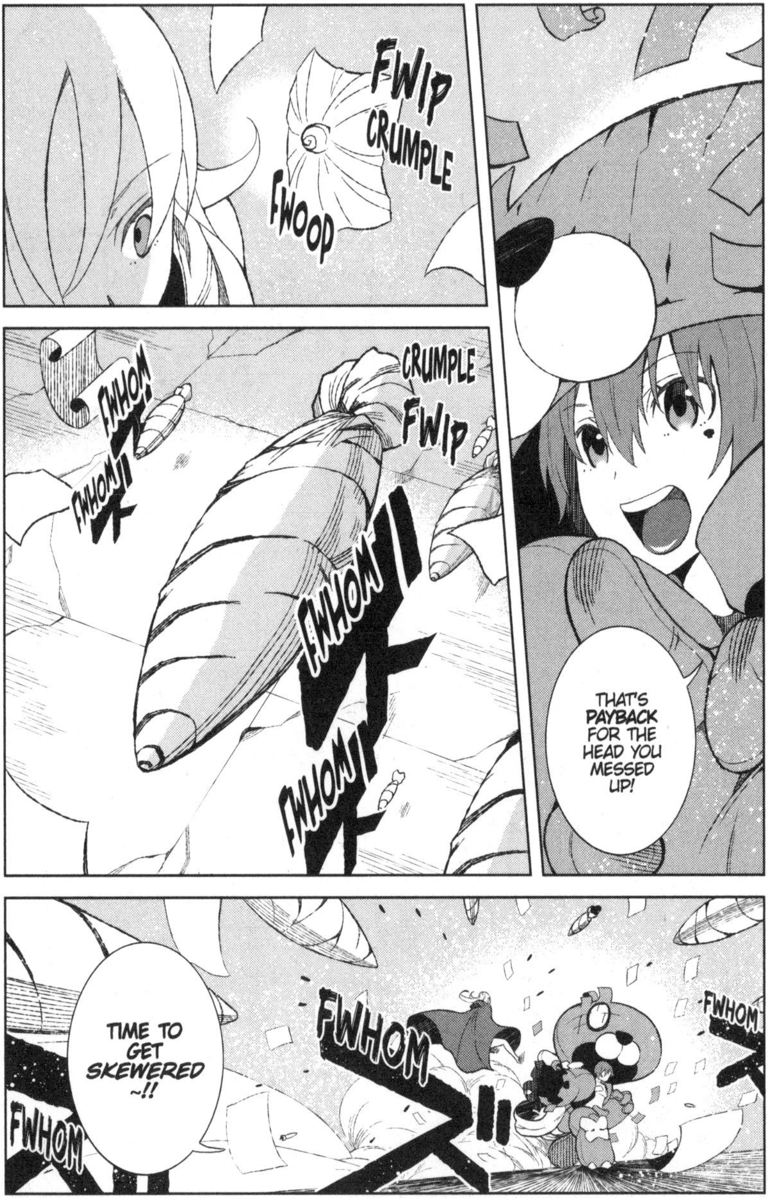
THAT'S PAYBACK FOR THE HEAD YOU MESSED UP!
FWIP
CRUMPLE
FWOOP
CRUMPLE
FWIP
FWHOM
FWHOM!!
FWHOM!
FWHOM!!
FWHOM
FWHOM!!
TIME TO GET SKEWERED ~!!
FWHOM

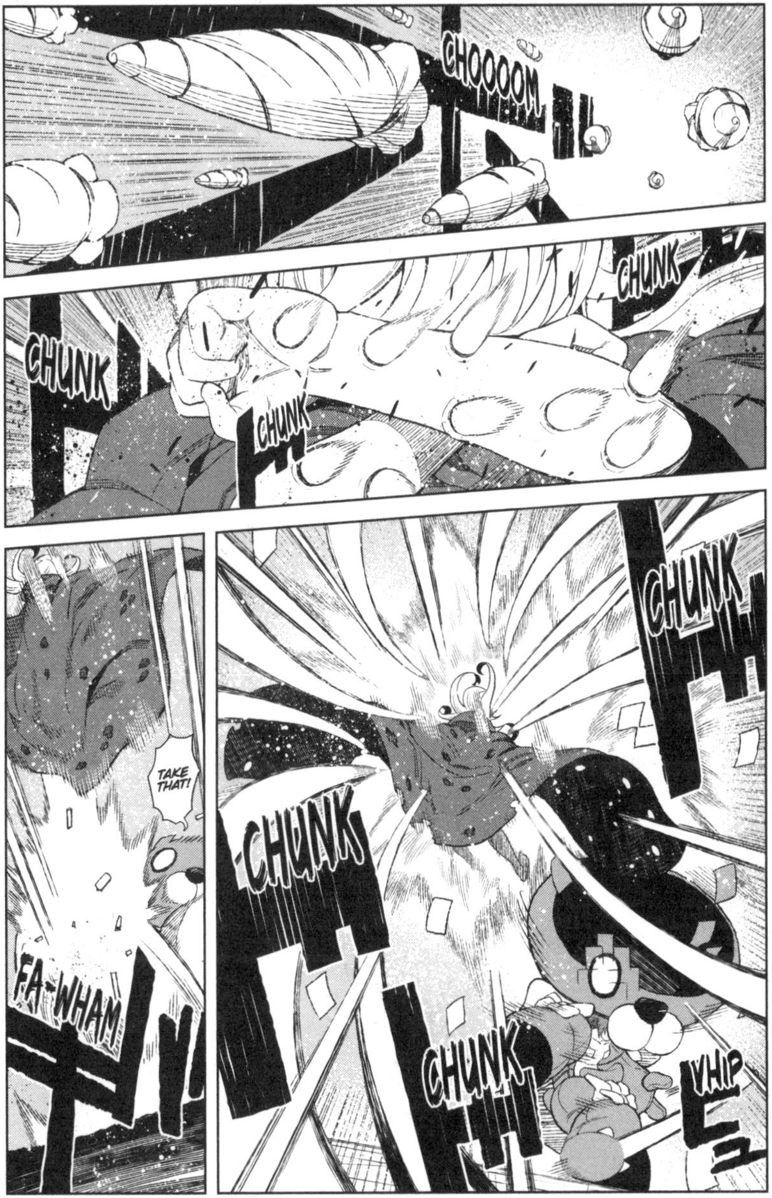
CHOOOOM
CHUNK
CHUNK
CHUNK
CHUNK
CHUNK
VHIP
CHUNK
TAKE THAT!
FA-WHAM

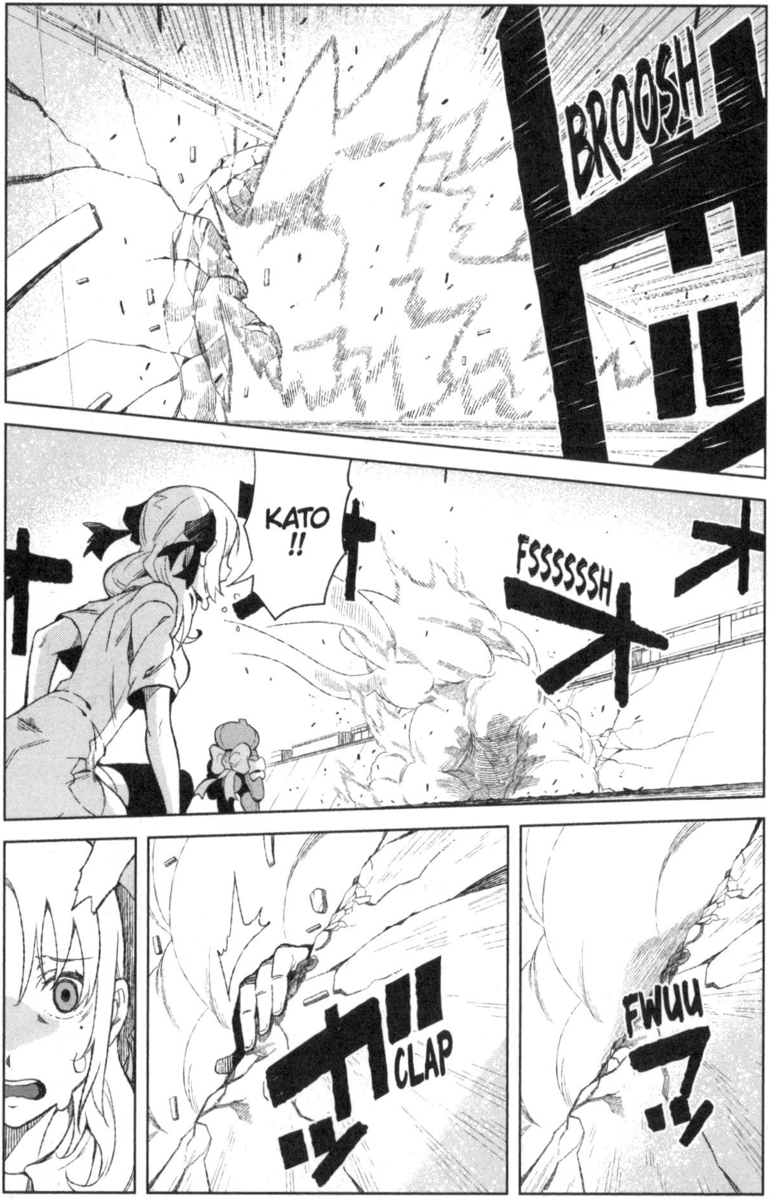
BROOSH
FSSSSSSH
KATO !!
FWUU
CLAP

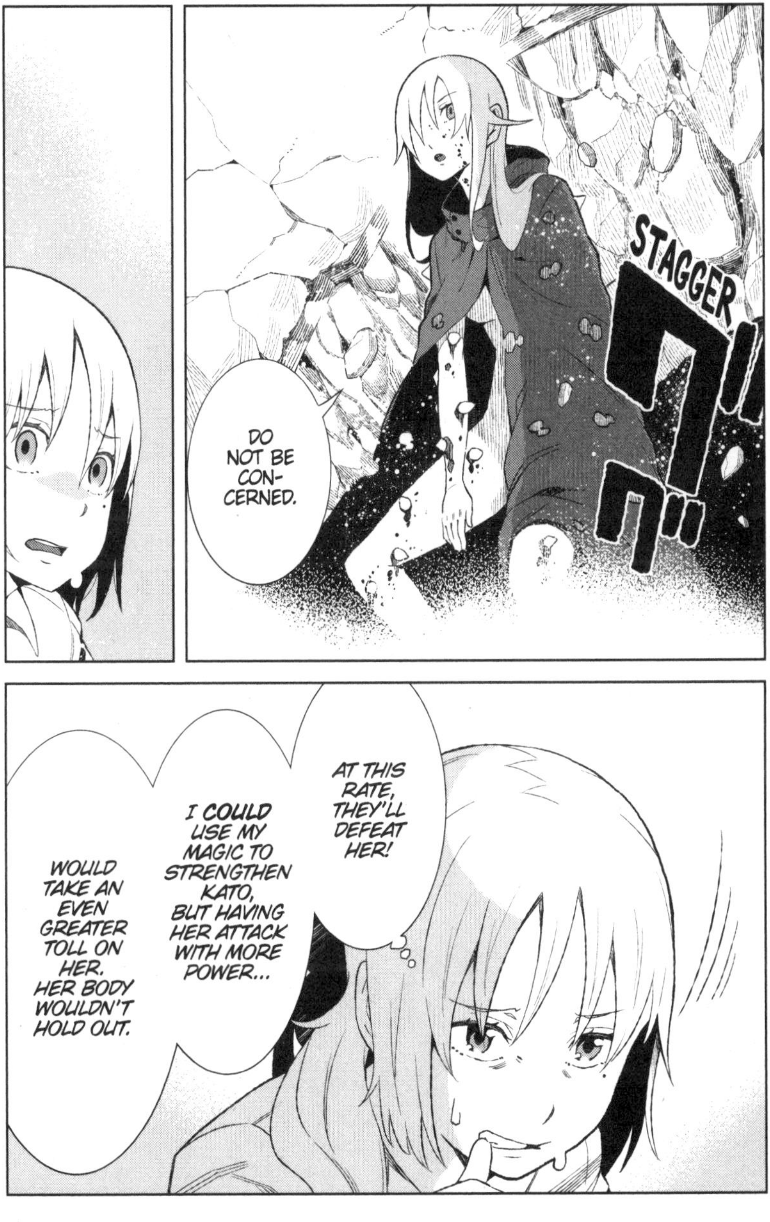
STAGGER
DO NOT BE CONCERNED.
AT THIS RATE, THEY'LL DEFEAT HER!
I **COULD** USE MY MAGIC TO STRENGTHEN KATO, BUT HAVING HER ATTACK WITH MORE POWER...
WOULD TAKE AN EVEN GREATER TOLL ON HER. HER BODY WOULDN'T HOLD OUT.

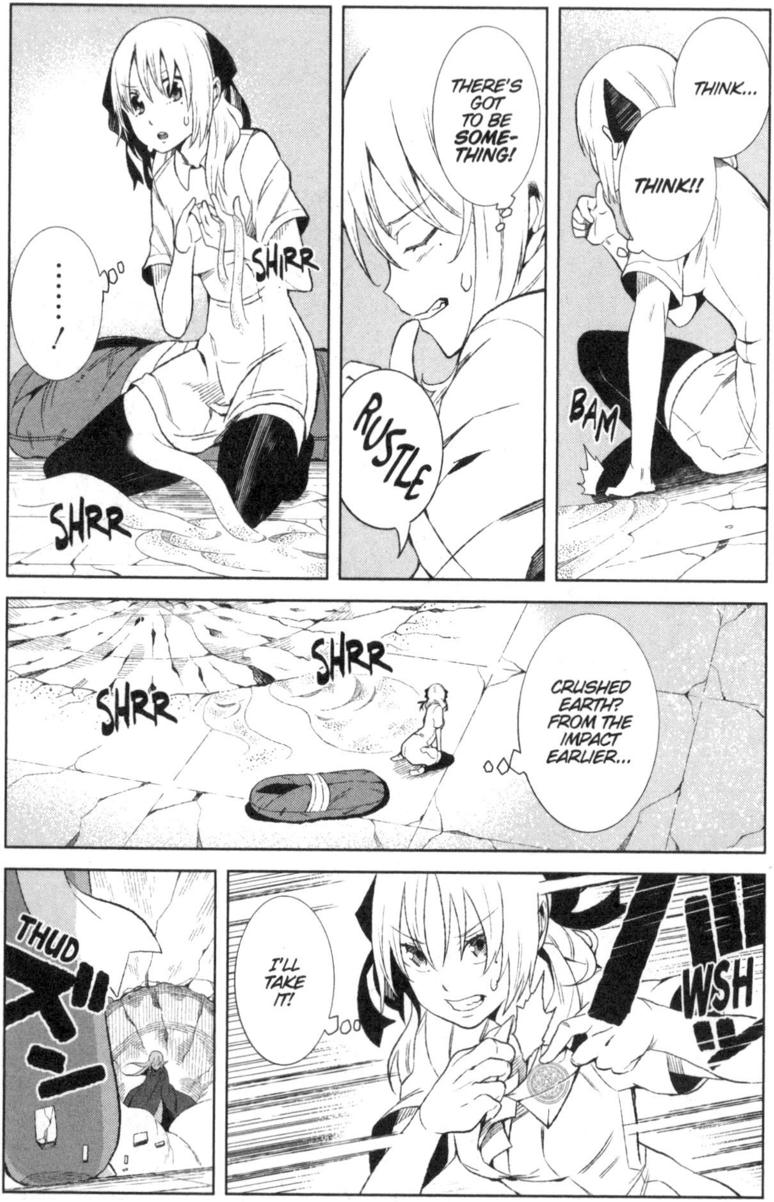
THINK...
THINK!!
BAM
THERE'S GOT TO BE SOME-THING!
RUSTLE
SHIRR
......!
SHRR
CRUSHED EARTH? FROM THE IMPACT EARLIER...
SHRR
SHRR
WSH!!
I'LL TAKE IT!
THUD

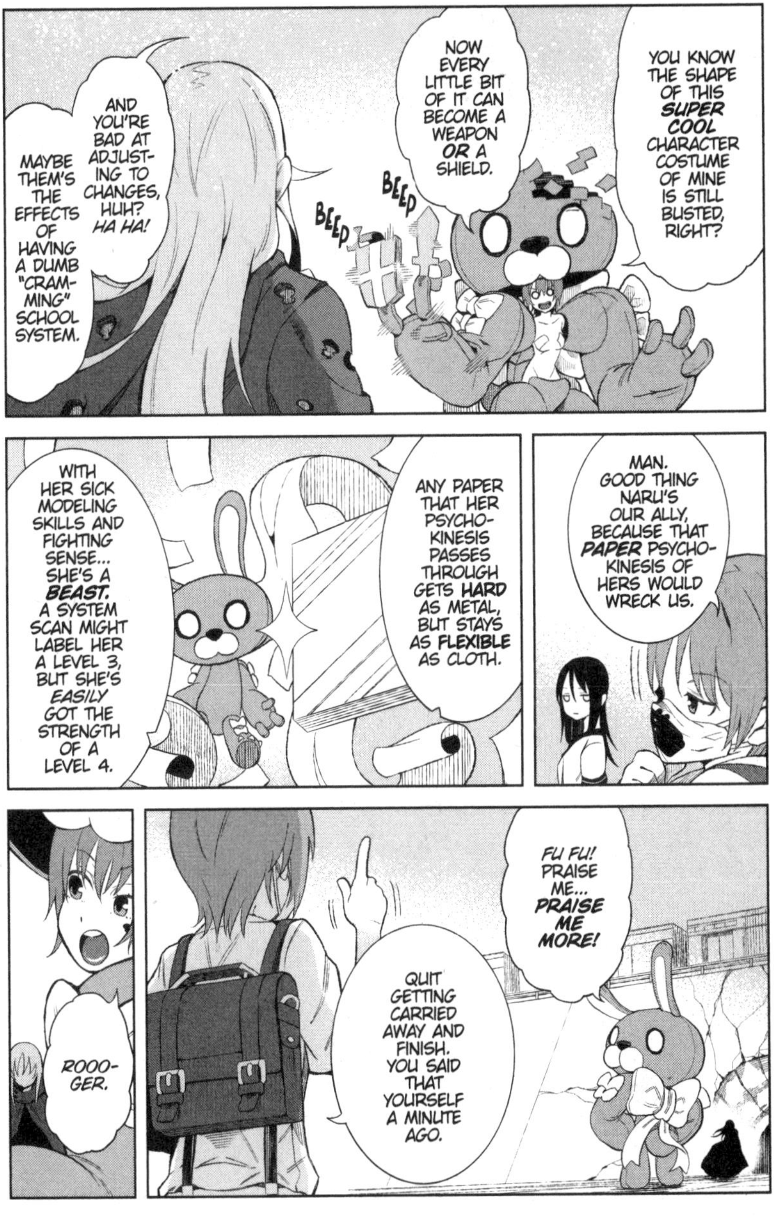
YOU KNOW THE SHAPE OF THIS SUPER COOL CHARACTER COSTUME OF MINE IS STILL BUSTED, RIGHT?
NOW EVERY LITTLE BIT OF IT CAN BECOME A WEAPON OR A SHIELD.
BEEP
BEEP
AND YOU'RE BAD AT ADJUSTING TO CHANGES, HUH? HA HA!
MAYBE THEM'S THE EFFECTS OF HAVING A DUMB "CRAMMING" SCHOOL SYSTEM.
MAN. GOOD THING NARU'S OUR ALLY, BECAUSE THAT PAPER PSYCHOKINESIS OF HERS WOULD WRECK US.
ANY PAPER THAT HER PSYCHOKINESIS PASSES THROUGH GETS HARD AS METAL, BUT STAYS AS FLEXIBLE AS CLOTH.
WITH HER SICK MODELING SKILLS AND FIGHTING SENSE... SHE'S A BEAST. A SYSTEM SCAN MIGHT LABEL HER A LEVEL 3, BUT SHE'S EASILY GOT THE STRENGTH OF A LEVEL 4.
FU FU! PRAISE ME... PRAISE ME MORE!
QUIT GETTING CARRIED AWAY AND FINISH. YOU SAID THAT YOURSELF A MINUTE AGO.
ROOOGER.

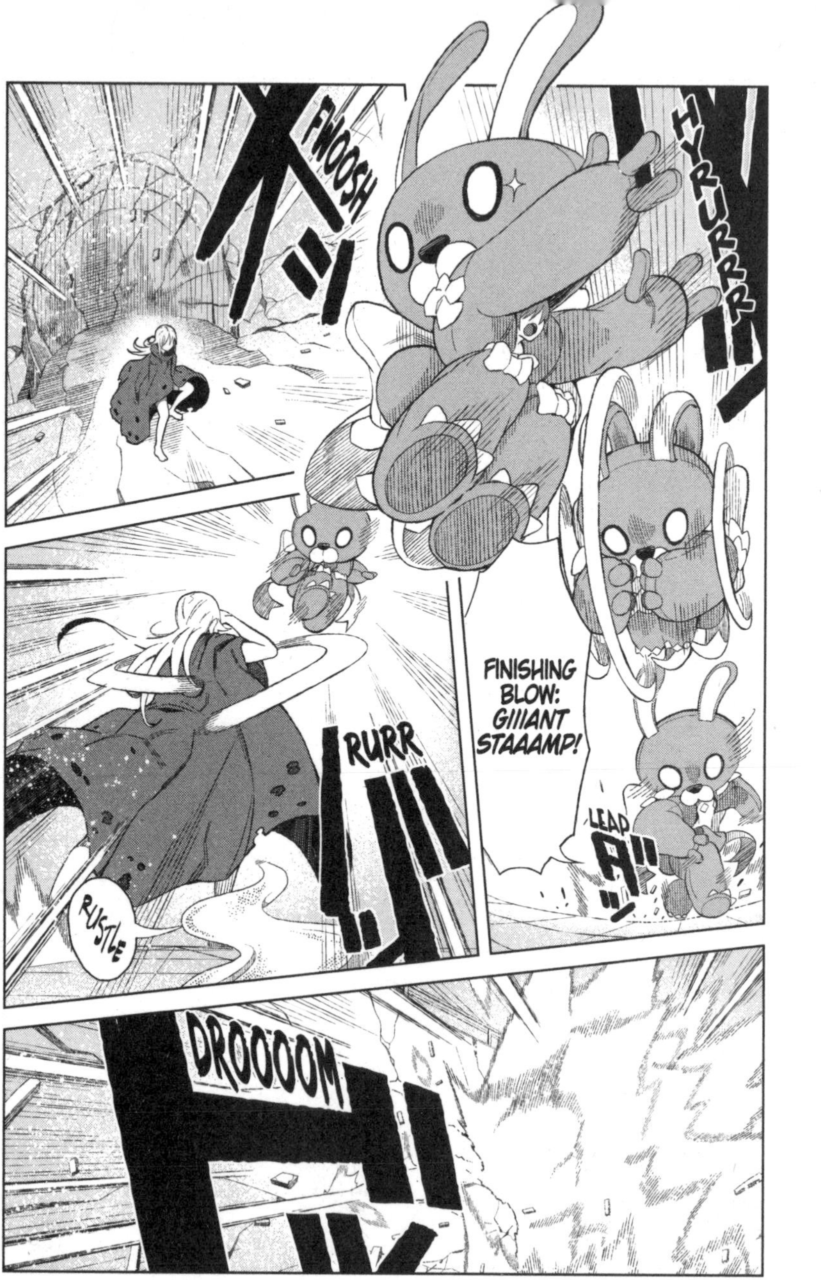
HYRURRR
FWOOSH
FINISHING BLOW: GIIIANT STAAAMP!
LEAP
RURR
RUSTLE
DROOOOM

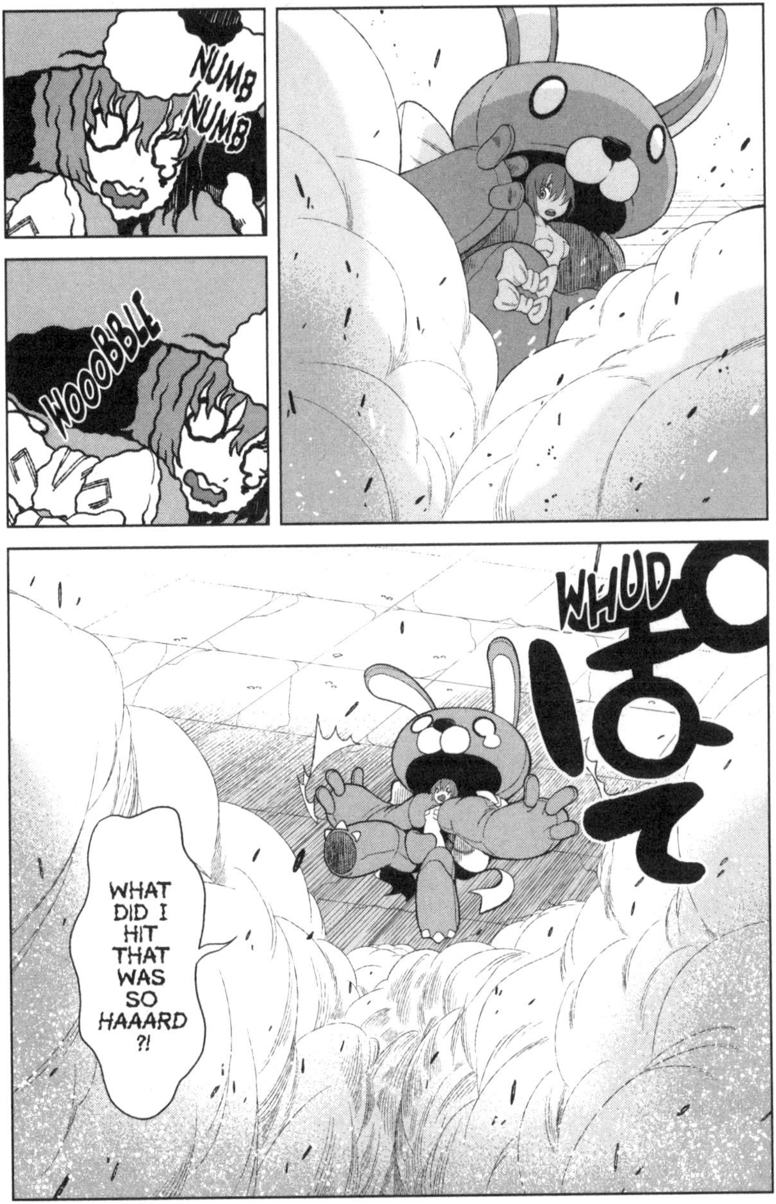
NUMB NUMB
WOOOBBLE
WHUD
ぽて
WHAT DID I HIT THAT WAS SO HAAARD?!

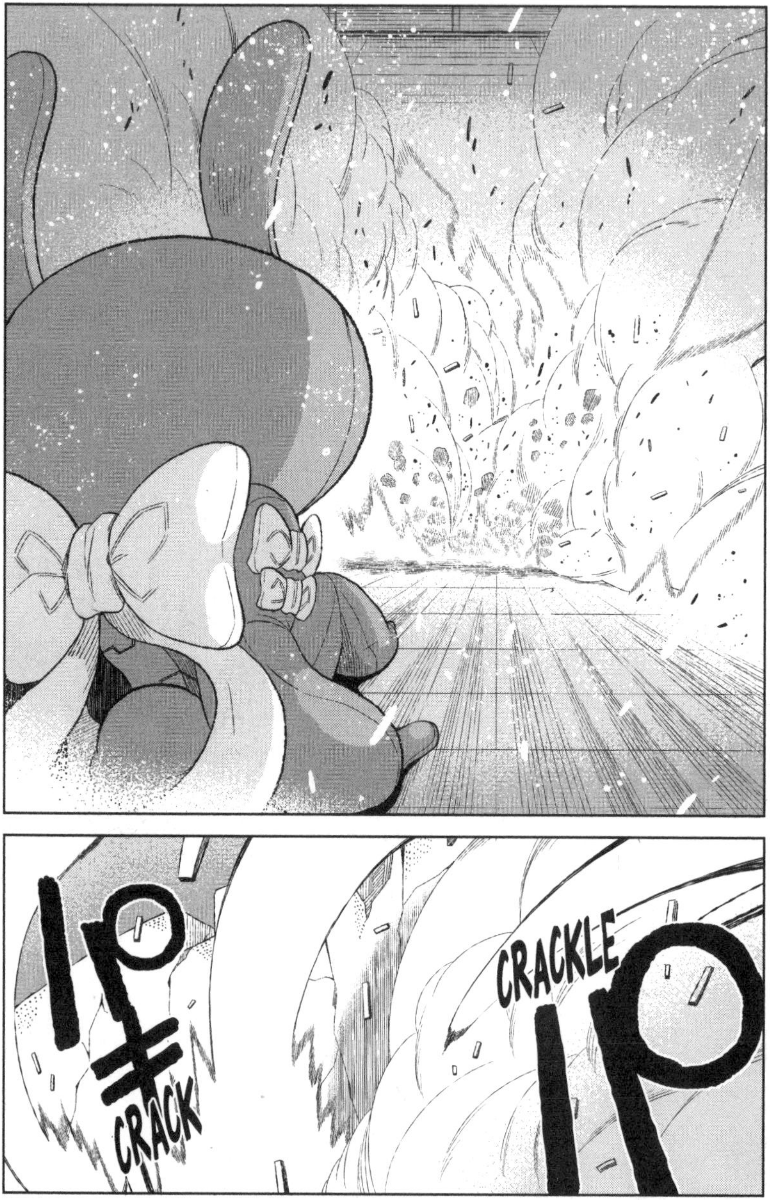
CRACKLE
CRACK

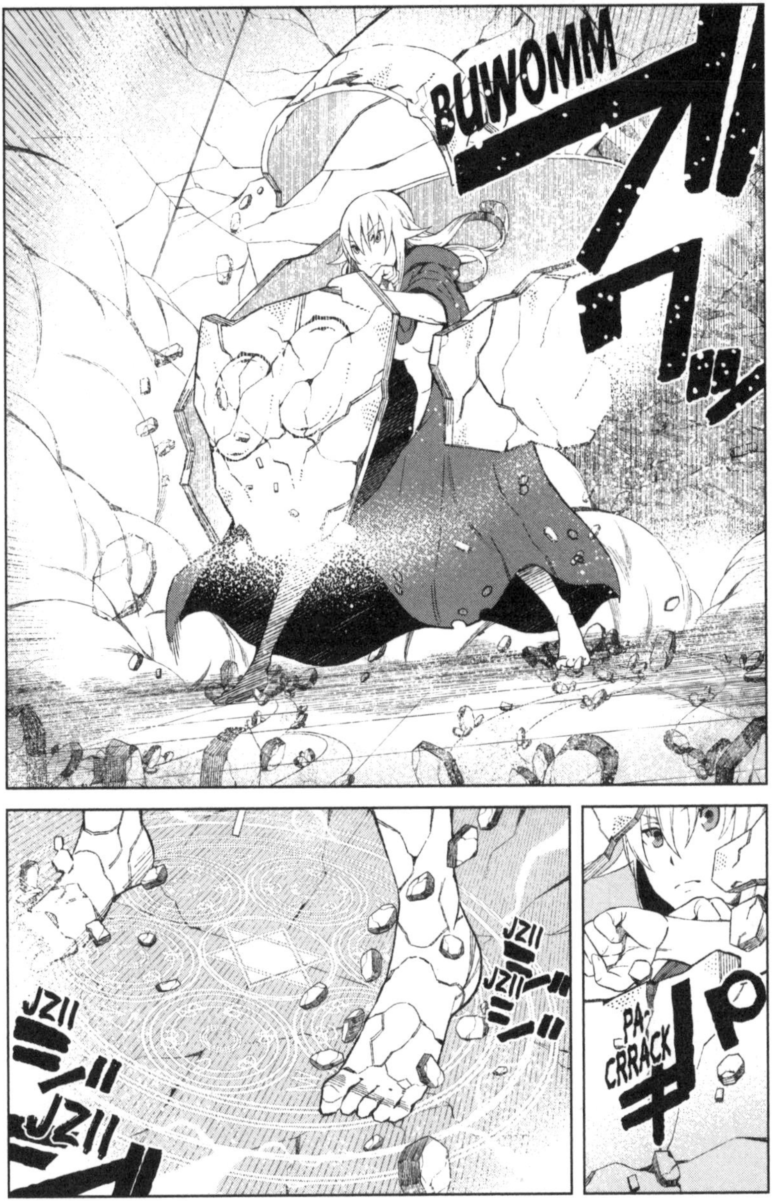
BUWOMM
PA-
CRRACK
JZII
JZII
JZII
JZII

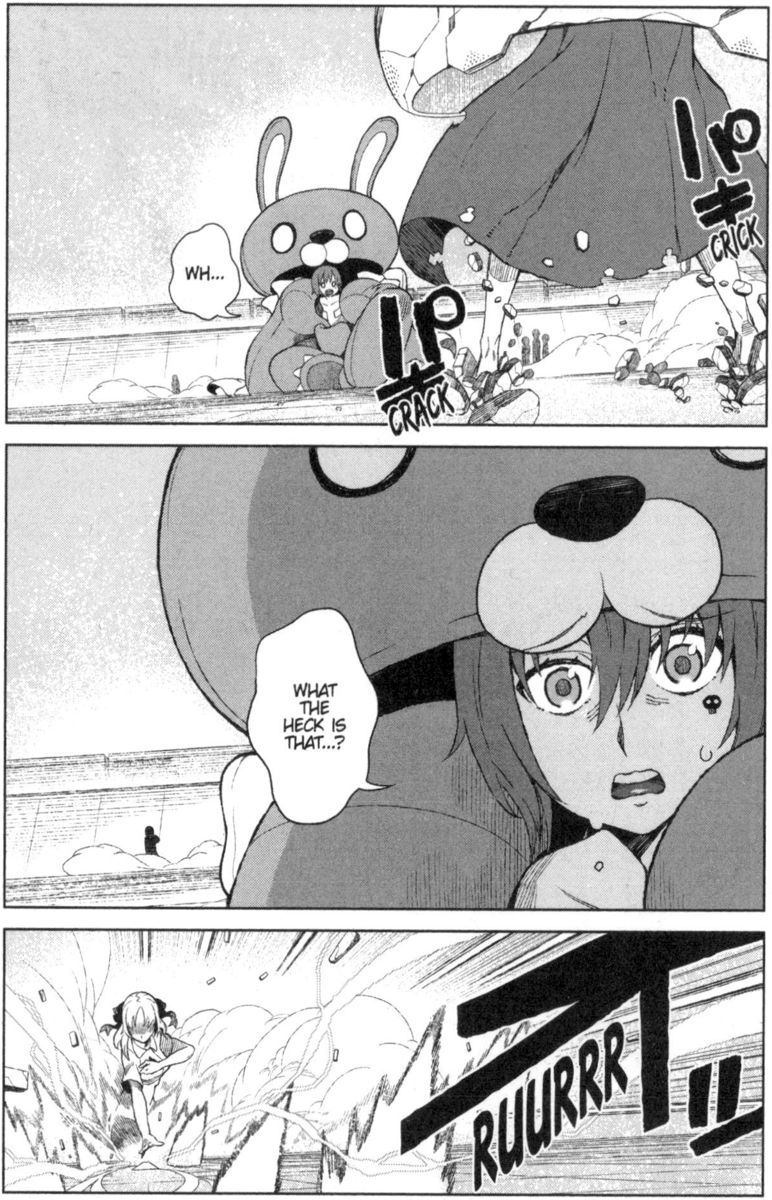
CRICK
WH...
CRACK
WHAT THE HECK IS THAT...?
RUURRR

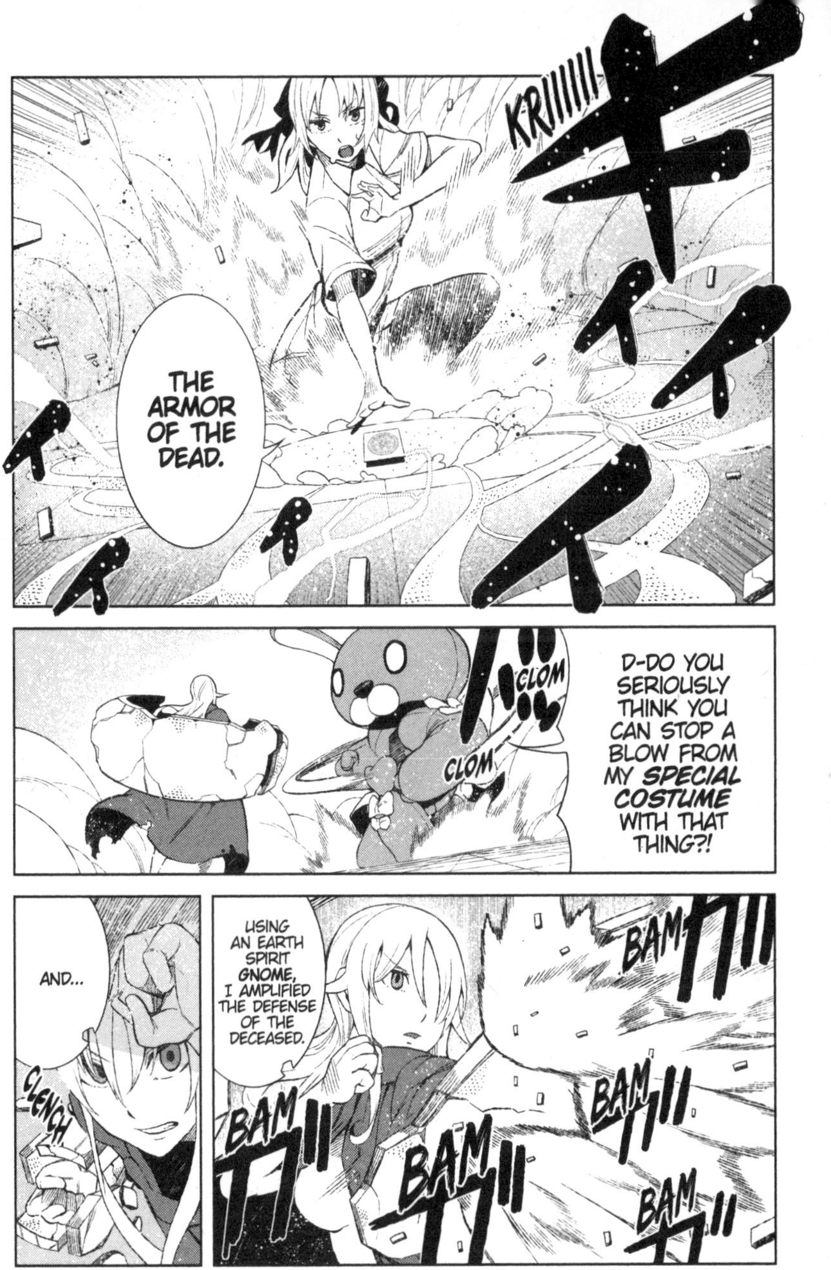
KRIIIIII
THE ARMOR OF THE DEAD.
D-DO YOU SERIOUSLY THINK YOU CAN STOP A BLOW FROM MY SPECIAL COSTUME WITH THAT THING?!
CLOM
CLOM
BAM
USING AN EARTH SPIRIT GNOME, I AMPLIFIED THE DEFENSE OF THE DECEASED.
BAM
BAM
BAM
BAM
AND...
CLENCH

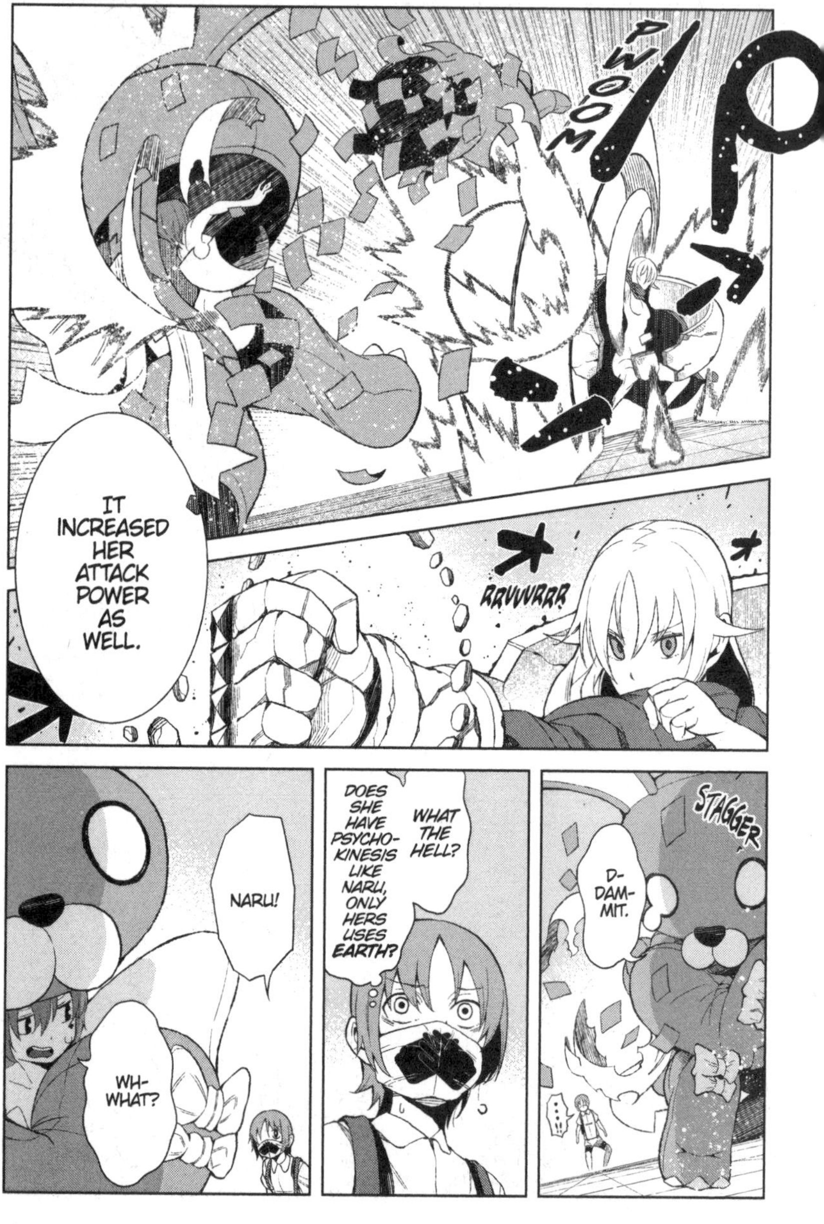
PWOOOM
P
IT INCREASED HER ATTACK POWER AS WELL.
RRVVVRRR
STAGGER
D-DAMMIT.
...!!
WHAT THE HELL?
DOES SHE HAVE PSYCHOKINESIS LIKE NARU, ONLY HERS USES EARTH?
NARU!
WH-WHAT?

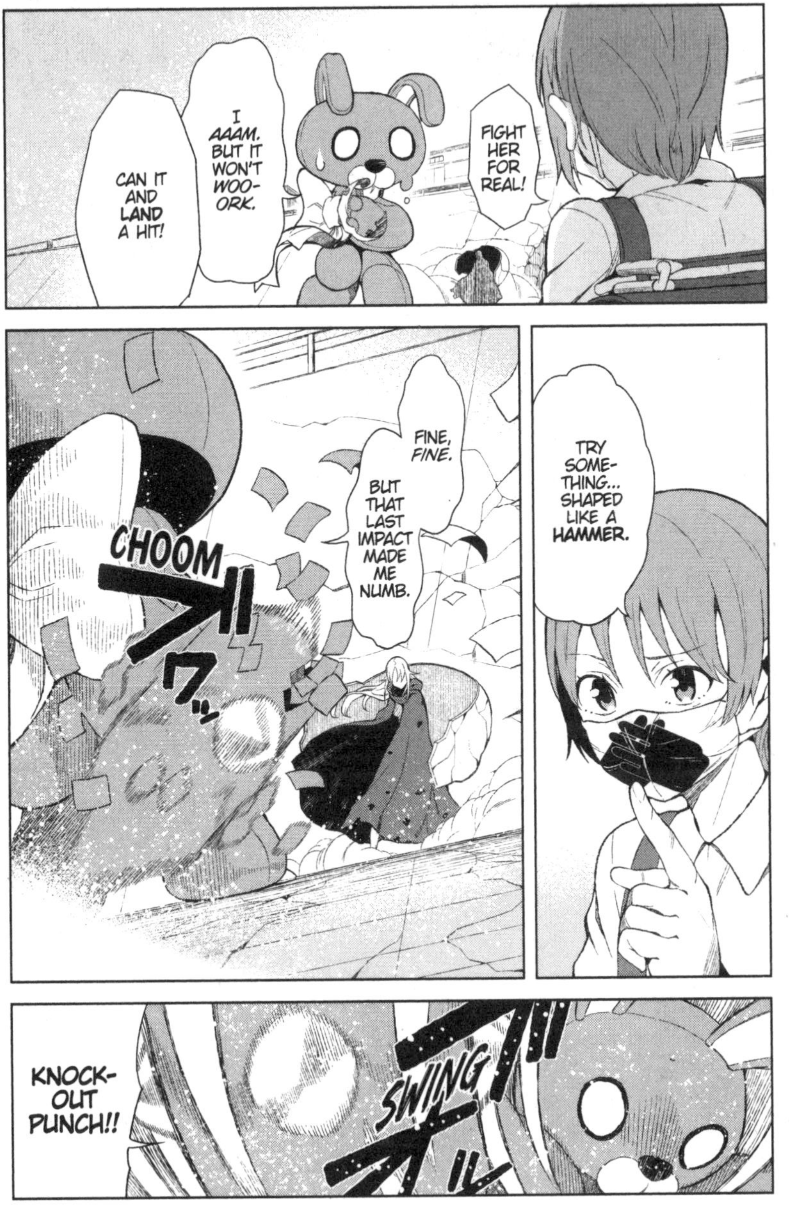
FIGHT HER FOR REAL!
I AAAM. BUT IT WON'T WOO-ORK.
CAN IT AND LAND A HIT!
TRY SOME-THING... SHAPED LIKE A HAMMER.
FINE, FINE.
BUT THAT LAST IMPACT MADE ME NUMB.
CHOOM
SWING
KNOCK-OUT PUNCH!!

WHAM!!

WHAM!!

WHAM!!

BOO, I KNEW IT!

IT'S SO HAAARD!

CRUMBLE

LEAN

CRUMBLE

LISTEN TO ME!

CRICK

CRACK

CRMBL

THBBT!

HOO BOY!

TAP

I DON'T KNOW WHO THE REST OF YOU GIRLS ARE, BUT I DON'T WANT TO HURT YOU, TOO! LEAVE!

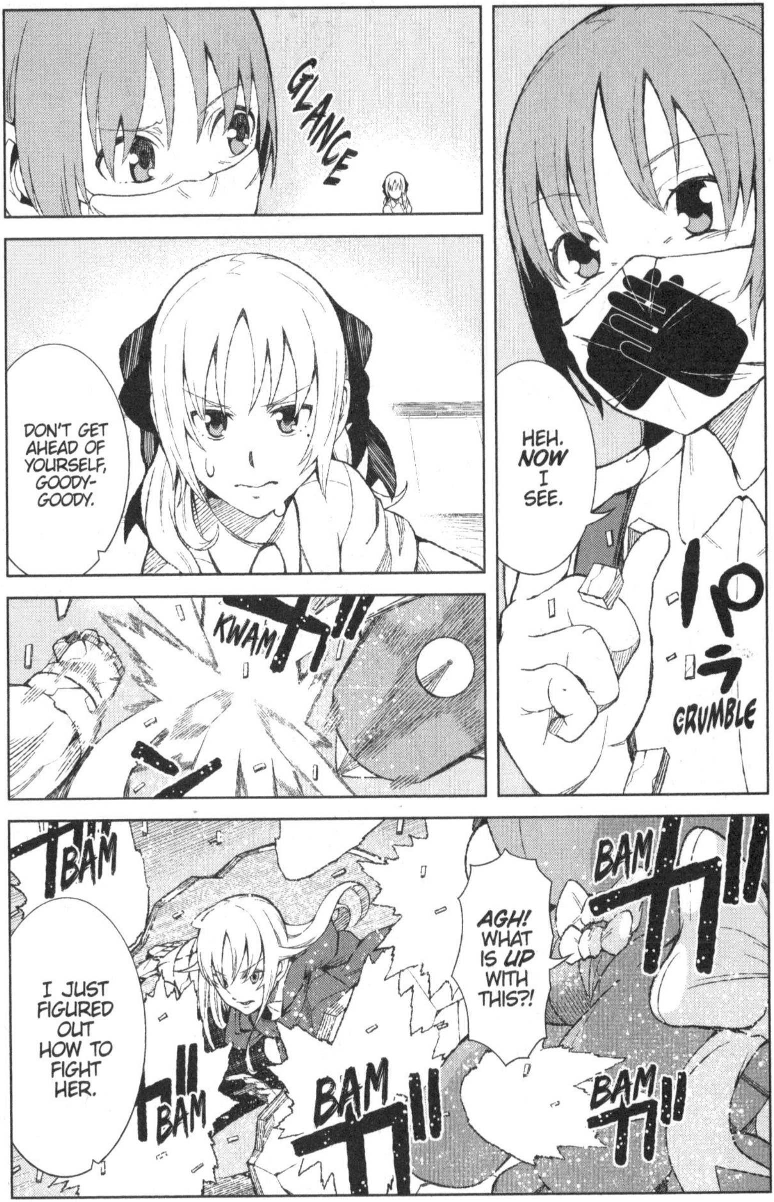
HEH. NOW I SEE.
CRUMBLE
GLANCE
DON'T GET AHEAD OF YOURSELF, GOODY-GOODY.
KWAM
BAM
AGH! WHAT IS UP WITH THIS?!
BAM
I JUST FIGURED OUT HOW TO FIGHT HER.
BAM
BAM
BAM
BAM

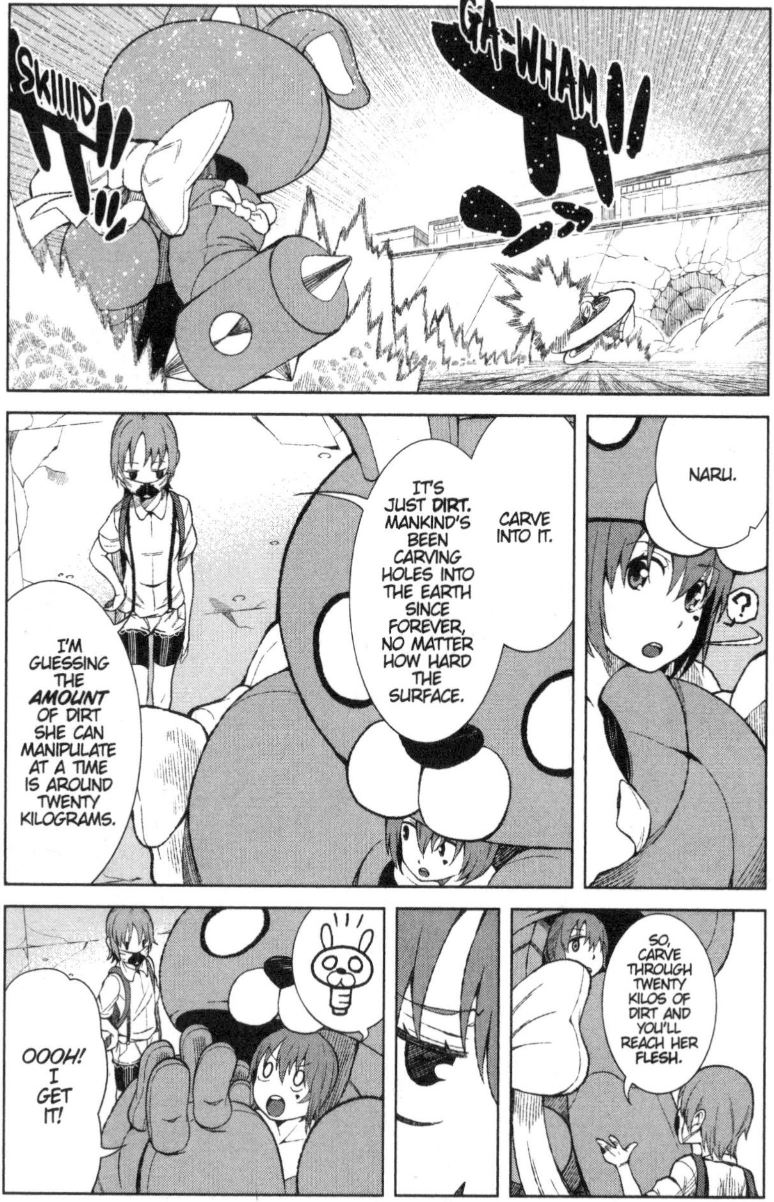
GA-WHAM!!
SKIIIID!!
NARU.
CARVE INTO IT.
IT'S JUST DIRT. MANKIND'S BEEN CARVING HOLES INTO THE EARTH SINCE FOREVER, NO MATTER HOW HARD THE SURFACE.
I'M GUESSING THE AMOUNT OF DIRT SHE CAN MANIPULATE AT A TIME IS AROUND TWENTY KILOGRAMS.
SO, CARVE THROUGH TWENTY KILOS OF DIRT AND YOU'LL REACH HER FLESH.
OOOH! I GET IT!

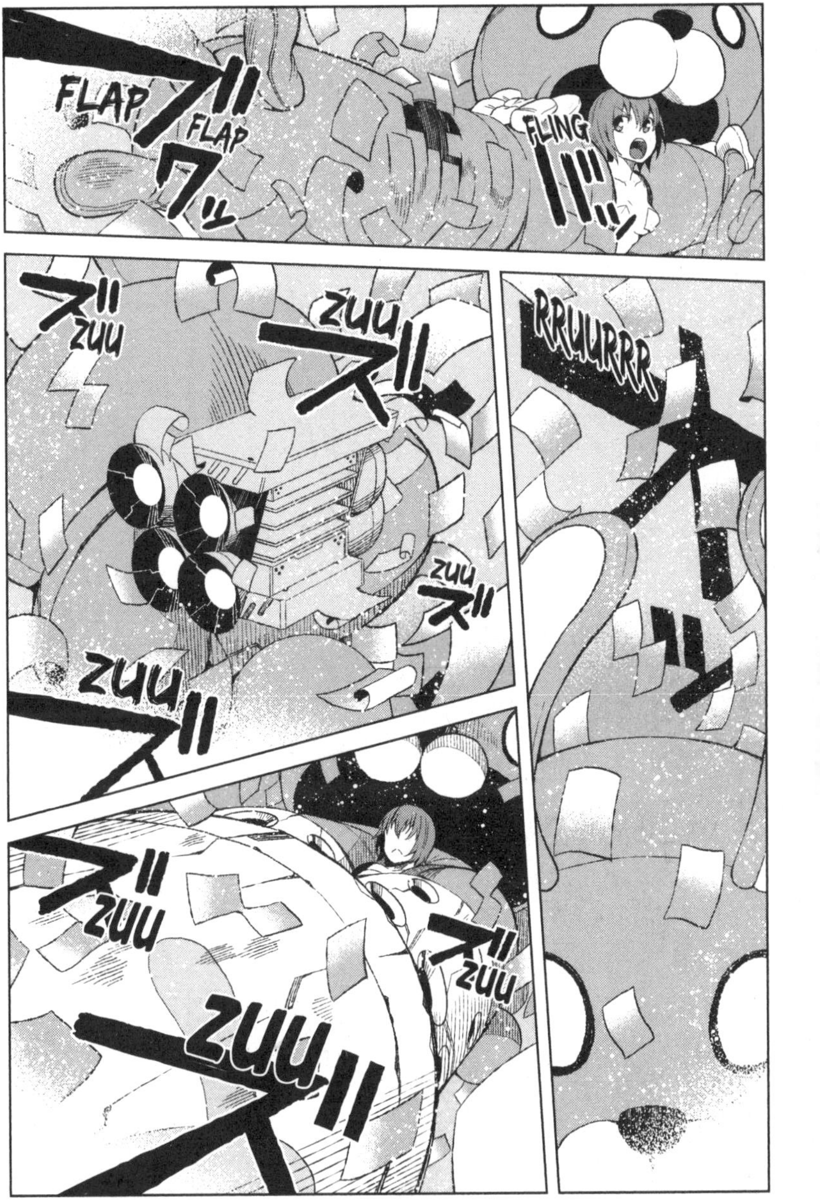
FLING
FLAP
FLAP
RRUURRRR
ZUU
ZUU
ZUU
ZUU
ZUU
ZUU
ZUU

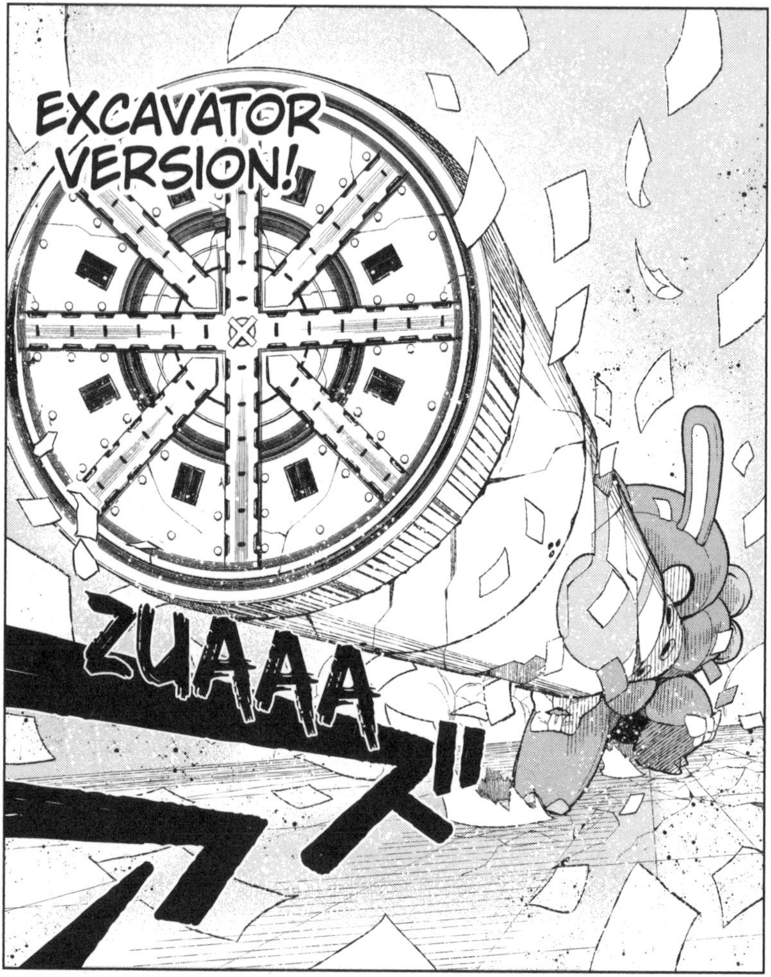
EXCAVATOR VERSION!
ZUAAA
ズ
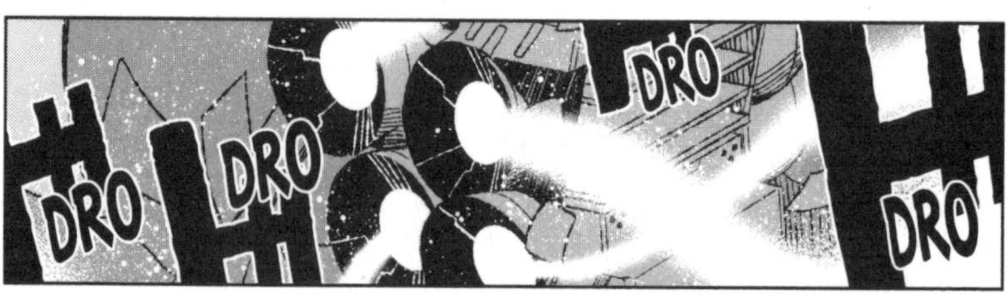
DRO
DRO
DRO
DRO

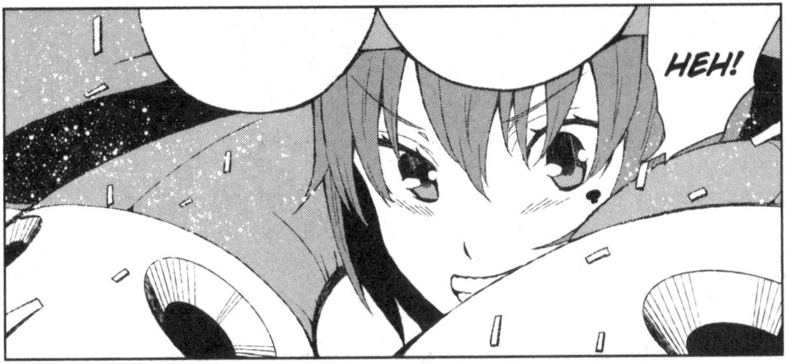
HEH!
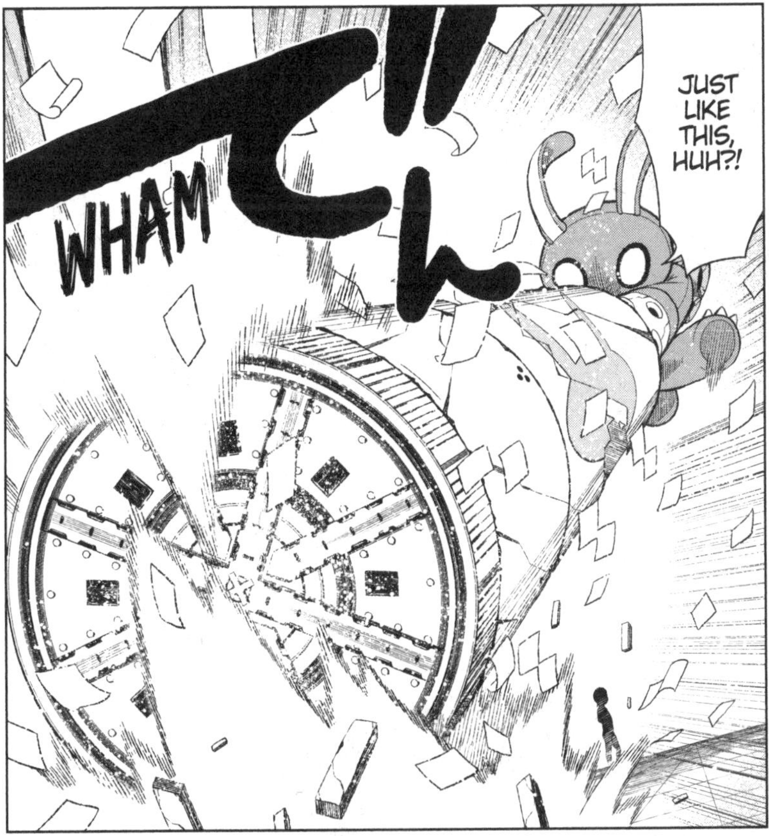
JUST LIKE THIS, HUH?!
WHAM

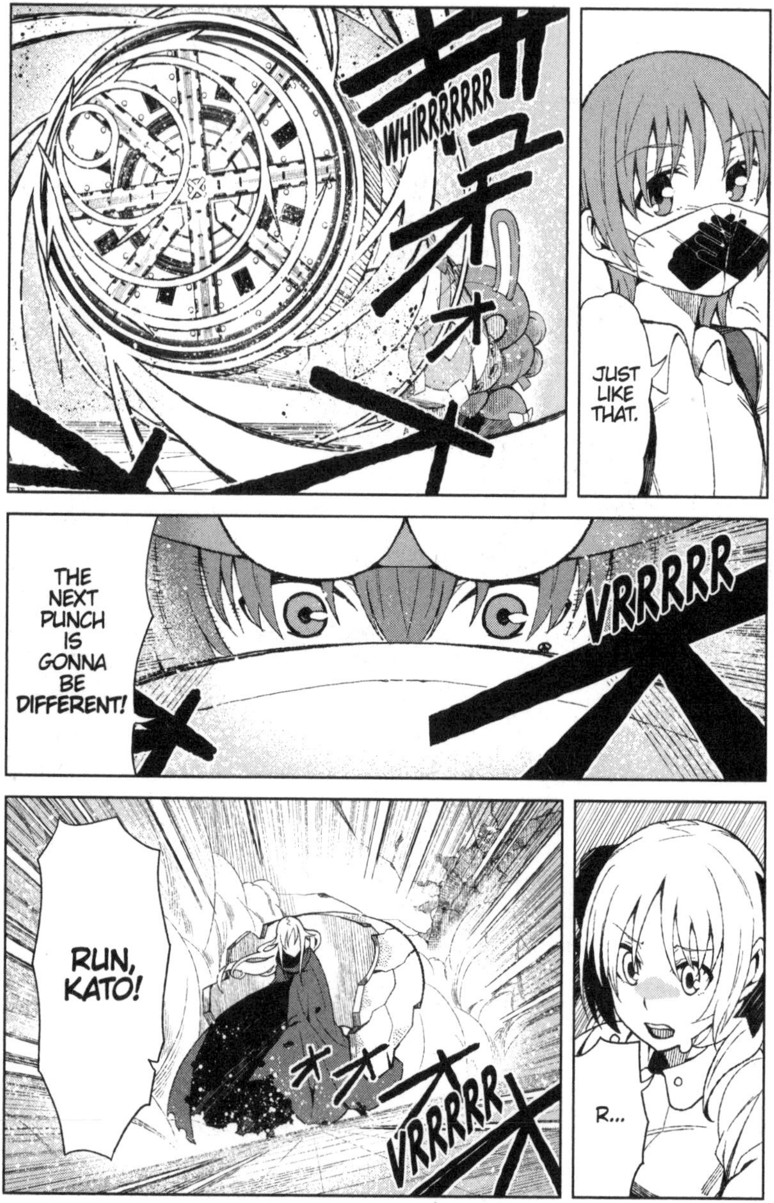
JUST LIKE THAT.
WHIRRRRRR
THE NEXT PUNCH IS GONNA BE DIFFERENT!
VRRRRR
R...
RUN, KATO!
VRRRRR

a certain
SCIENTIFIC
ACCELERATOR

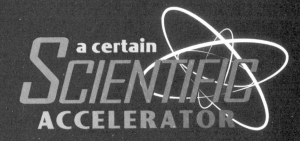

CHAPTER 15

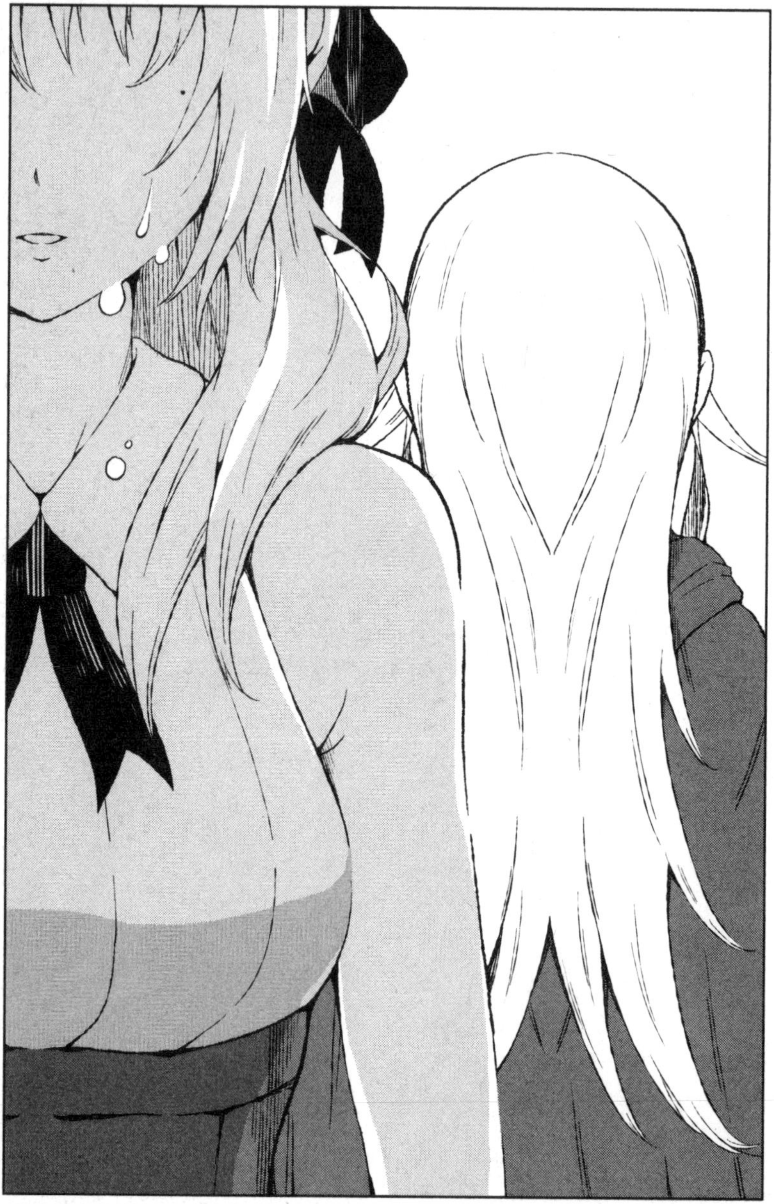

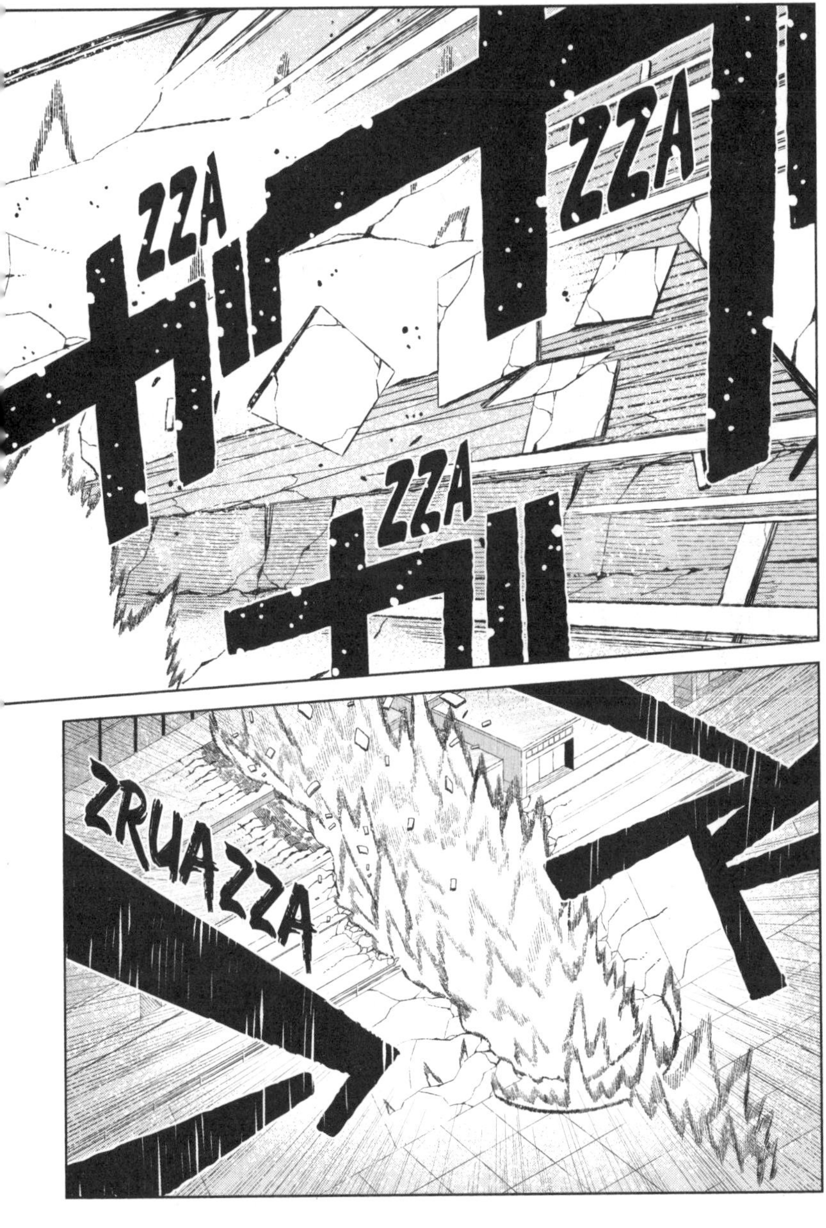
ZZA
ZZA
ZZA
ZRUAZZA

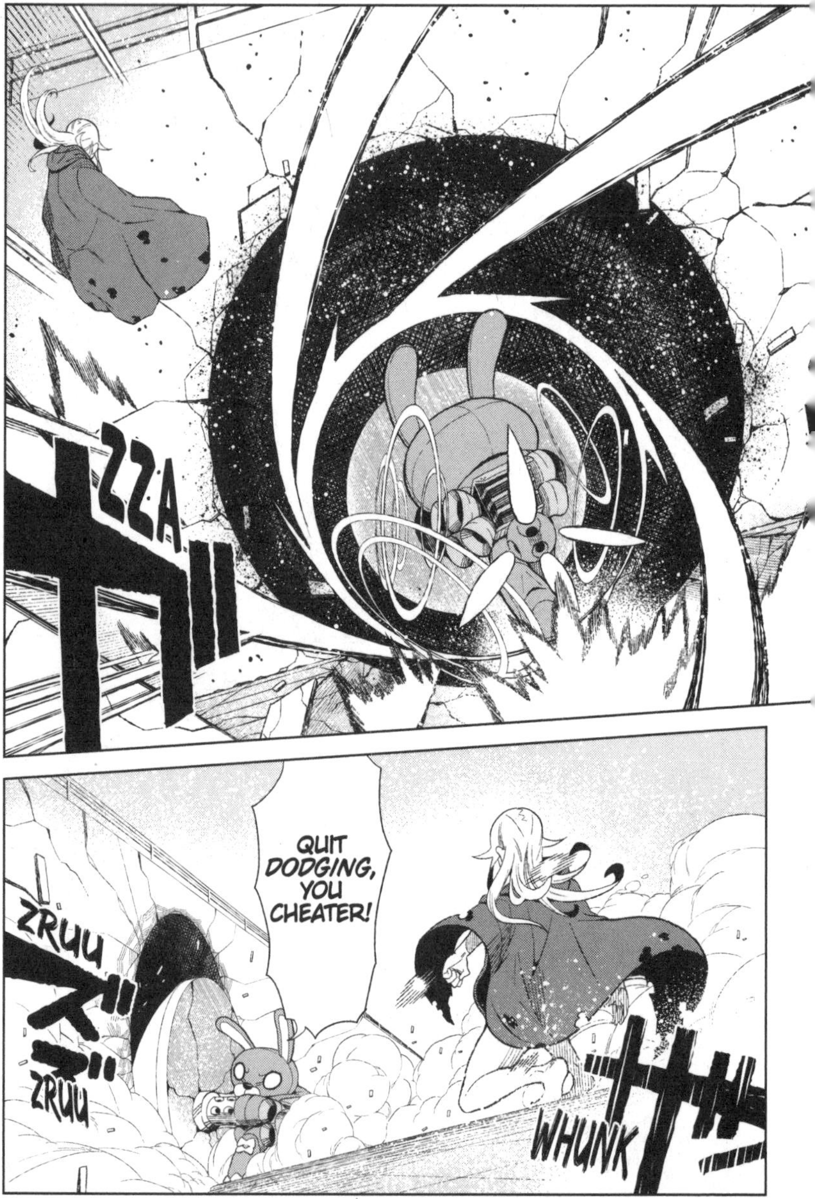
ZZA
QUIT DODGING, YOU CHEATER!
WHUNK
ZRUU
ZRUU

RIIZZ

ブブブ

ブブブ

YOU!

DAM-MIT!

RIIZZ IZZ IZZ IZZ

ARGH! QUIT RUNNING!

GYRIZZZ

DROOM

JUST ONCE... JUST ONCE, WOULD YOU PLEASE LET ME HIT YOU?!

HUFF!

HUFF!

SLIDE

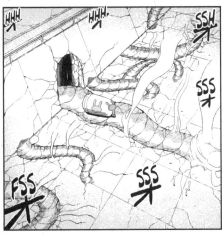

HHH.

HHH.

SSH

SSS

SSS

FSS

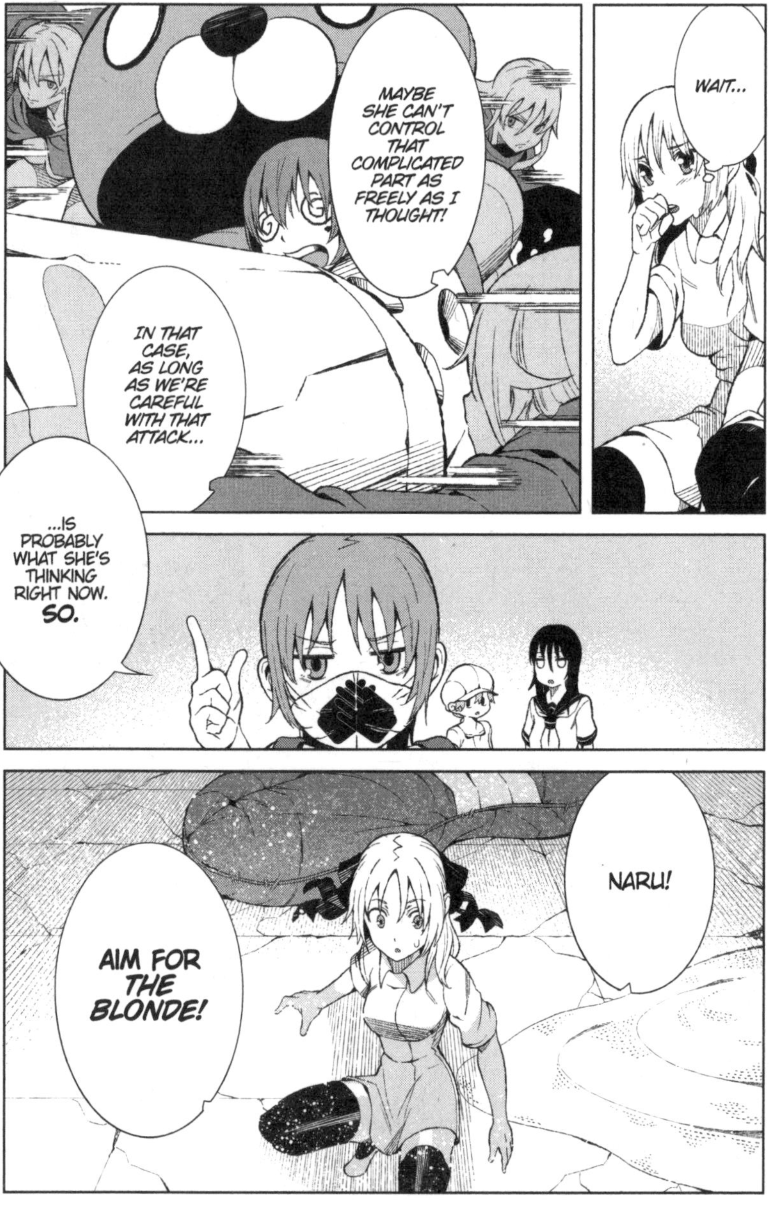
WAIT...
MAYBE SHE CAN'T CONTROL THAT COMPLICATED PART AS FREELY AS I THOUGHT!
IN THAT CASE, AS LONG AS WE'RE CAREFUL WITH THAT ATTACK...
...IS PROBABLY WHAT SHE'S THINKING RIGHT NOW. SO.
NARU!
AIM FOR THE BLONDE!

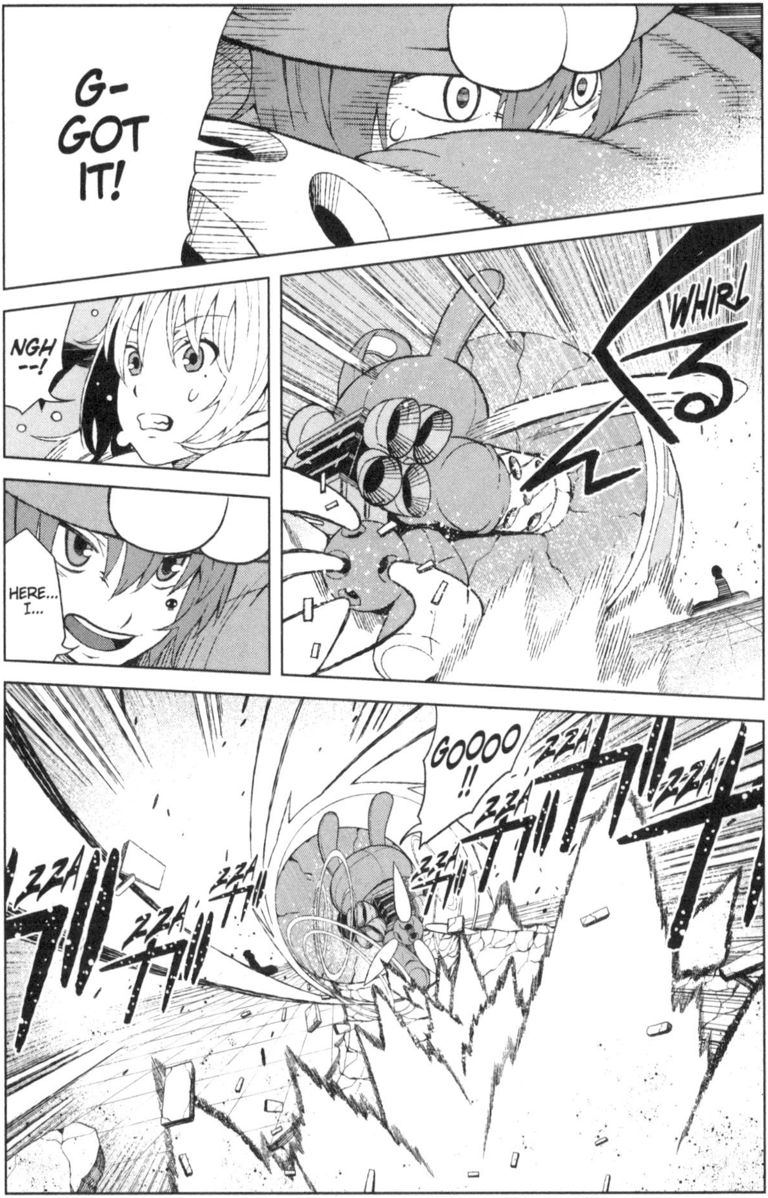
G-GOT IT!
WHIRL
NGH--!
HERE... I...
GOOOO!!
ZZA
ZZA
ZZA
ZZA
ZZA
ZZA
ZZA

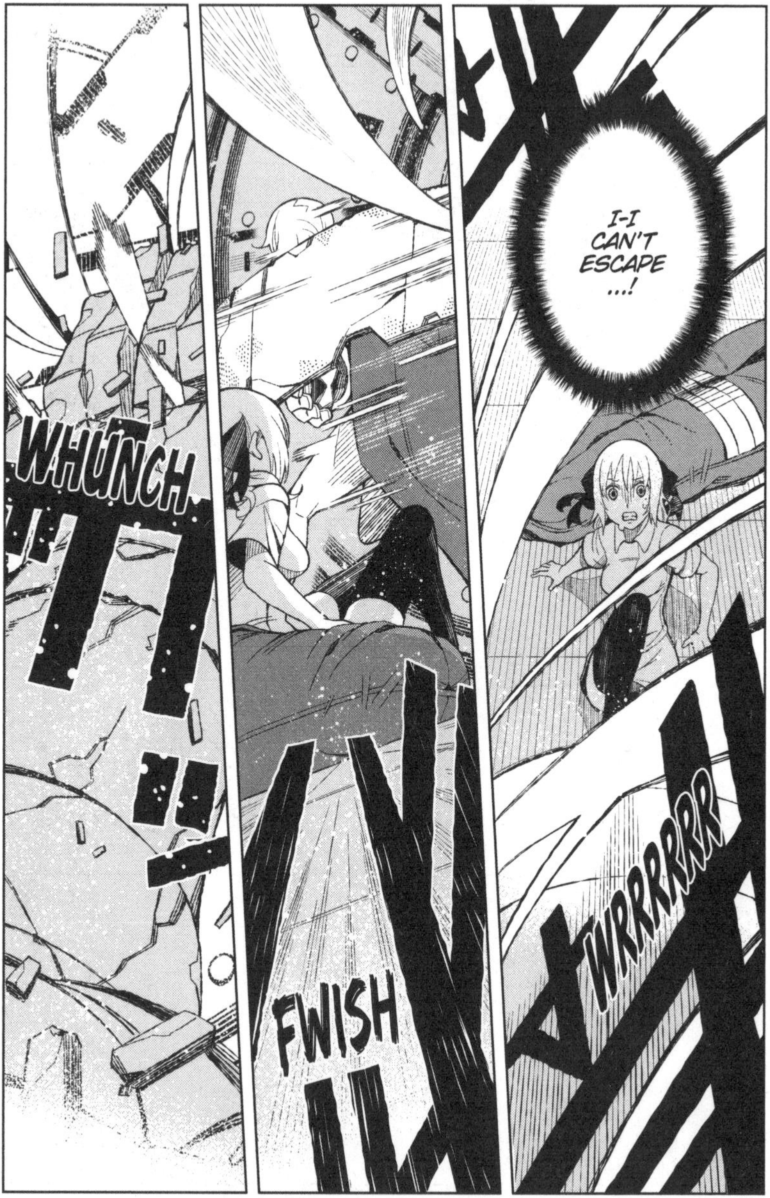
I-I CAN'T ESCAPE ...!
TWRRRRRR
FWISH
WHUNCH

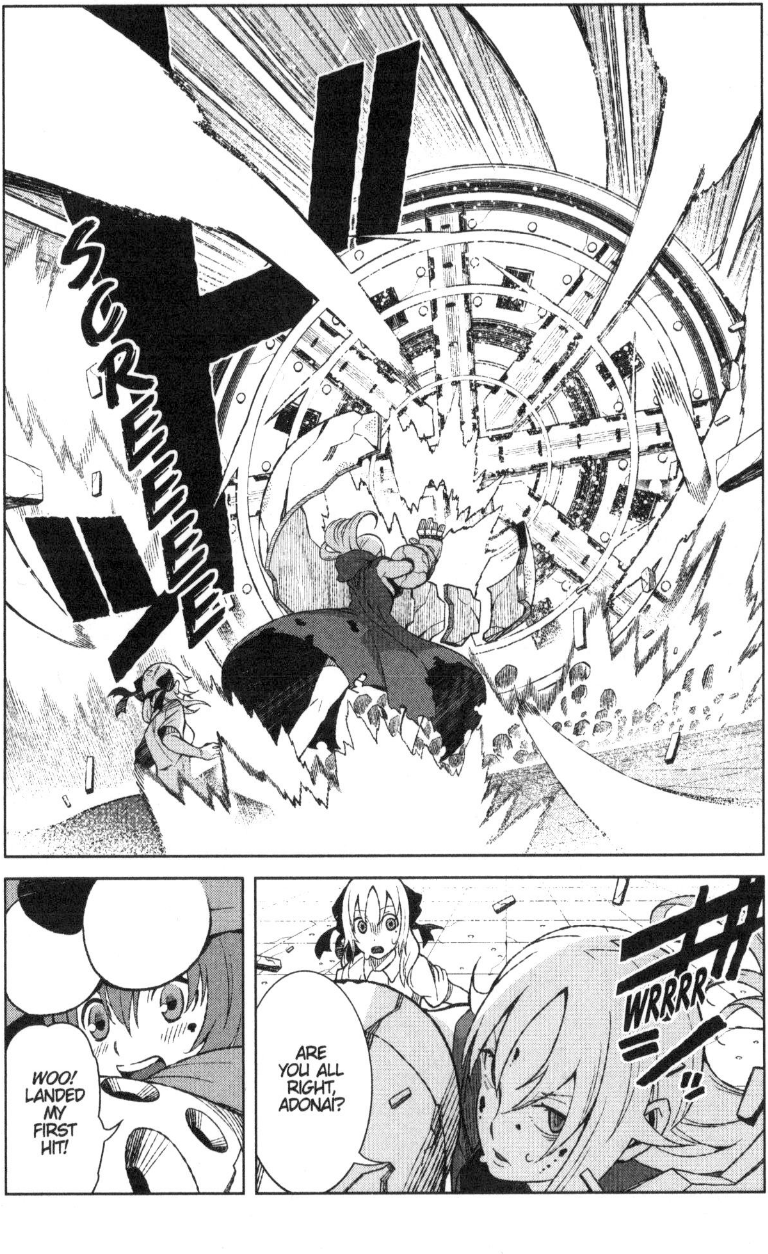
SCREEEEEE
WRRRR
ARE YOU ALL RIGHT, ADONAI?
WOO! LANDED MY FIRST HIT!

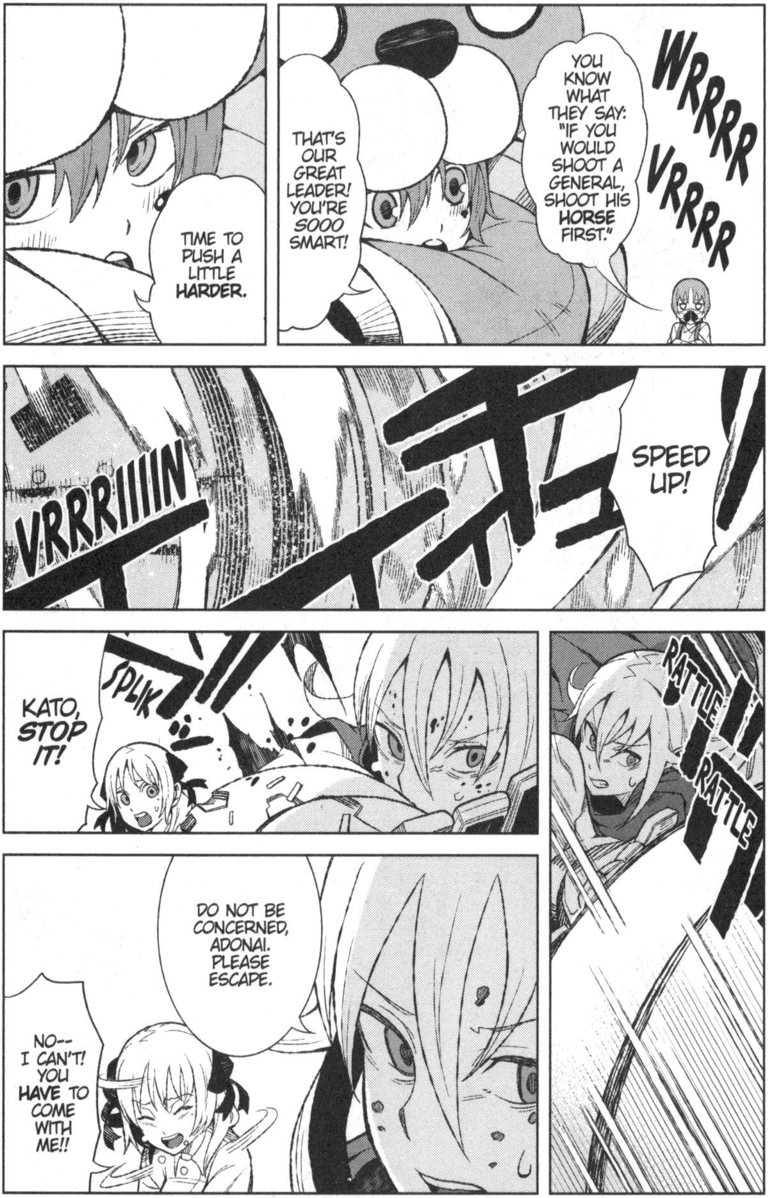
WRRRRR VRRRRR
YOU KNOW WHAT THEY SAY: "IF YOU WOULD SHOOT A GENERAL, SHOOT HIS **HORSE** FIRST."
THAT'S OUR GREAT LEADER! YOU'RE SOOO SMART!
TIME TO PUSH A LITTLE **HARDER.**
SPEED UP!
VRRRIIIIN
RATTLE RATTLE
SPLIK
KATO, ***STOP IT!***
DO NOT BE CONCERNED, ADONAI. PLEASE ESCAPE.
NO-- I CAN'T! YOU **HAVE** TO COME WITH ME!!

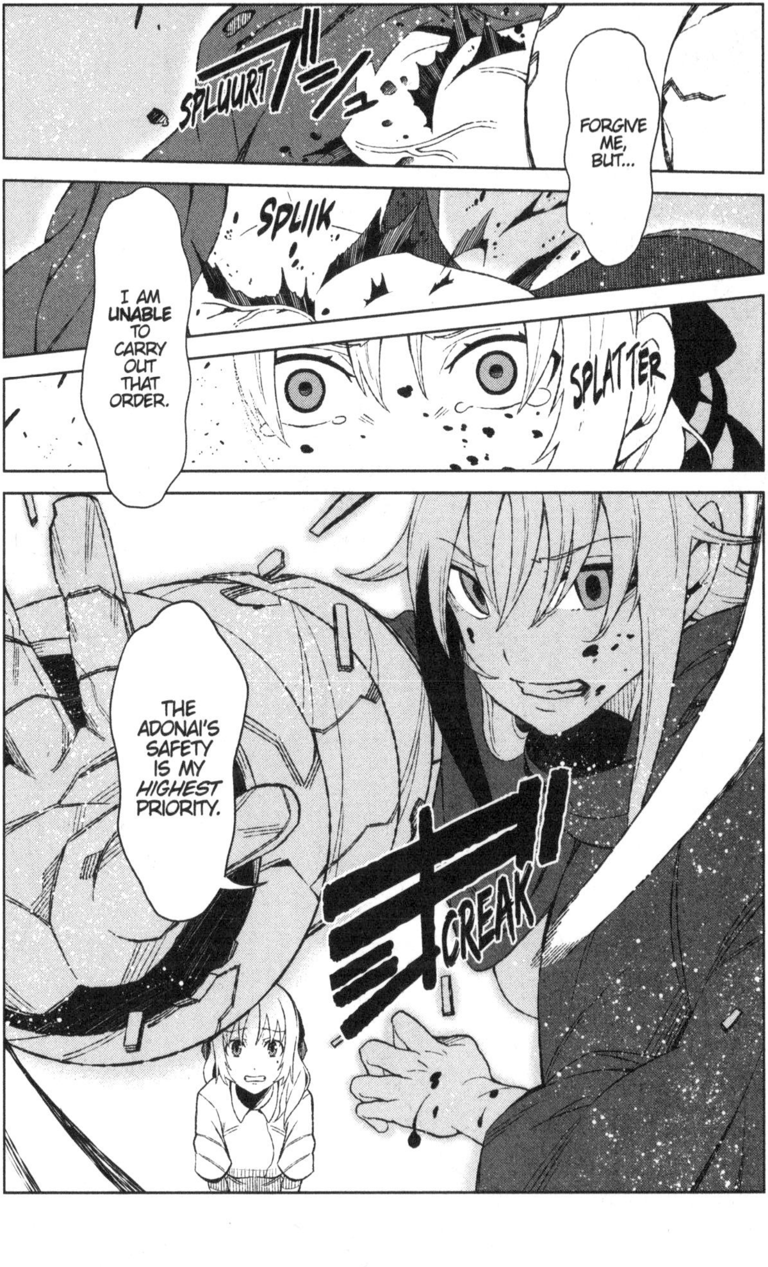
FORGIVE ME, BUT...
SPLUURT
SPLIIK
I AM UNABLE TO CARRY OUT THAT ORDER.
SPLATTER
THE ADONAI'S SAFETY IS MY *HIGHEST* PRIORITY.
CREAK

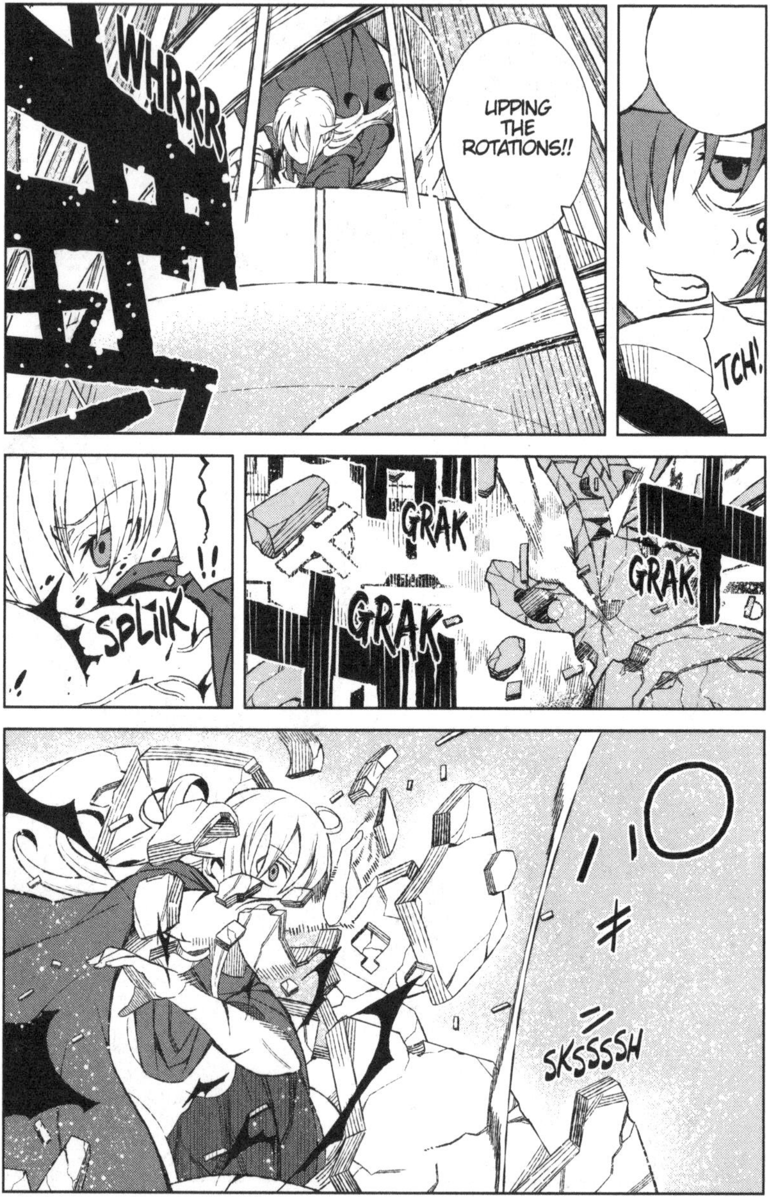
TCH!
UPPING THE ROTATIONS!!
WHRRR
GRAK
GRAK
GRAK
!!
SPLIIK
SKSSSSH

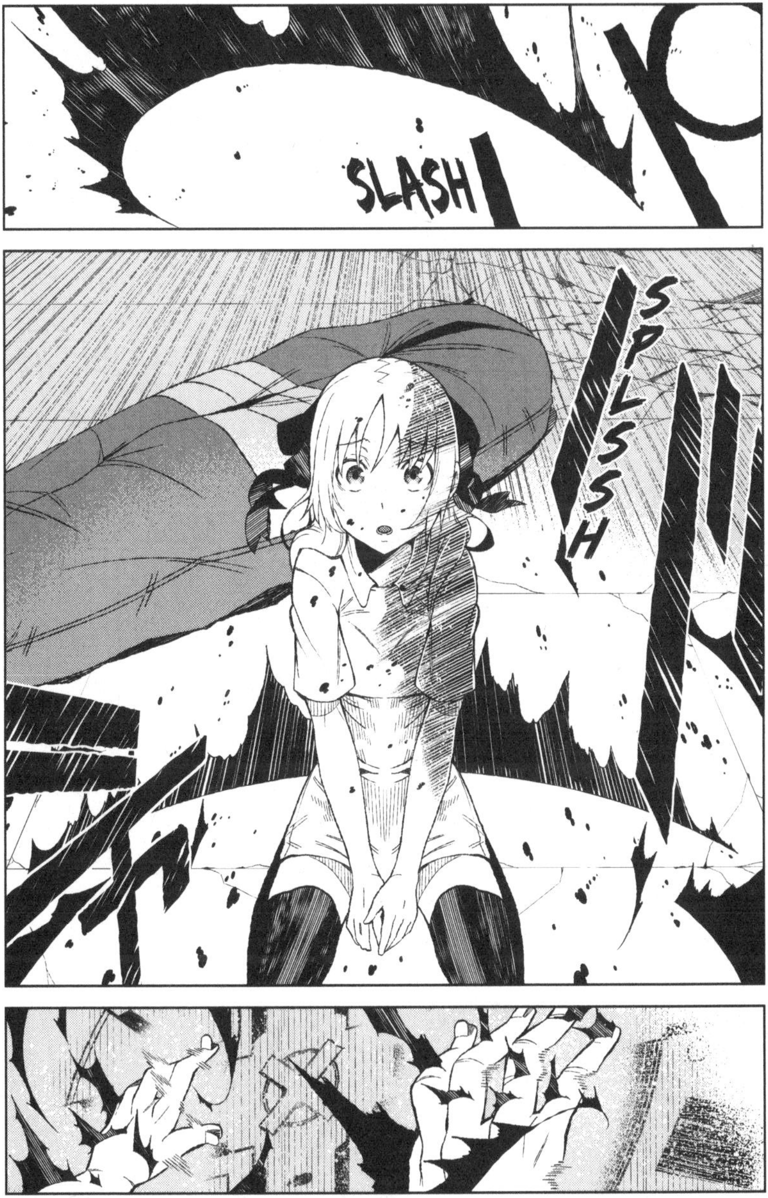
SLASH
SPLSSH

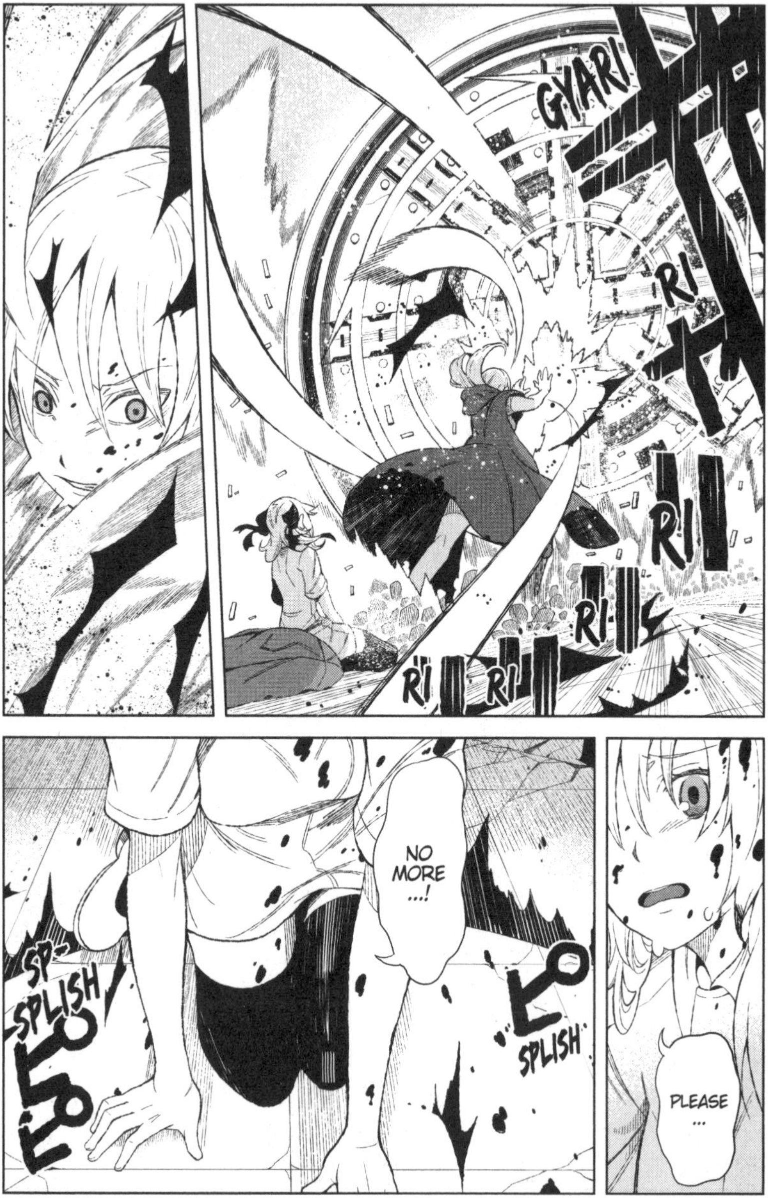
GYARI
RI
RI
RI
RI
RI
PLEASE ...
NO MORE ...!
SPLISH
SP-SPLISH

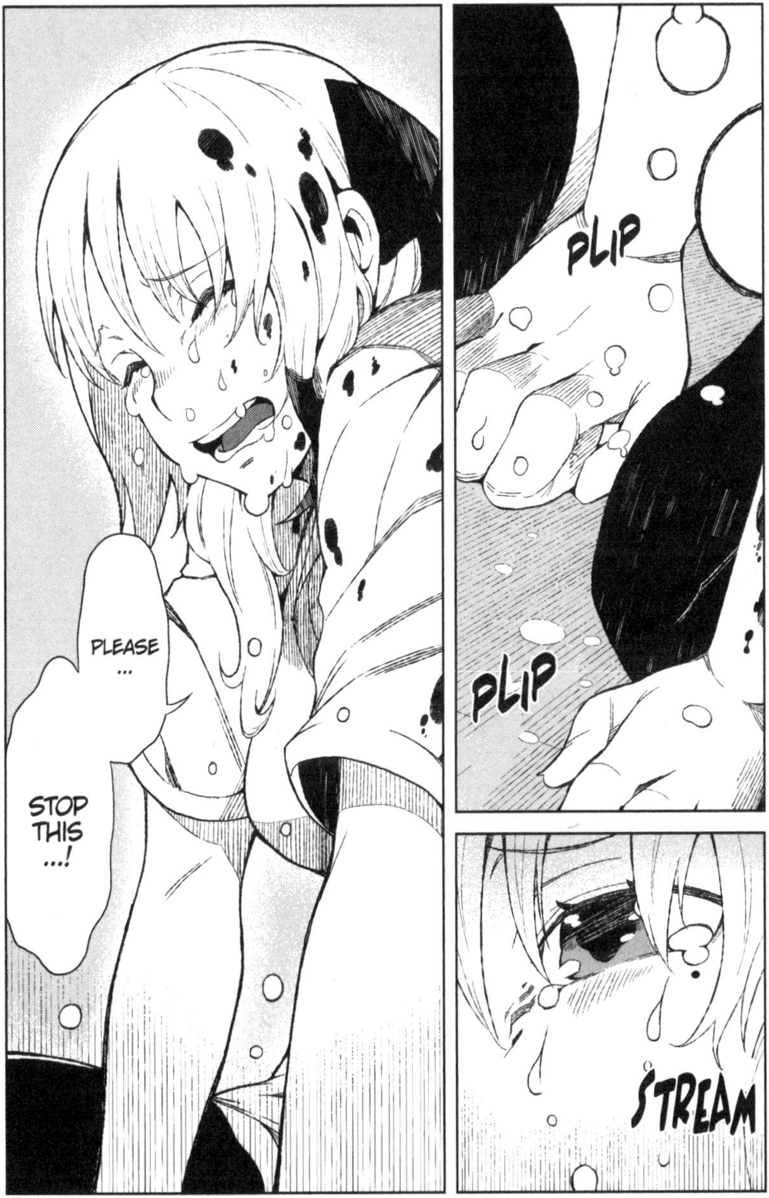
PLIP
PLIP
STREAM
PLEASE ...
STOP THIS ...!

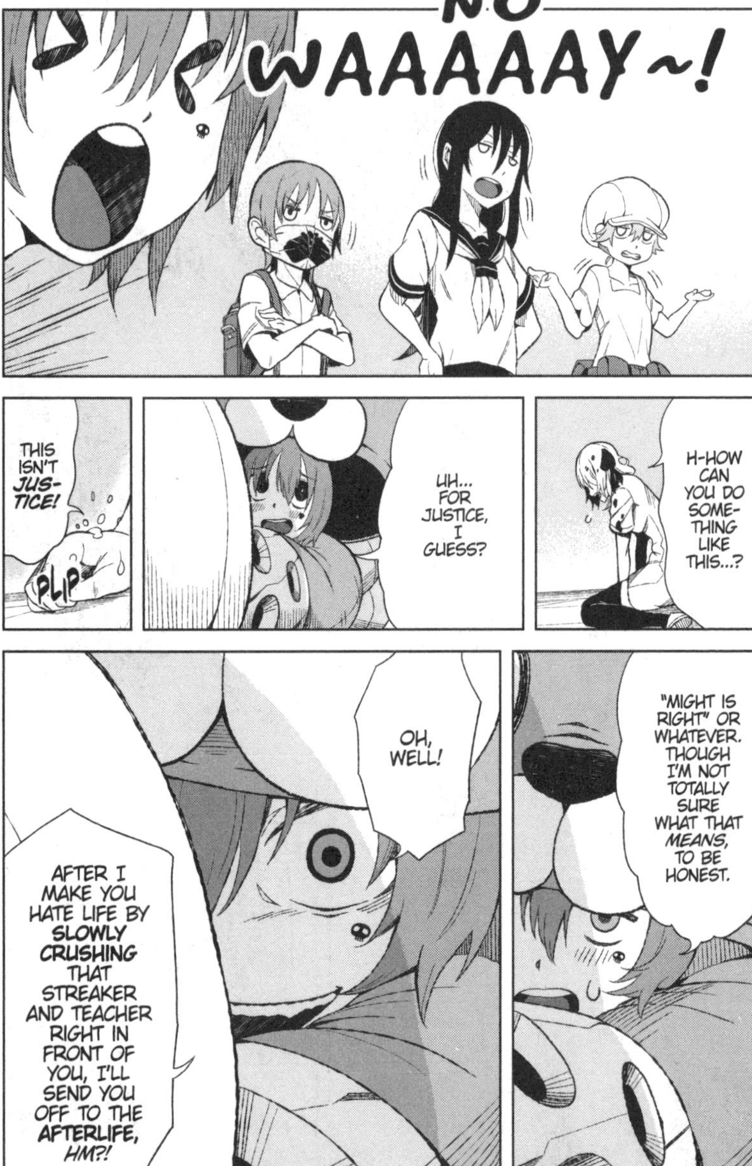
NO WAAAAAY~!
H-HOW CAN YOU DO SOMETHING LIKE THIS...?
UH... FOR JUSTICE, I GUESS?
THIS ISN'T **JUSTICE!**
PLIP
"MIGHT IS RIGHT" OR WHATEVER. THOUGH I'M NOT TOTALLY SURE WHAT THAT *MEANS,* TO BE HONEST.
OH, WELL!
AFTER I MAKE YOU HATE LIFE BY **SLOWLY CRUSHING** THAT STREAKER AND TEACHER RIGHT IN FRONT OF YOU, I'LL SEND YOU OFF TO THE **AFTERLIFE,** *HM?!*

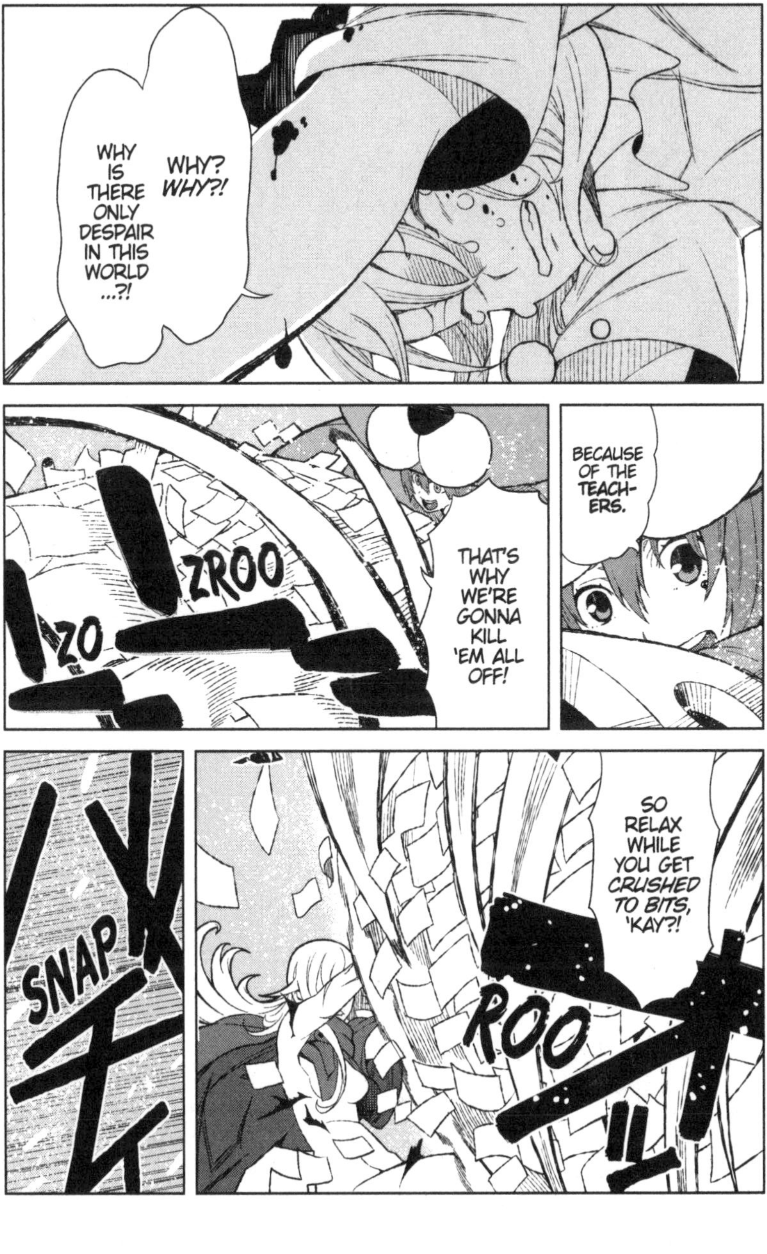
WHY? WHY?!
WHY IS THERE ONLY DESPAIR IN THIS WORLD ...?!
BECAUSE OF THE TEACHERS.
THAT'S WHY WE'RE GONNA KILL 'EM ALL OFF!
ZROO
ZO
SO RELAX WHILE YOU GET CRUSHED TO BITS, 'KAY?!
ROO
SNAP

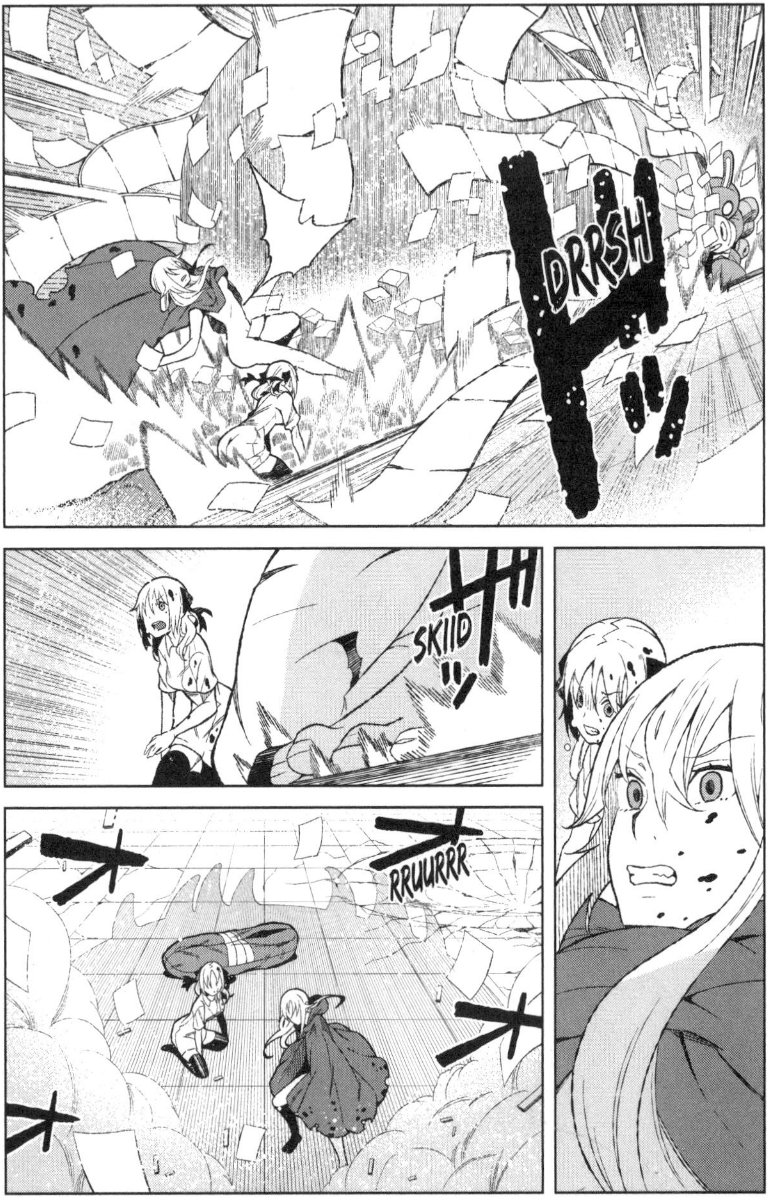
DRRSH
SKIID
RRUURRR

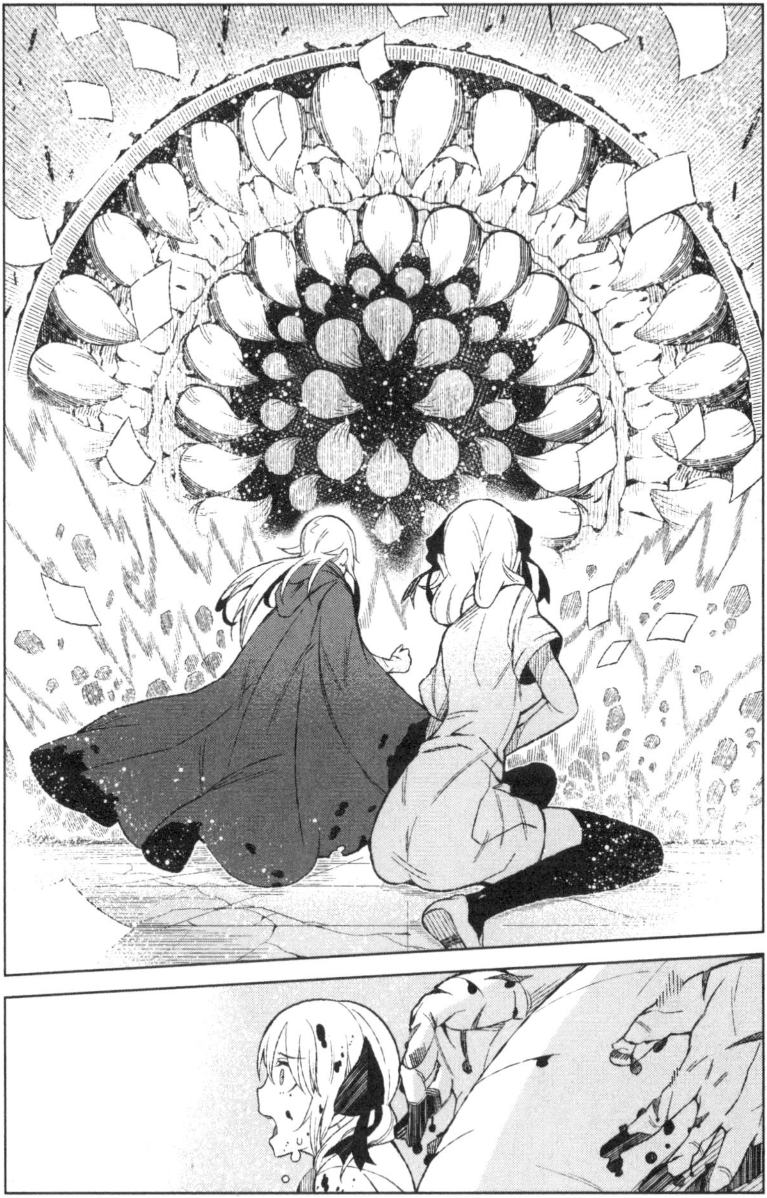

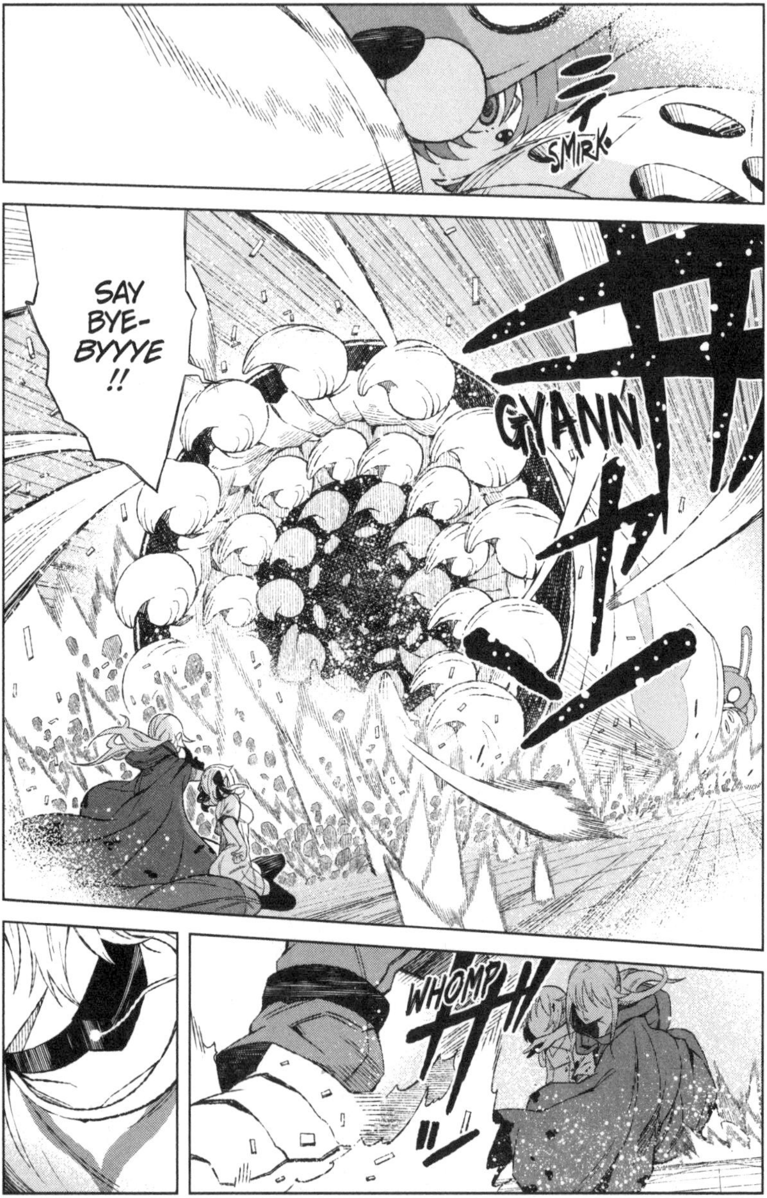
SMIRK
SAY BYE-BYYYE!!
GYANN
WHOMP

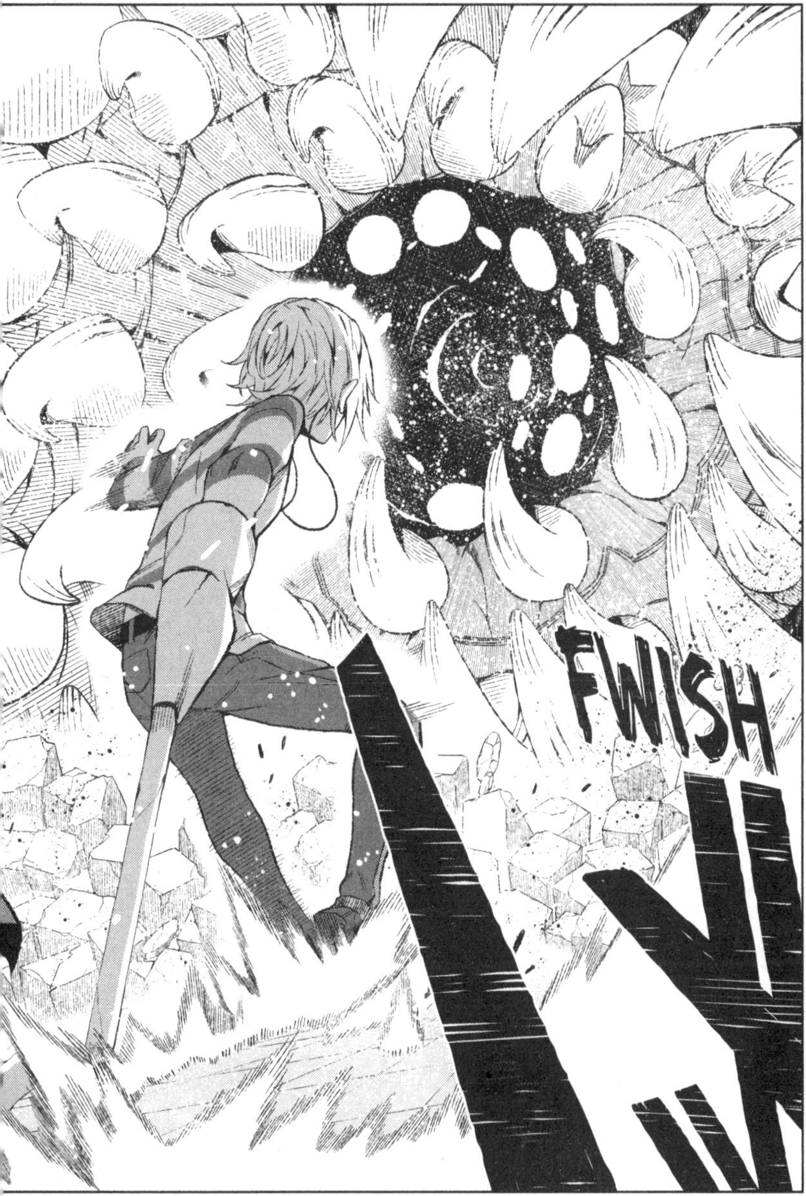
FWISH

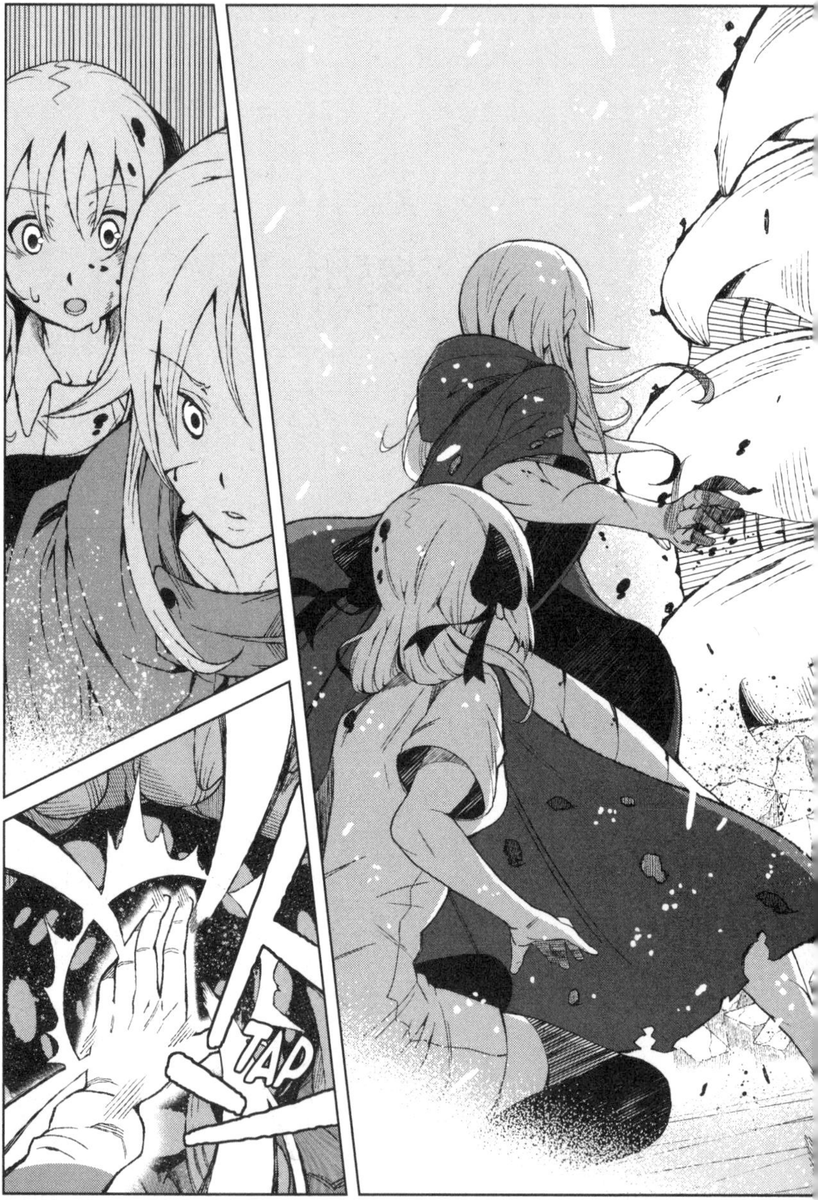
TAP

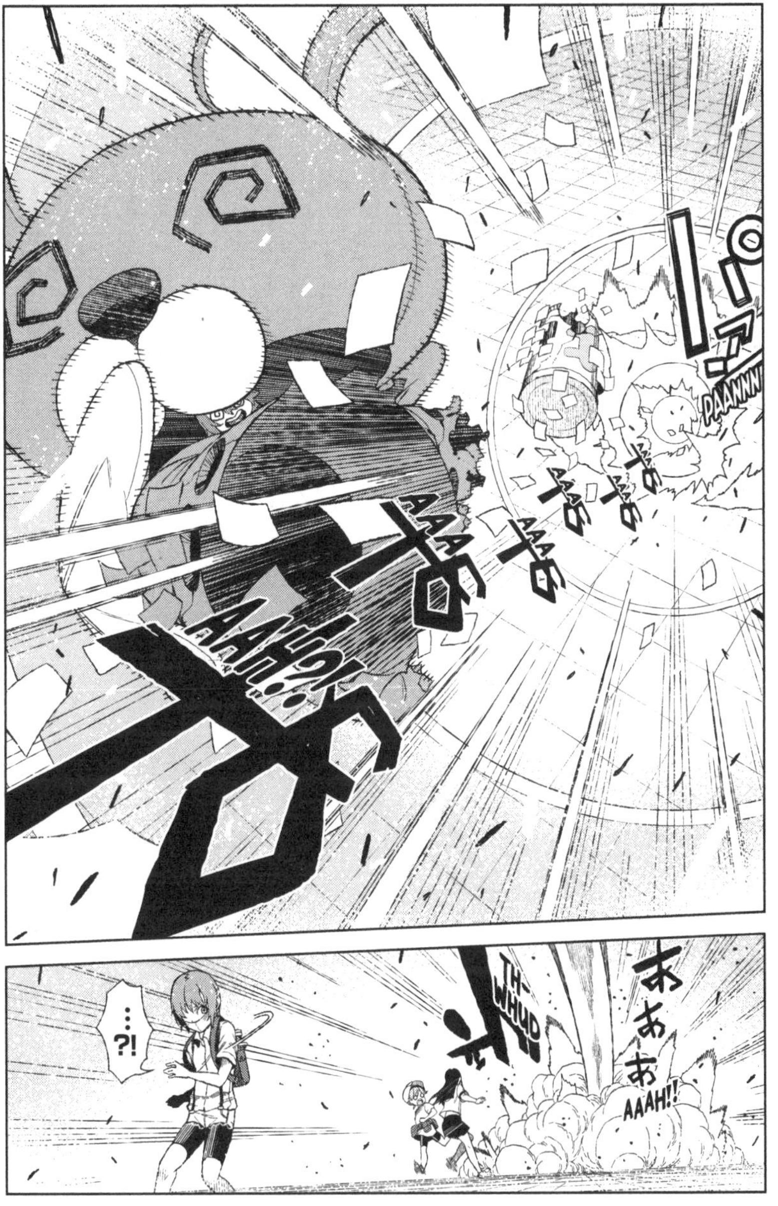
PAANNN
AAA
AAA
AAA
AAA
AAH?!
AAAH!!
TH-WHUD
...?!

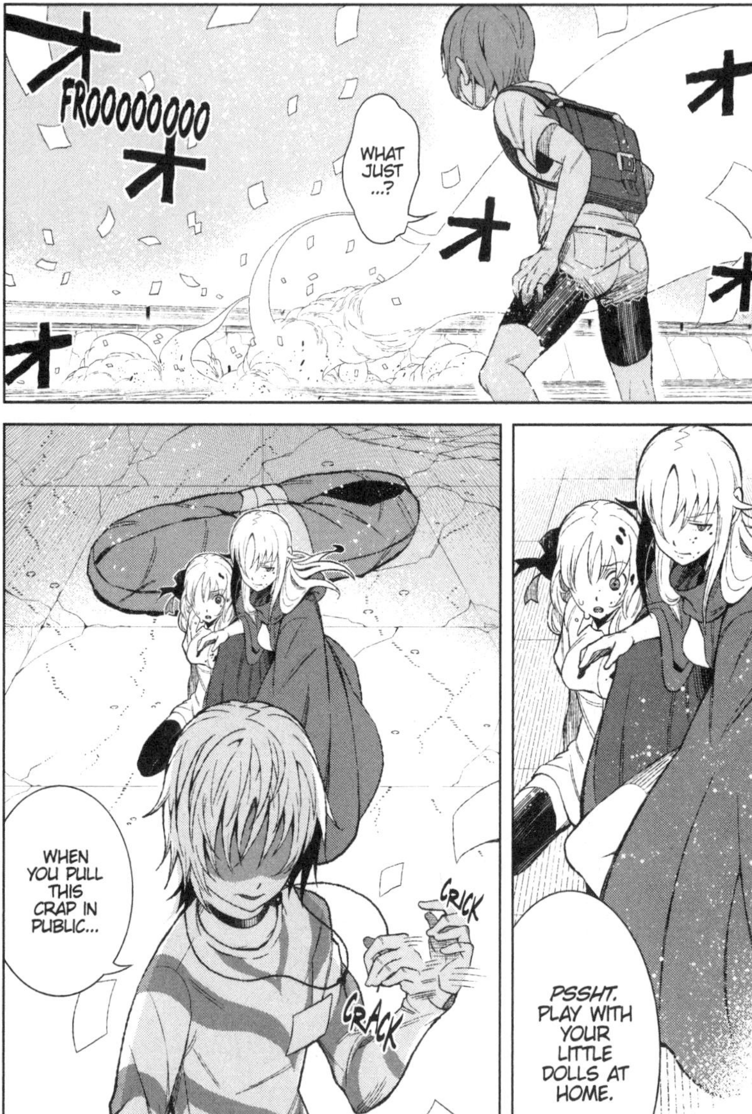
WHAT JUST ...?
FROOOOOOOOO
PSSHT. PLAY WITH YOUR LITTLE DOLLS AT HOME.
WHEN YOU PULL THIS CRAP IN PUBLIC...
CRICK
CRACK

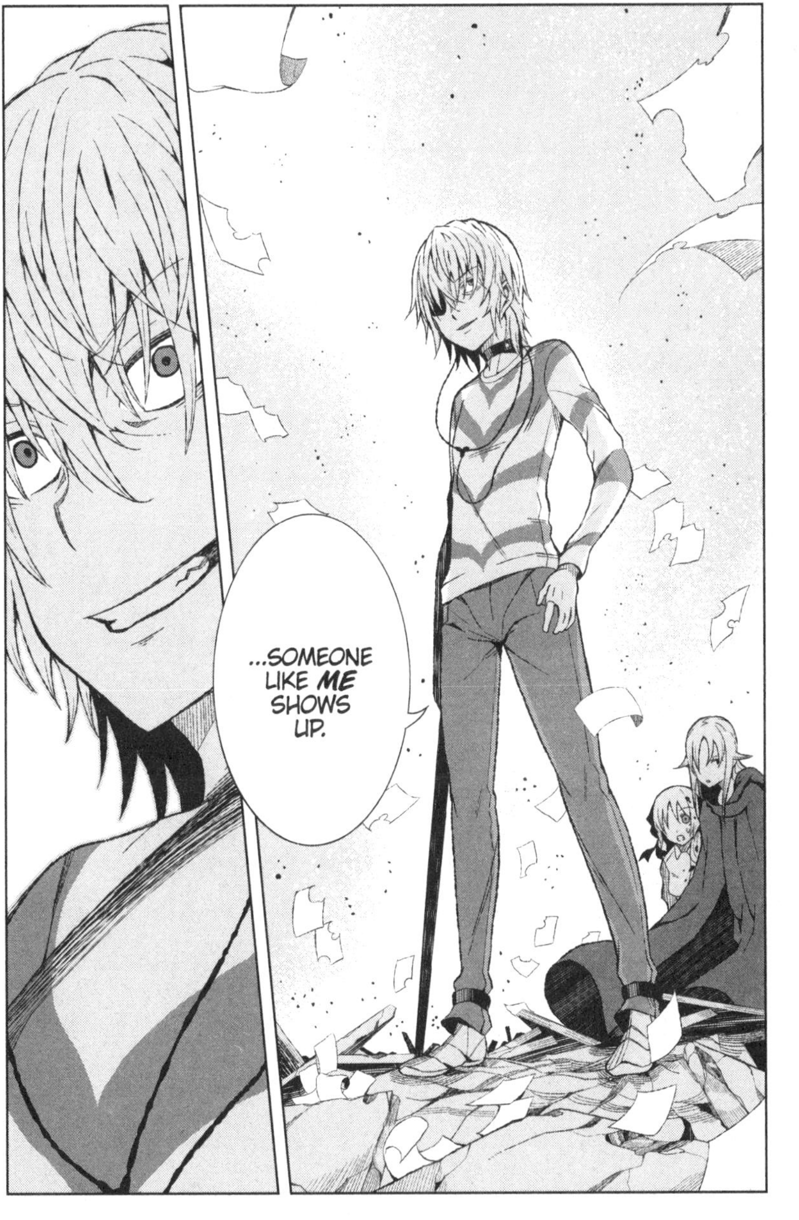
...SOMEONE LIKE ME SHOWS UP.

CHAPTER 16

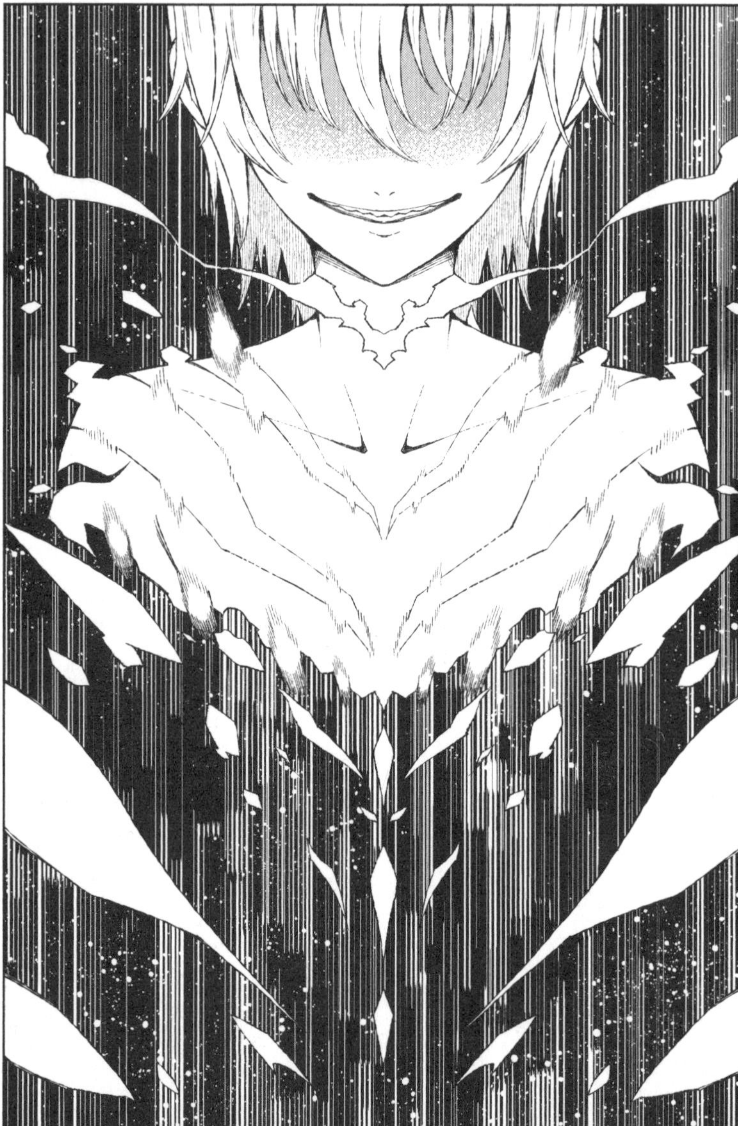

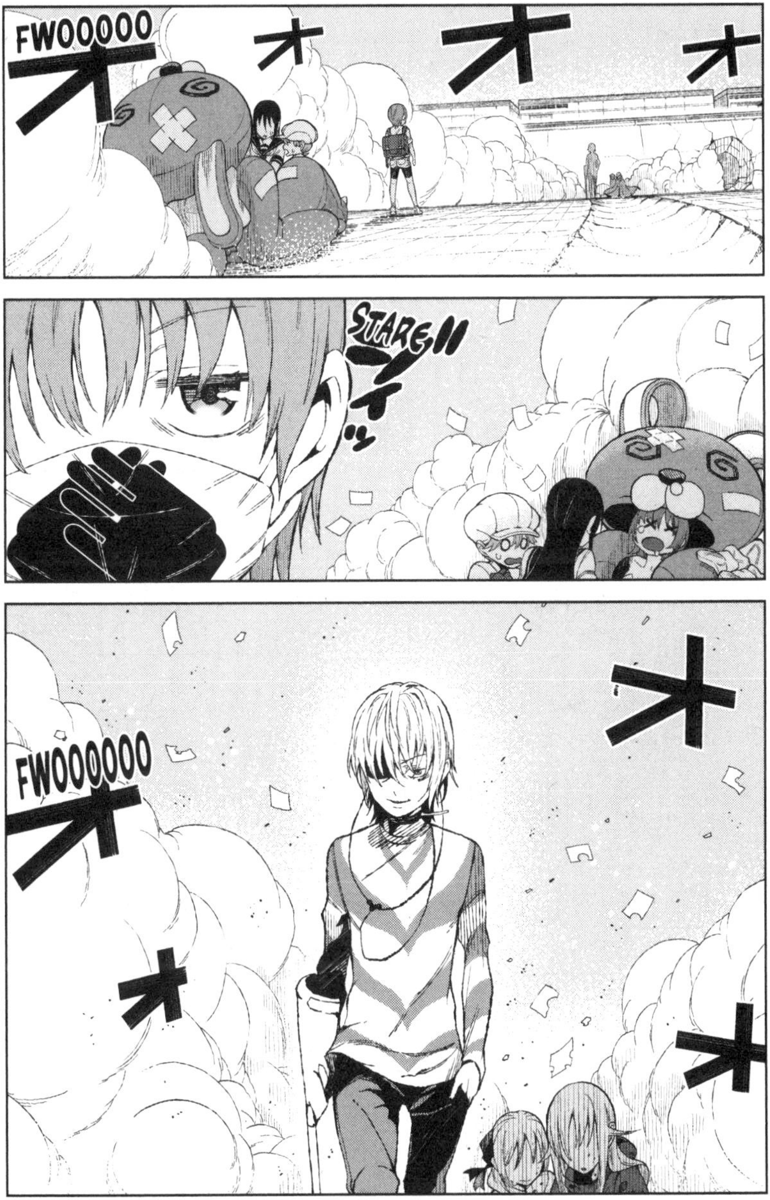
FWOOOOO
STARE!!
FWOOOOOO

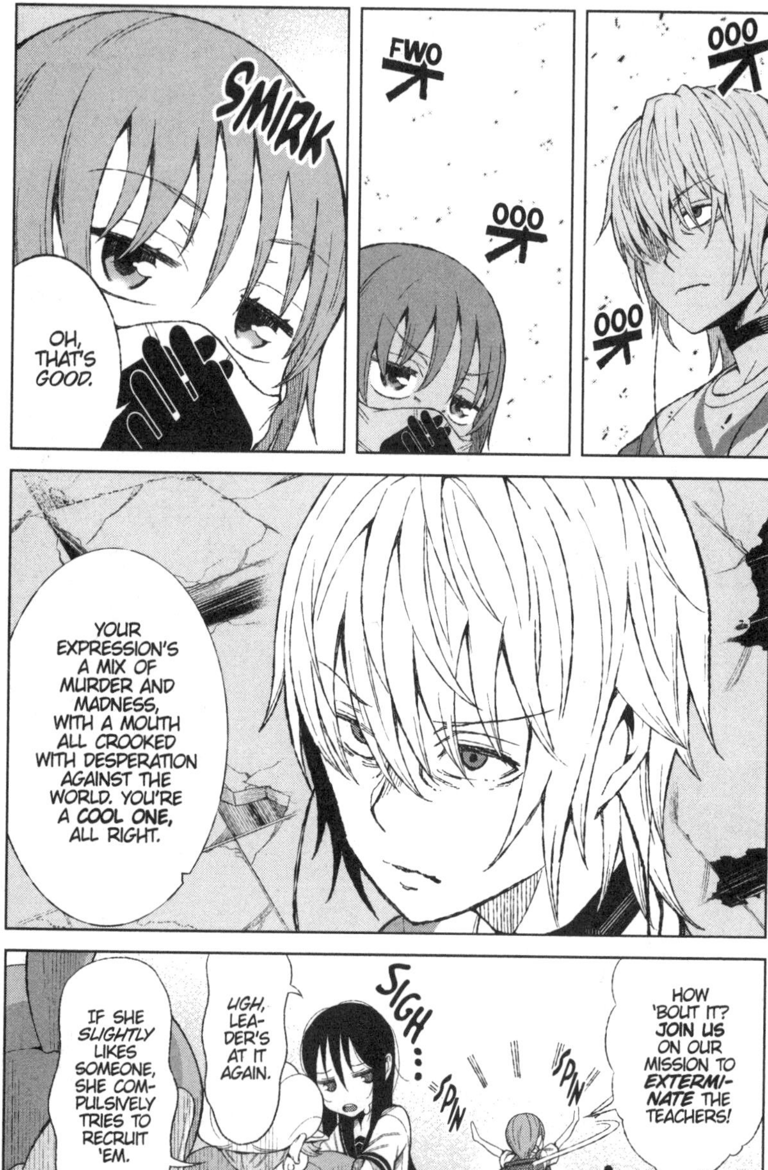
OOO
OOO
FWO
OOO
SMIRK
OH, THAT'S GOOD.
YOUR EXPRESSION'S A MIX OF MURDER AND MADNESS, WITH A MOUTH ALL CROOKED WITH DESPERATION AGAINST THE WORLD. YOU'RE A COOL ONE, ALL RIGHT.
HOW 'BOUT IT? JOIN US ON OUR MISSION TO EXTERMINATE THE TEACHERS!
SPIN
SPIN
SIGH...
UGH, LEADER'S AT IT AGAIN.
IF SHE SLIGHTLY LIKES SOMEONE, SHE COMPULSIVELY TRIES TO RECRUIT 'EM.

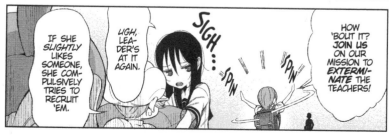

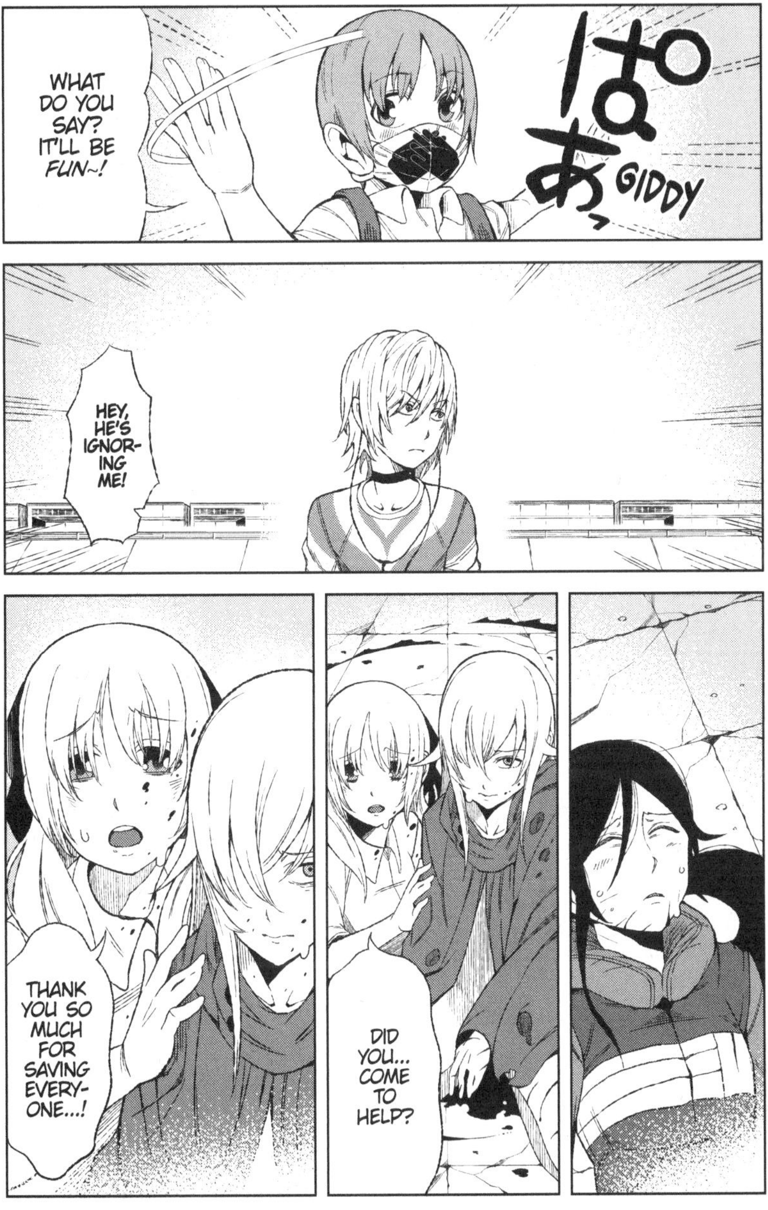
ぱあっ
GIDDY
WHAT DO YOU SAY? IT'LL BE *FUN*~!
HEY, HE'S IGNORING ME!
DID YOU... COME TO HELP?
THANK YOU SO MUCH FOR SAVING EVERYONE...!

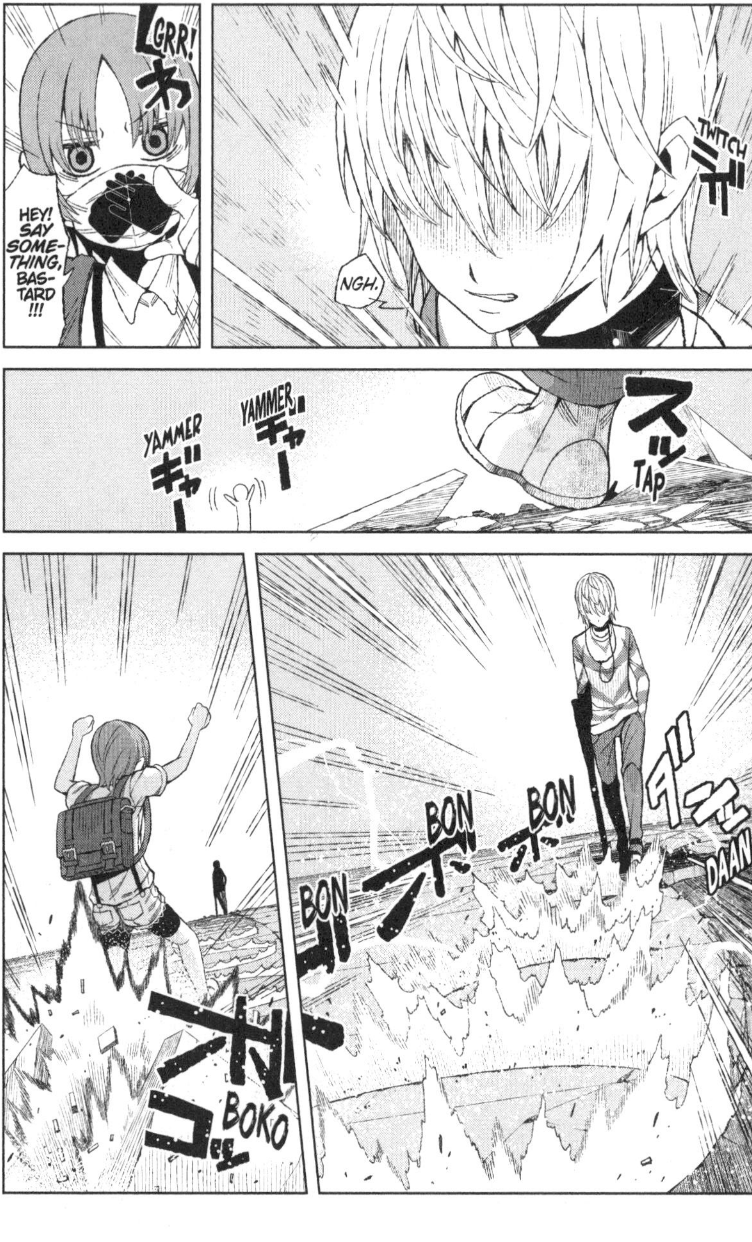
TWITCH
NGH.
GRR!
HEY! SAY SOMETHING, BASTARD!!!
TAP
YAMMER
YAMMER
DAAN
BON
BON
BON
BOKO

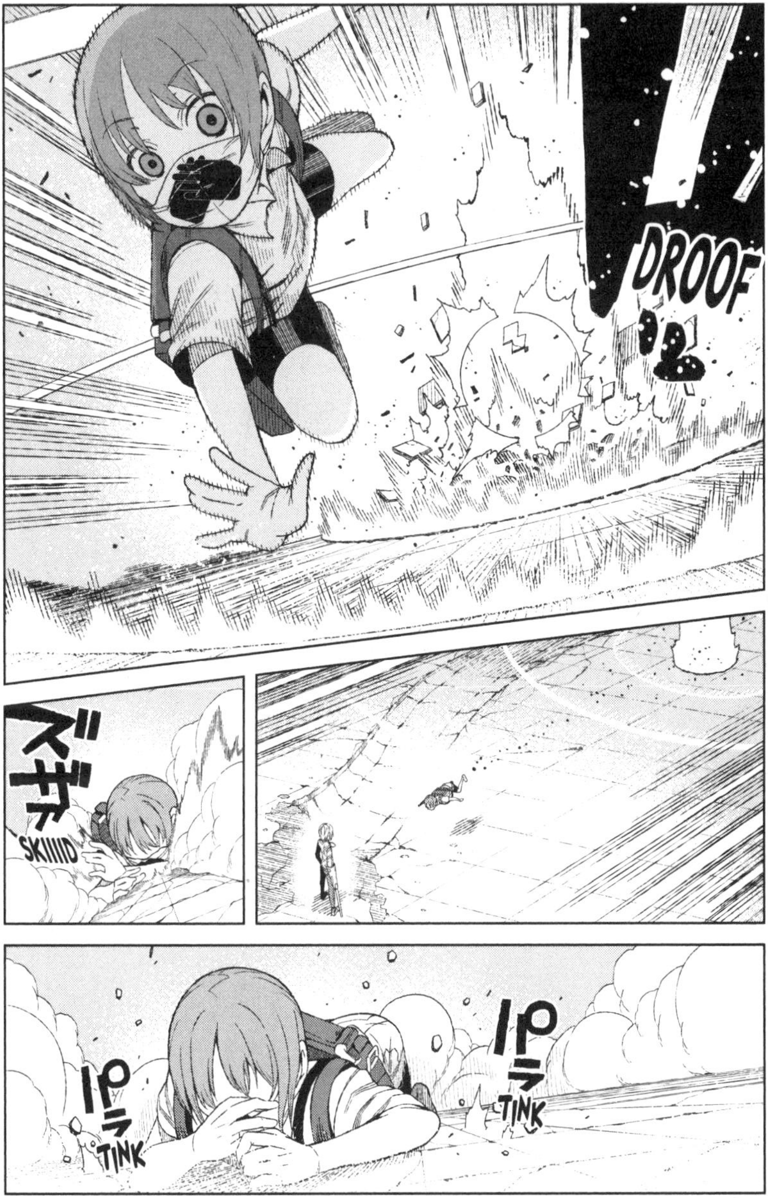
DROOF
ズザァ
SKIIIID
TINK
TINK

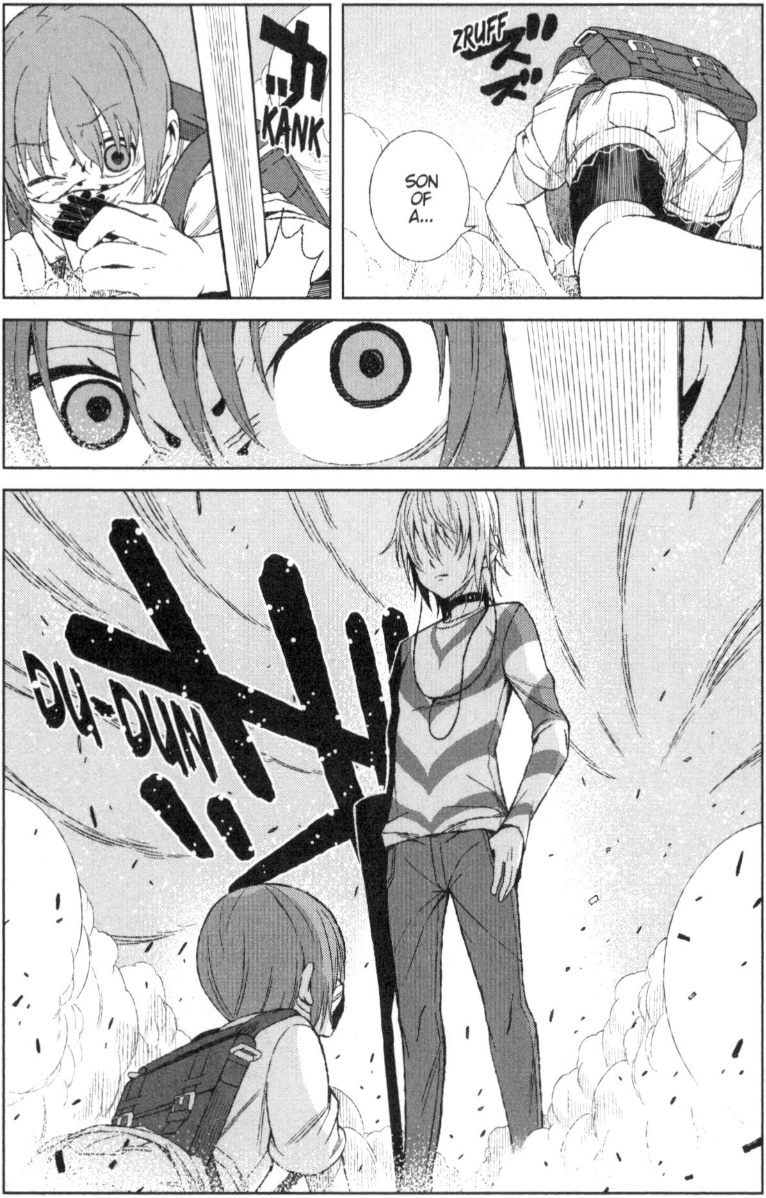
ZRUFF
ズズ
SON OF A...
カッ
KANK
DU-DUN

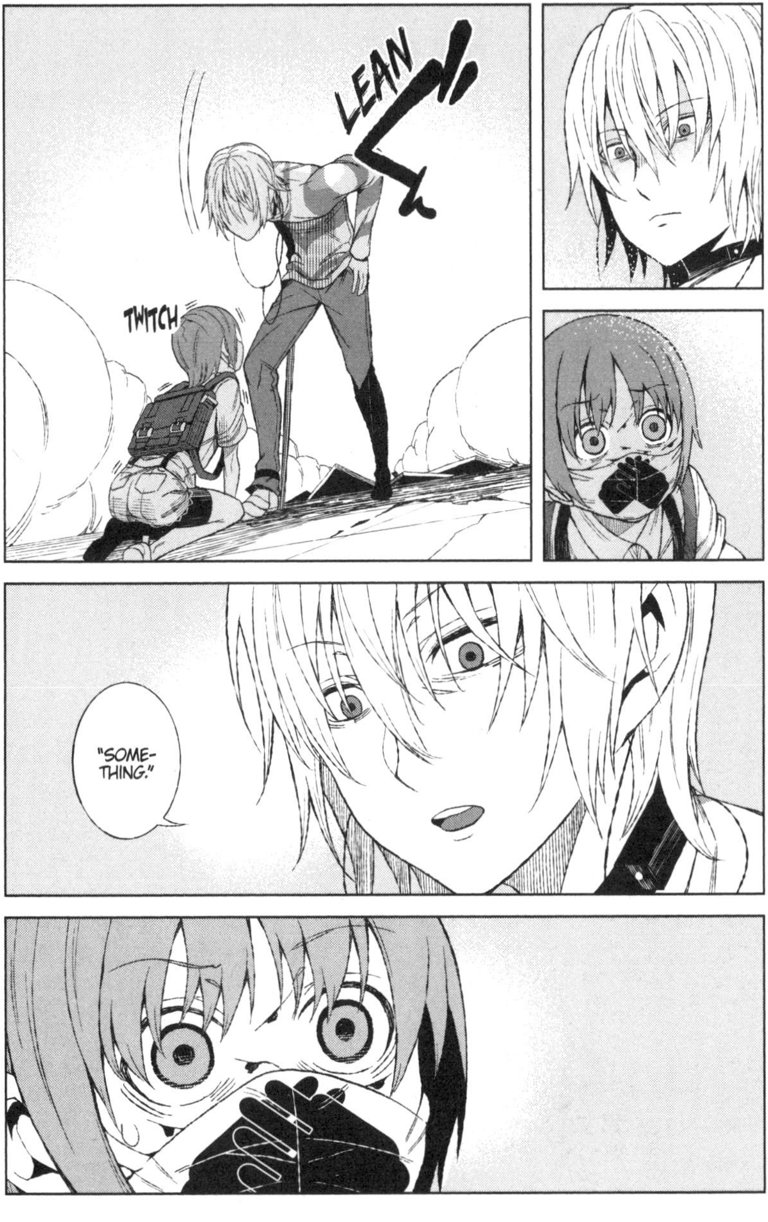
LEAN
TWITCH
"SOME-THING."

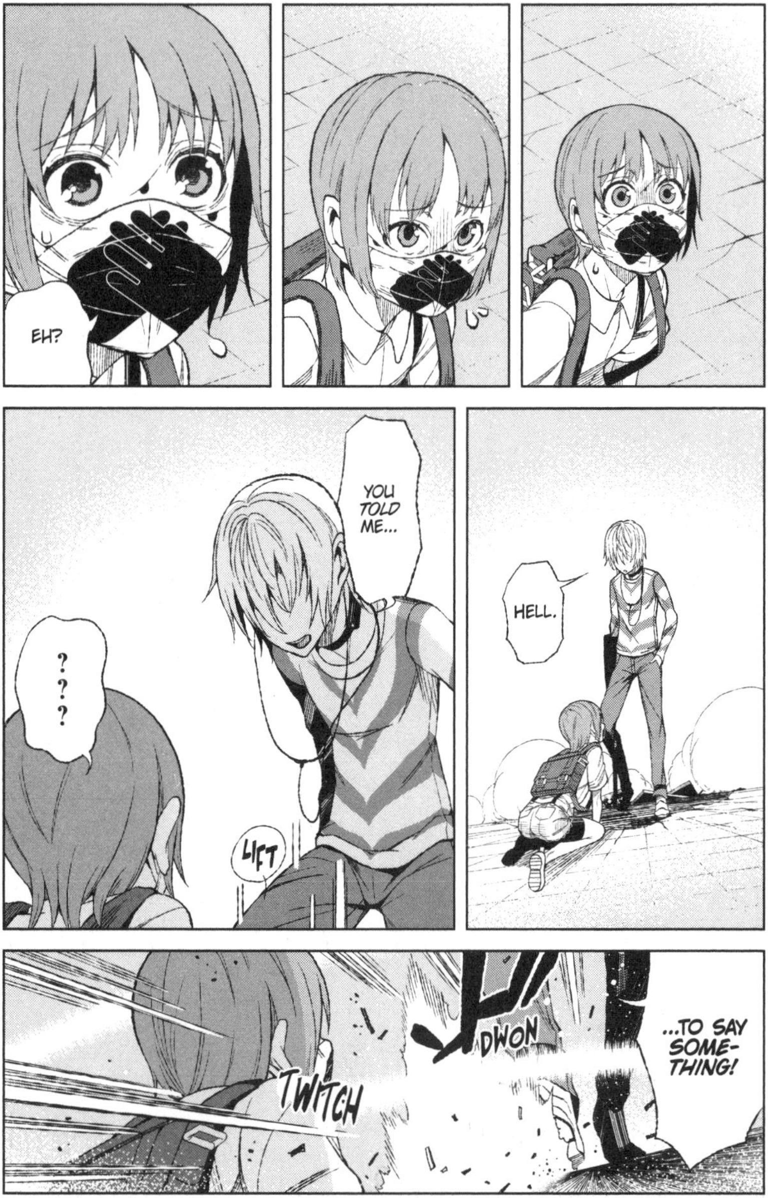
EH?
HELL.
YOU TOLD ME...
???
LIFT
...TO SAY SOME-THING!
DWON
TWITCH

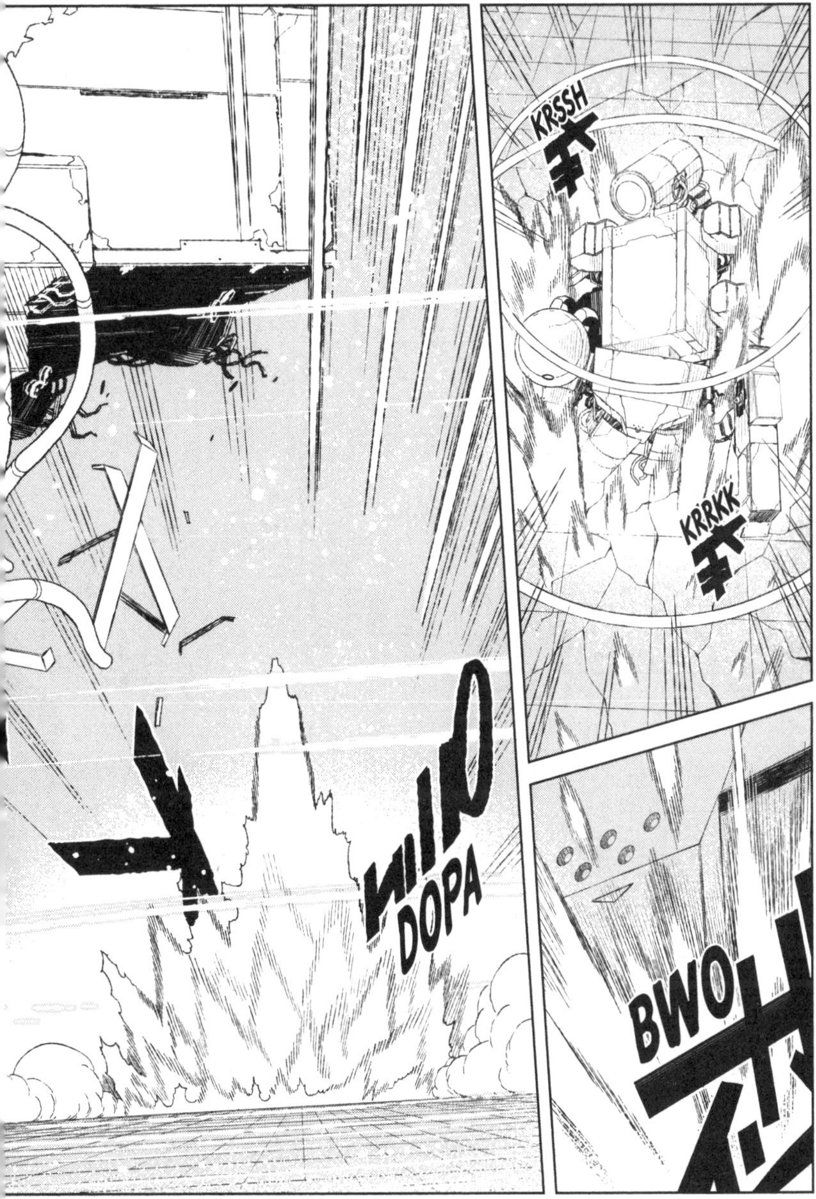
KRSSH
KRRKK
BWO
DOPA

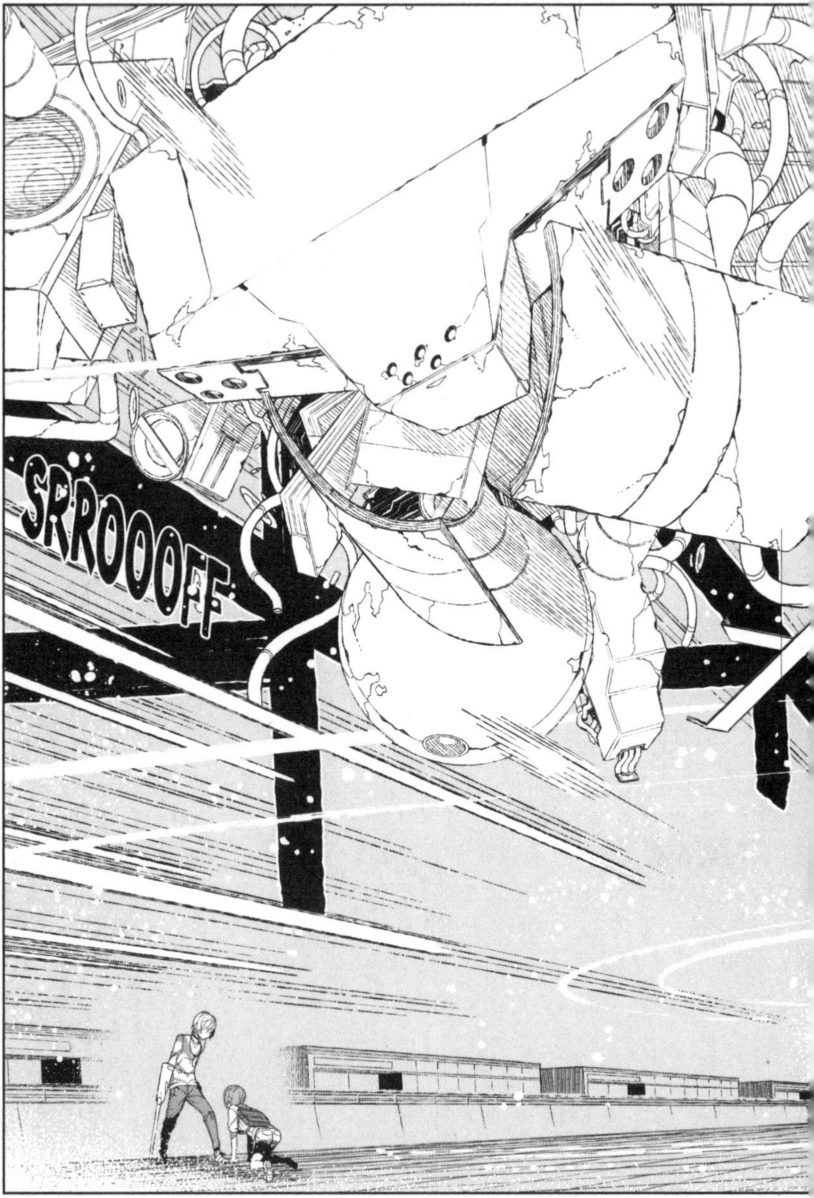
SRROOOFF

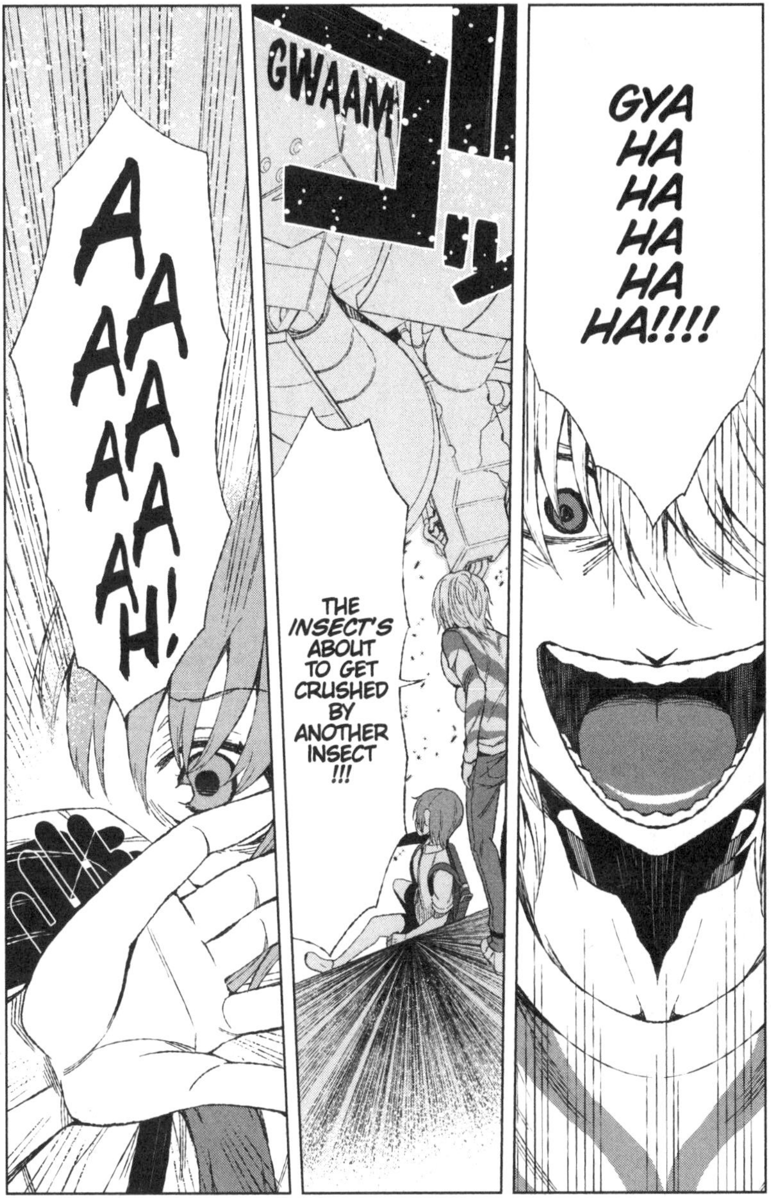
GYA HA HA HA HA HA!!!!
GWAAM
THE INSECT'S ABOUT TO GET CRUSHED BY ANOTHER INSECT!!!
AAAAAAAAH!

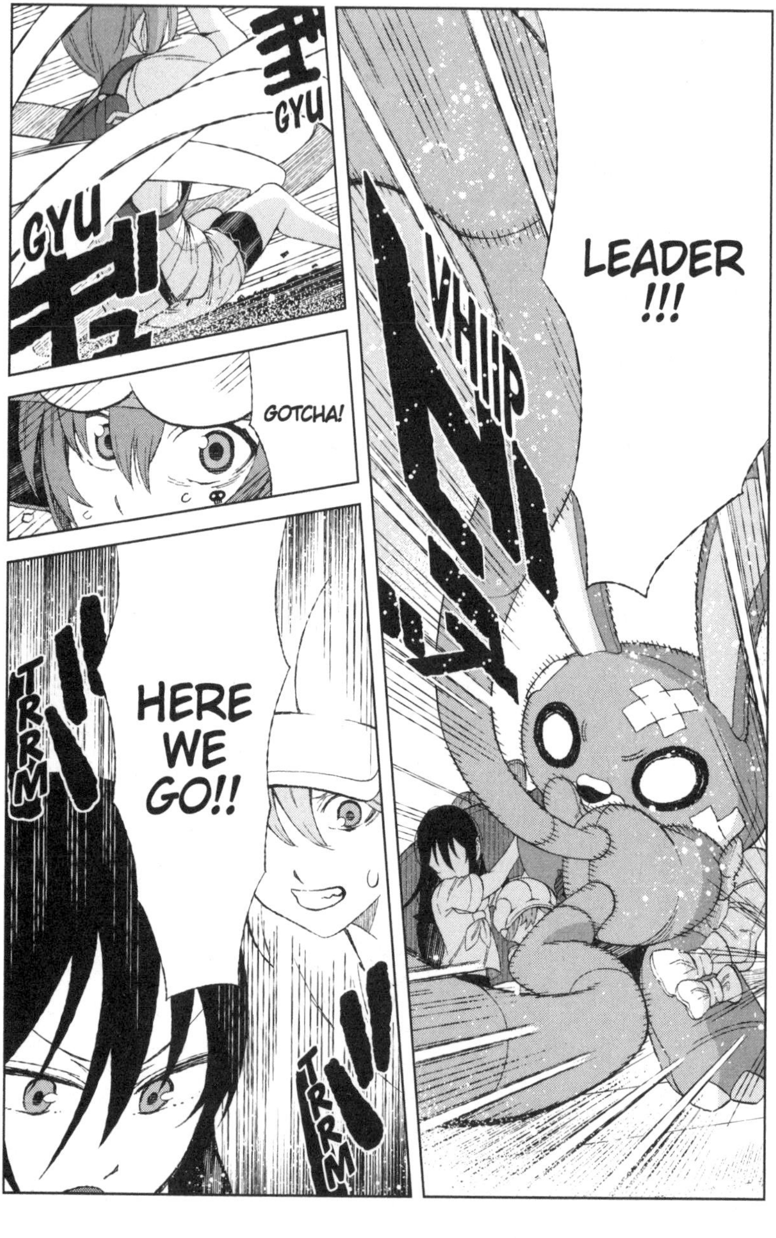
LEADER !!!
WHIP
GYU
GYU
GOTCHA!
HERE WE GO!!
TRRM
TRRM

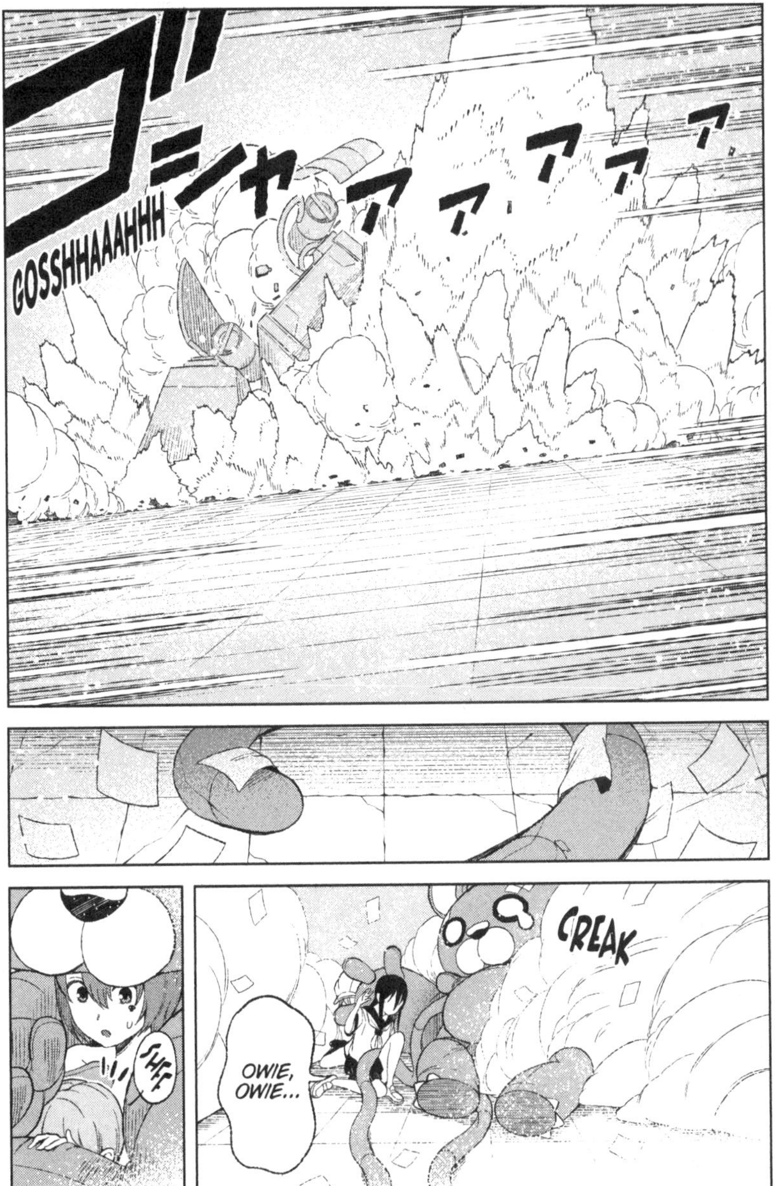
ゴシャアアアアア
GOSSHHAAAHHH
CREAK
OWIE, OWIE...
SHFF

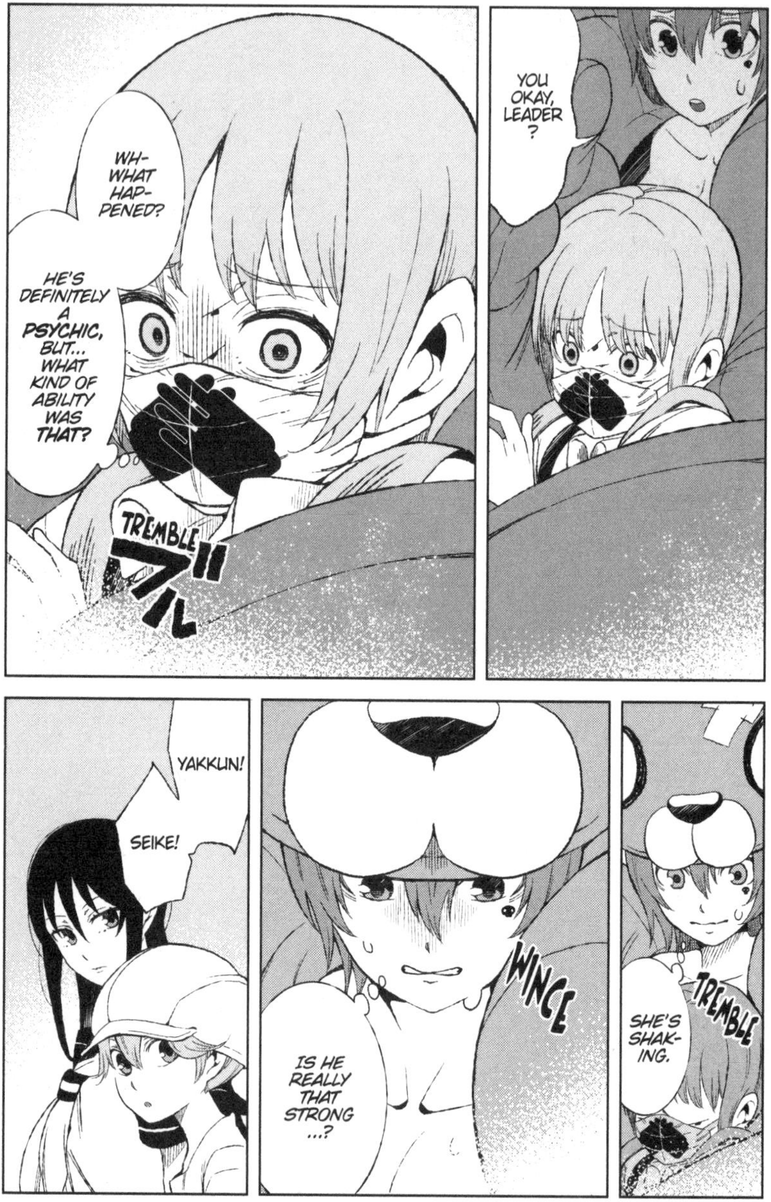
YOU OKAY, LEADER?
WH-WHAT HAPPENED?
HE'S DEFINITELY A PSYCHIC, BUT... WHAT KIND OF ABILITY WAS THAT?
TREMBLE
ブル
TREMBLE
SHE'S SHAKING.
WINCE
IS HE REALLY THAT STRONG ...?
YAKKUN!
SEIKE!

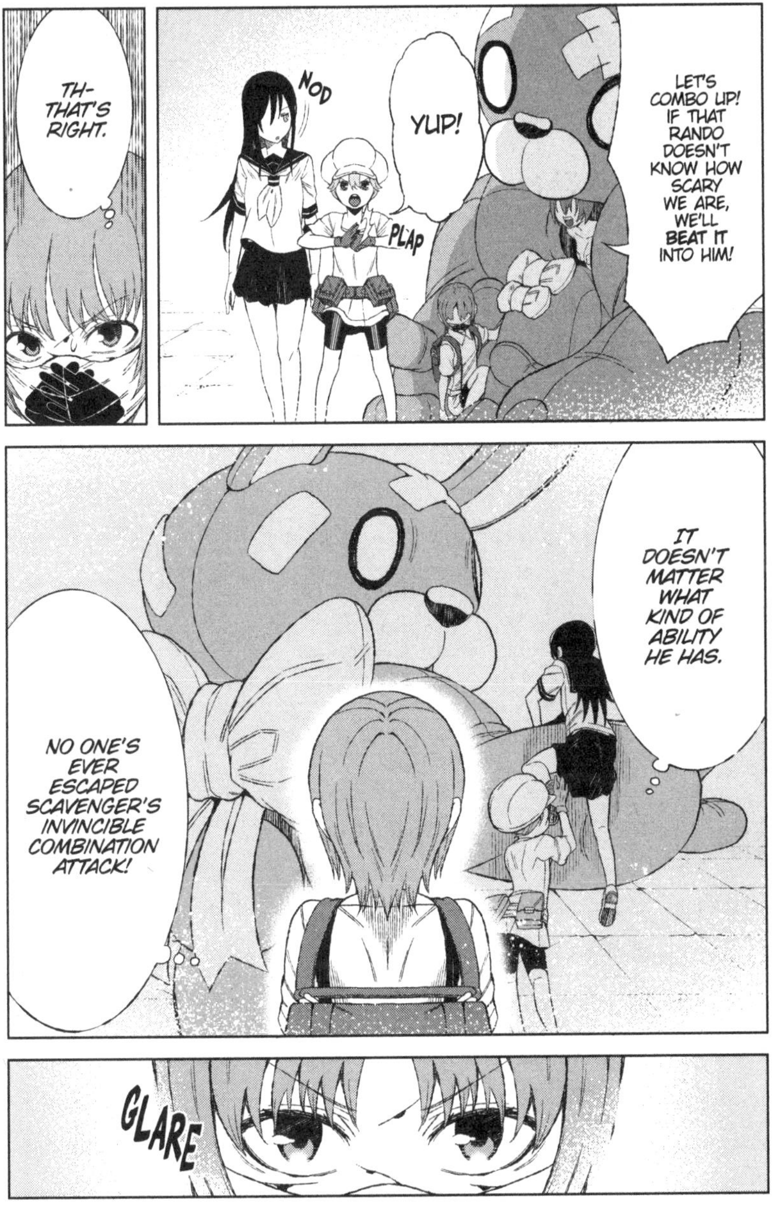
LET'S COMBO UP! IF THAT RANDO DOESN'T KNOW HOW SCARY WE ARE, WE'LL BEAT IT INTO HIM!
YUP!
NOD
PLAP
TH-THAT'S RIGHT.
IT DOESN'T MATTER WHAT KIND OF ABILITY HE HAS.
NO ONE'S EVER ESCAPED SCAVENGER'S INVINCIBLE COMBINATION ATTACK!
GLARE

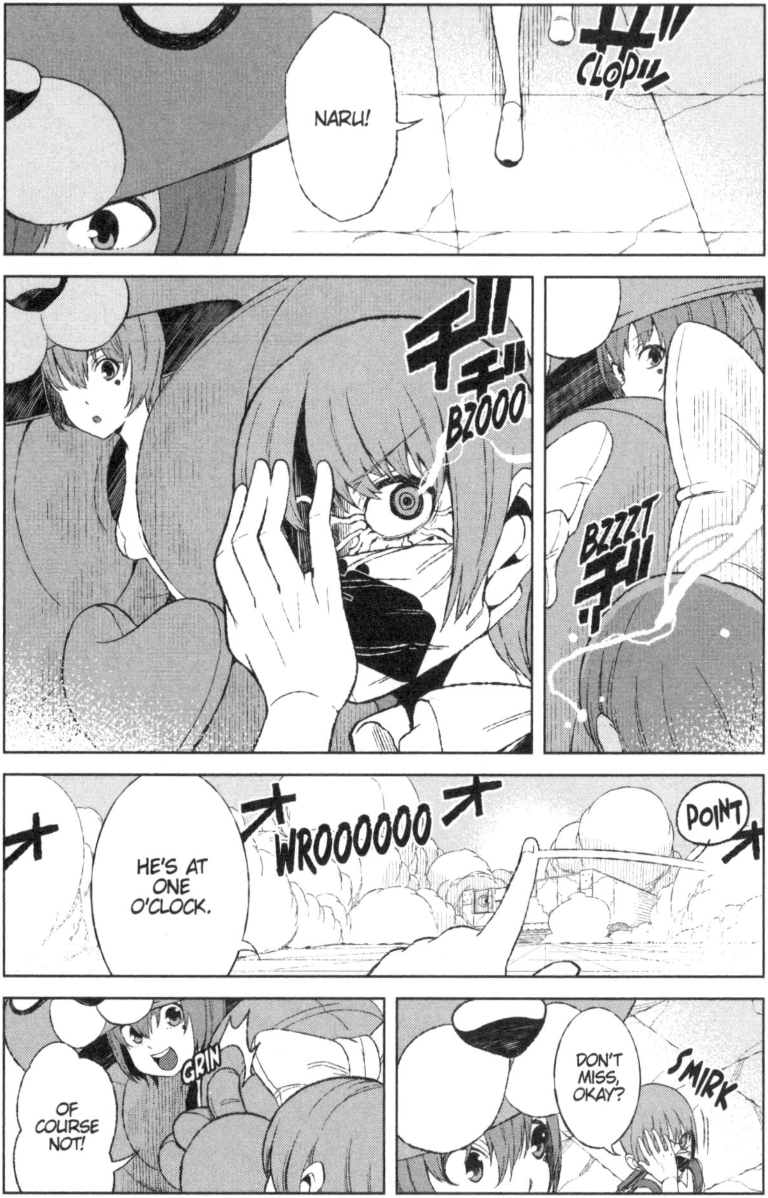
CLOP
NARU!
BZZZT
BZOOO
POINT
WROOOOOO
HE'S AT ONE O'CLOCK.
SMIRK
DON'T MISS, OKAY?
GRIN
OF COURSE NOT!

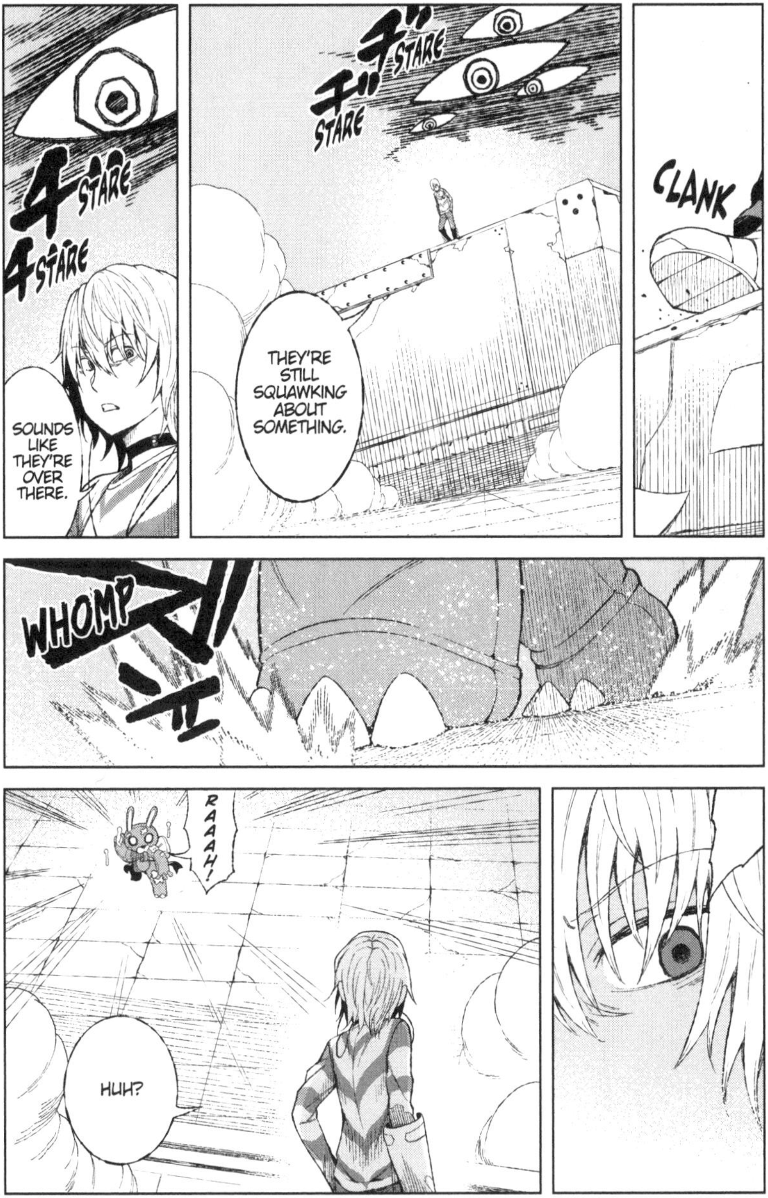
CLANK
STARE
STARE
THEY'RE STILL SQUAWKING ABOUT SOMETHING.
STARE
STARE
SOUNDS LIKE THEY'RE OVER THERE.
WHOMP
RAAAH!
HUH?

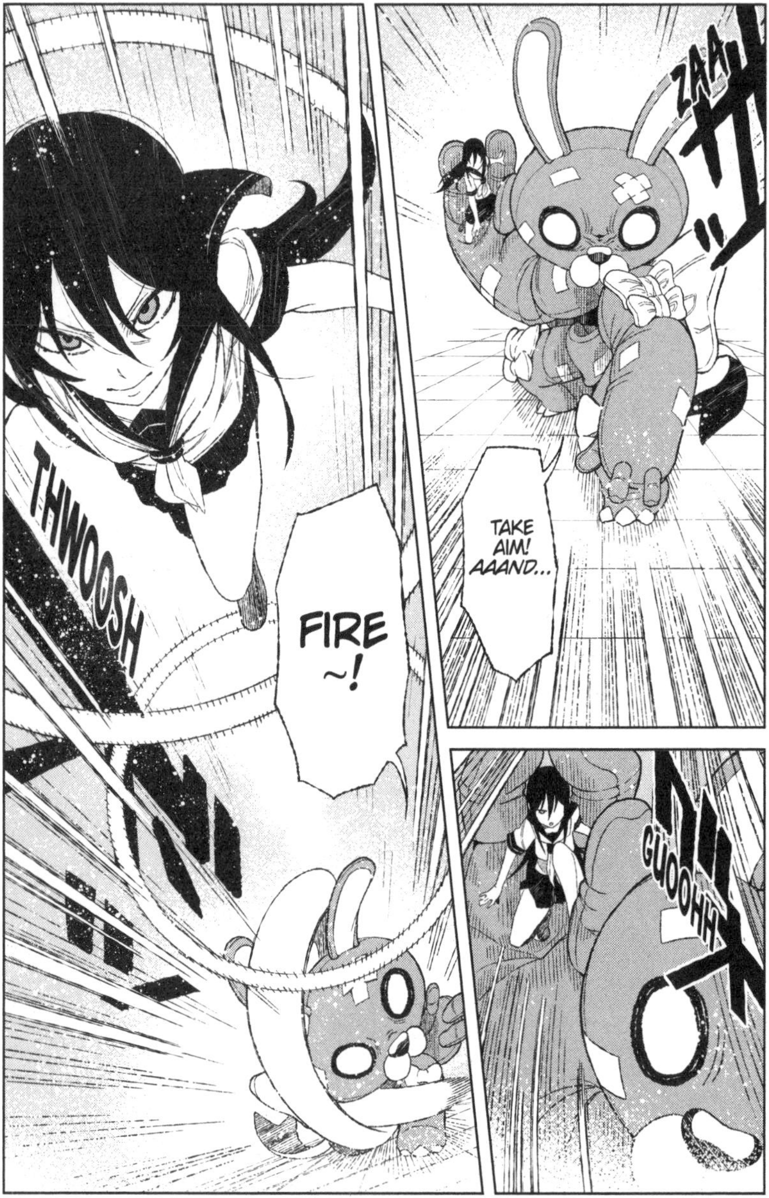
ZAA
TAKE AIM! AAAND...
GUOOHH
THWOOSH
FIRE ~!

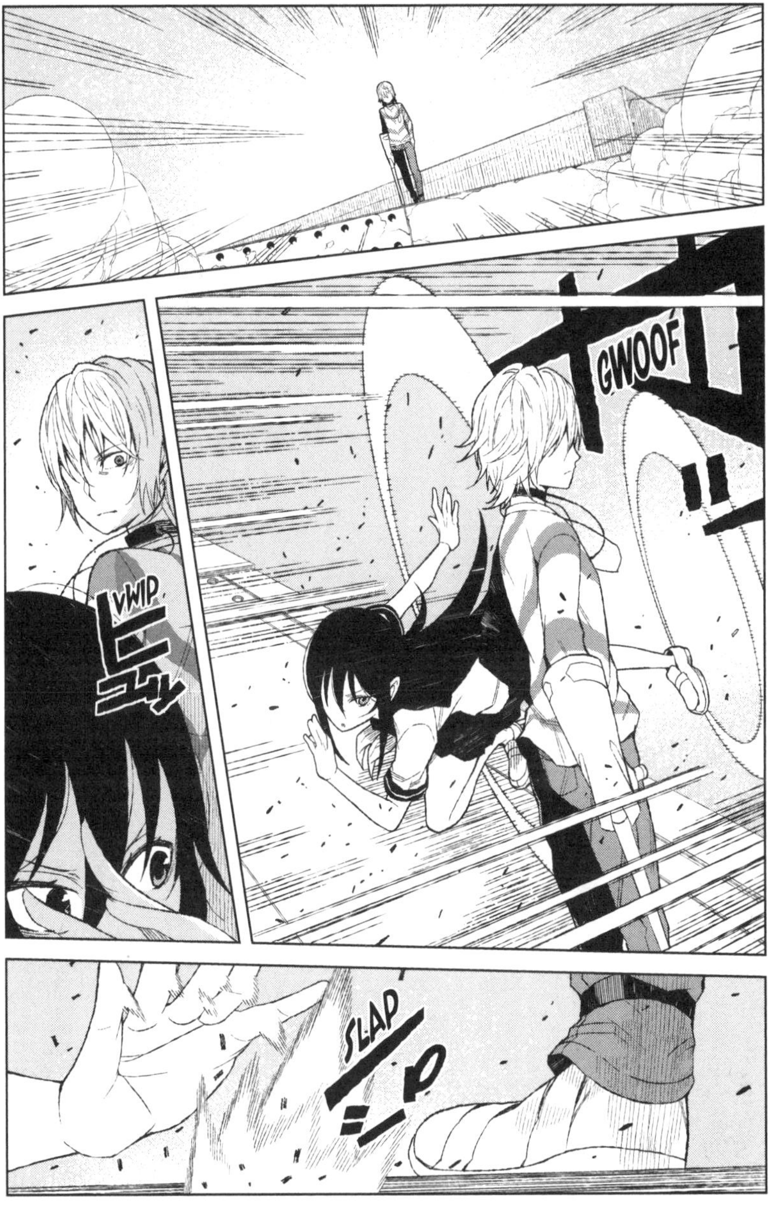
GWOOF
VWIP
SLAP

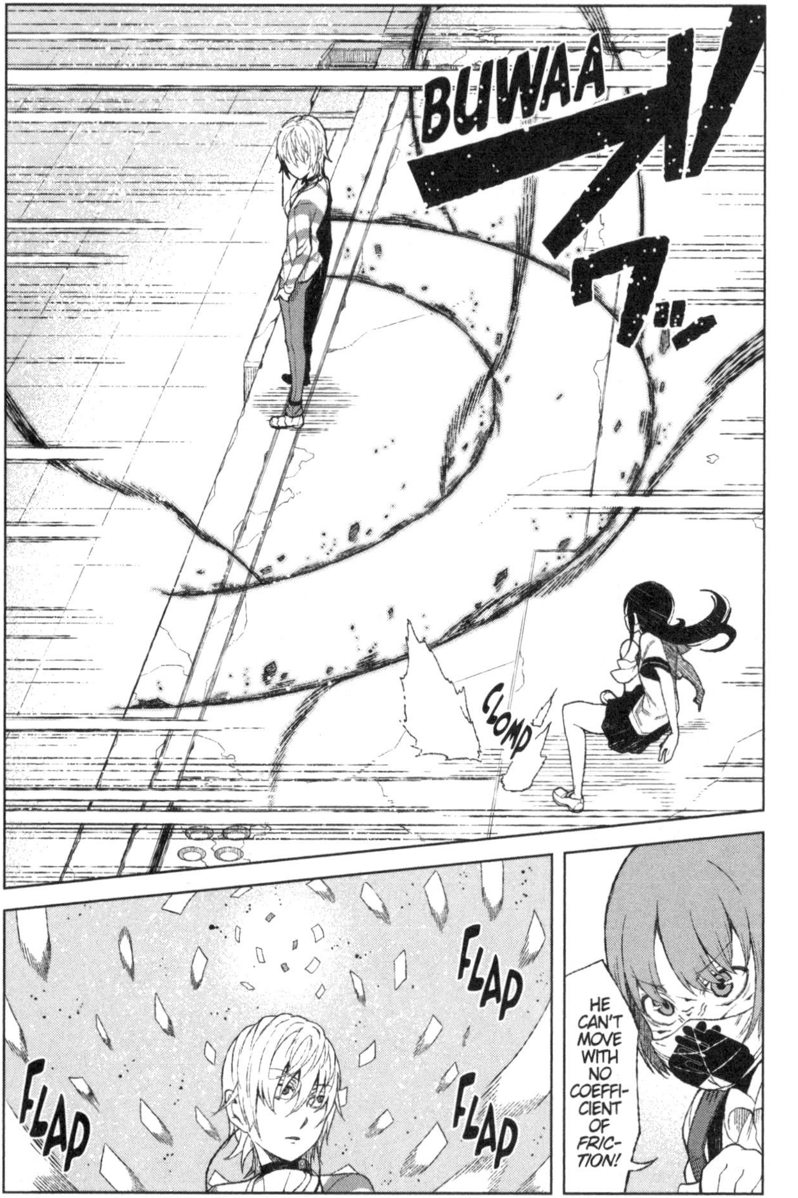
BUWAA
CLOMP
HE CAN'T MOVE WITH NO COEFFICIENT OF FRICTION!
FLAP
FLAP
FLAP

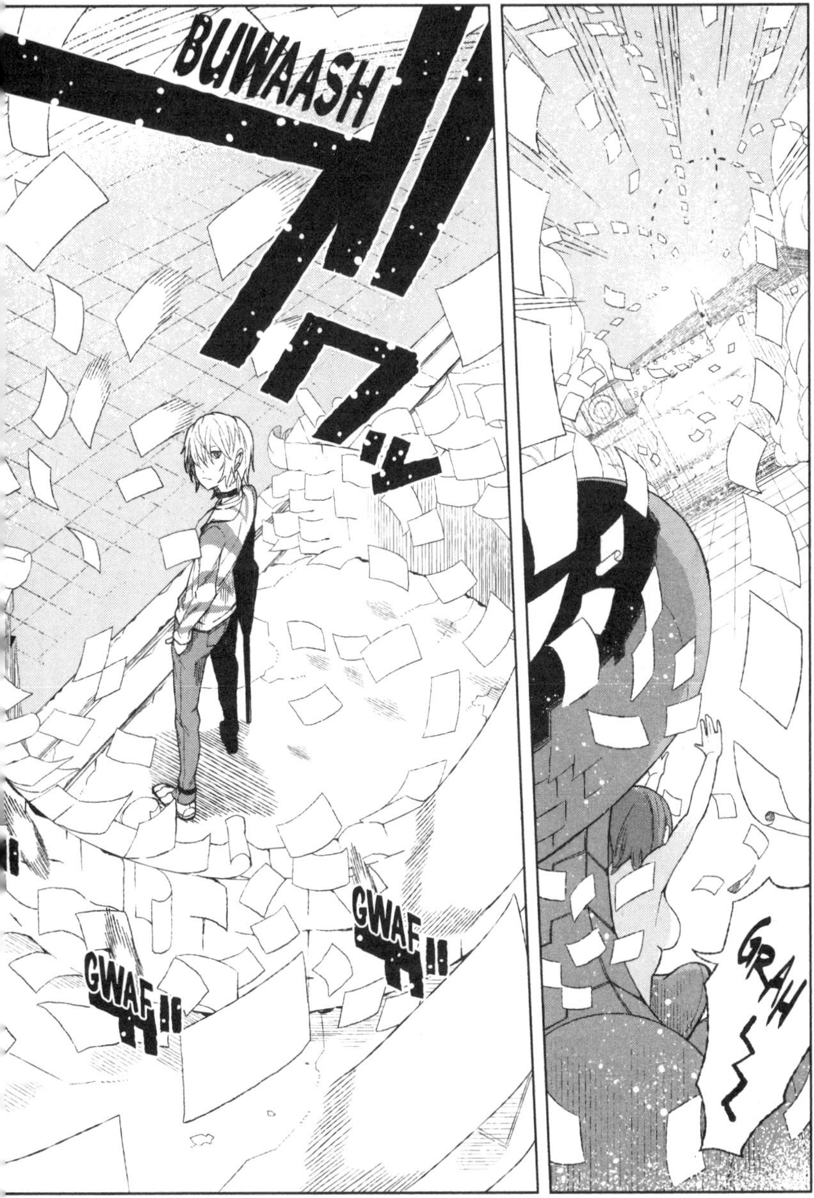
GRAH
BUWAASH
GWAF!!
GWAF!!

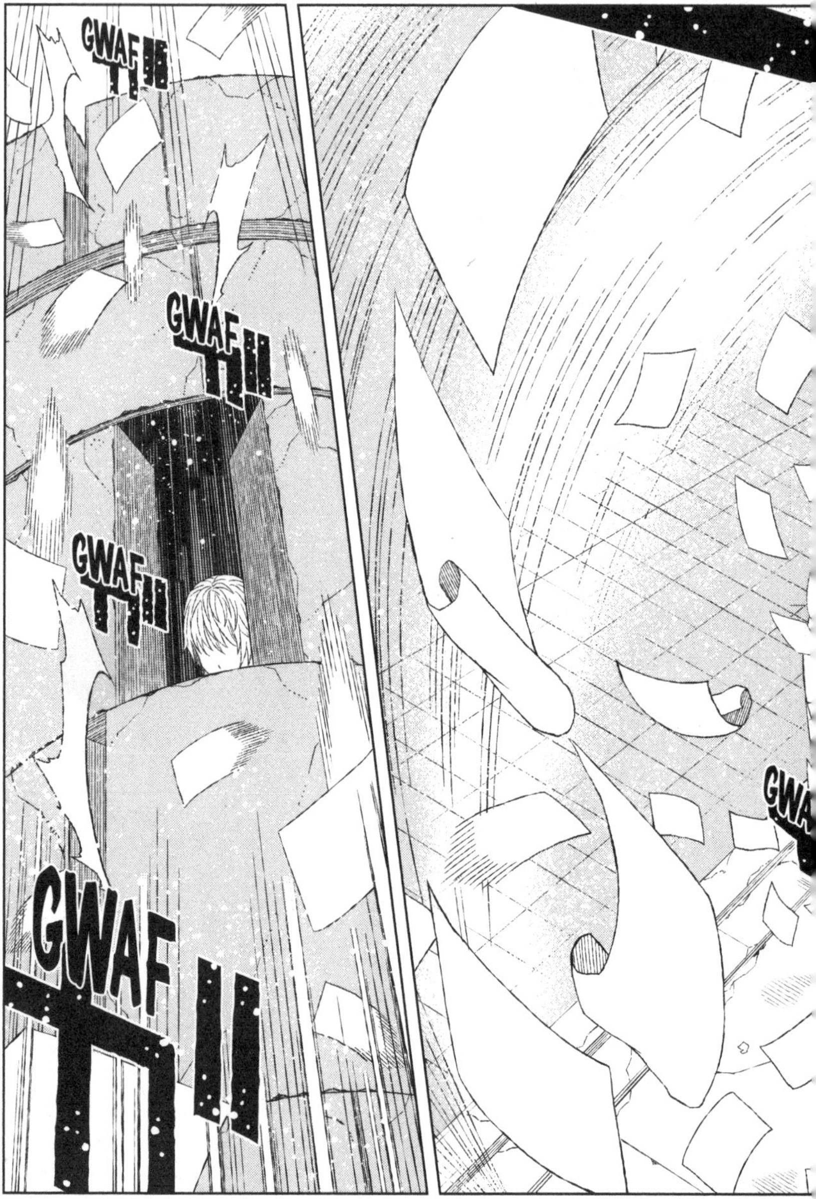
GWA
GWAF
GWAF
GWAF
GWAF

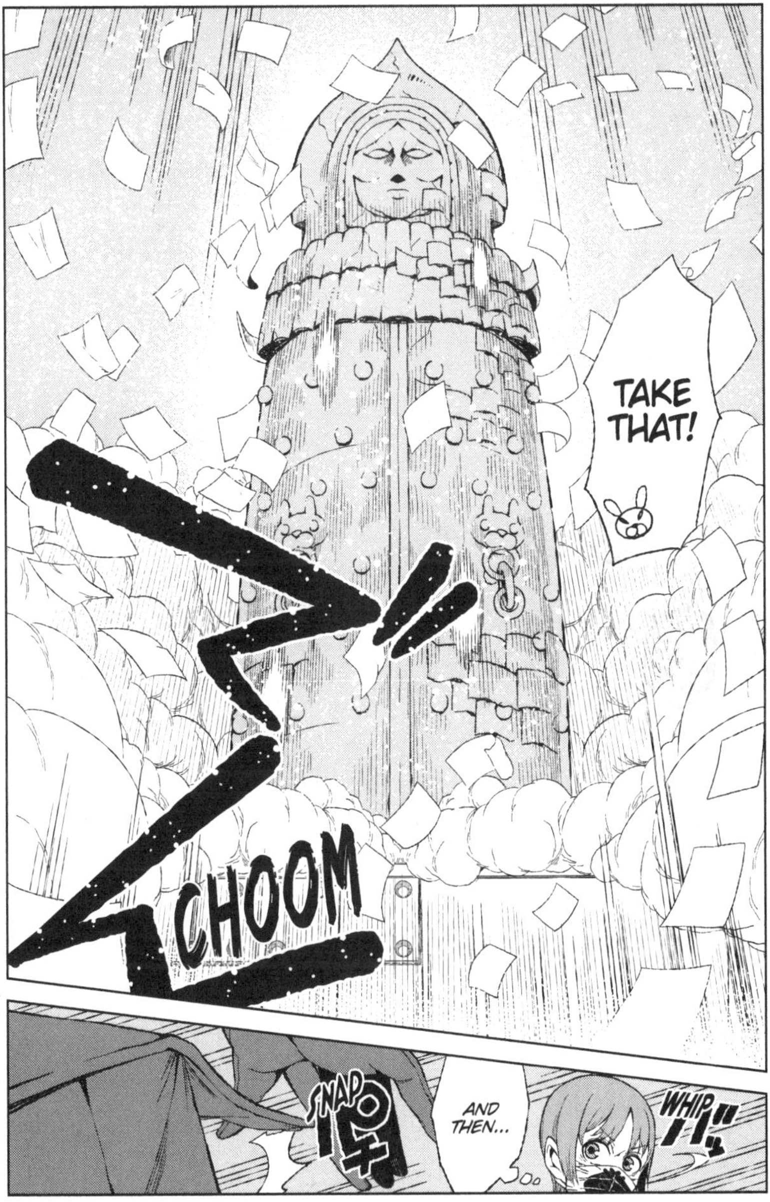
TAKE THAT!
CHOOM
WHIP
AND THEN...
SNAP

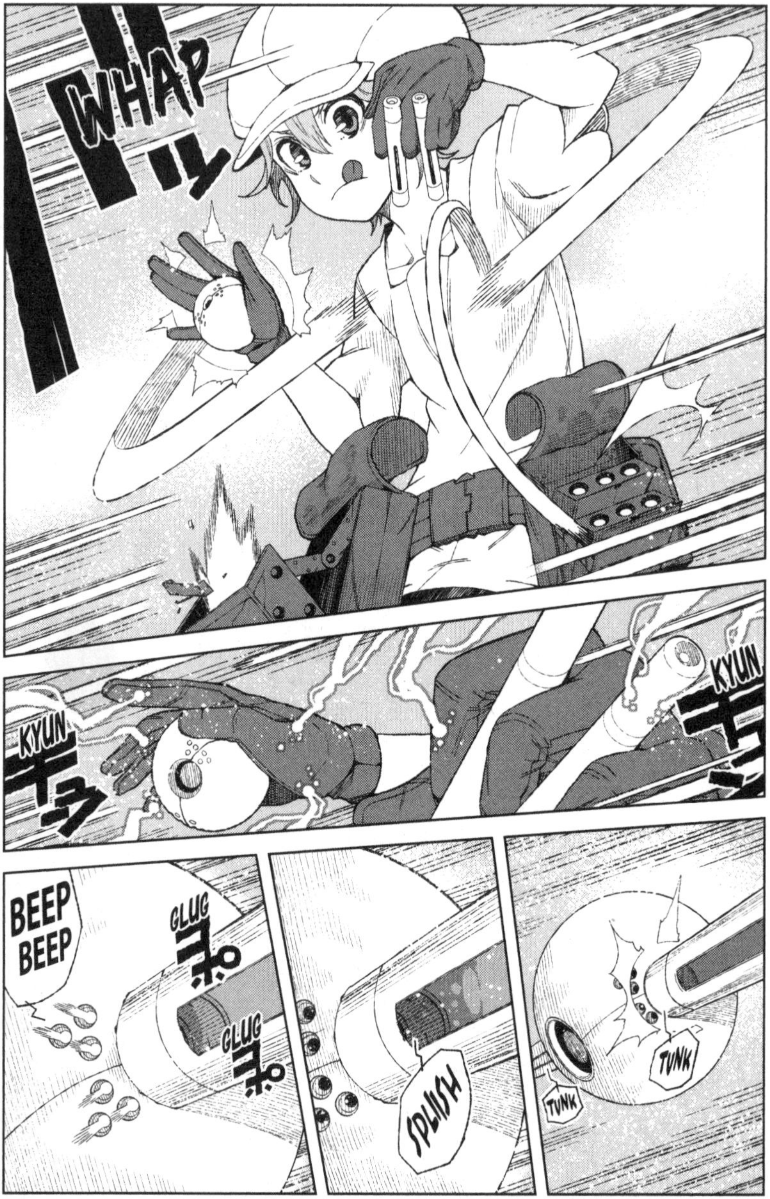
WHAP
KYUN
KYUN
TUNK
TUNK
SPLISH
BEEP BEEP
GLUG
GLUG

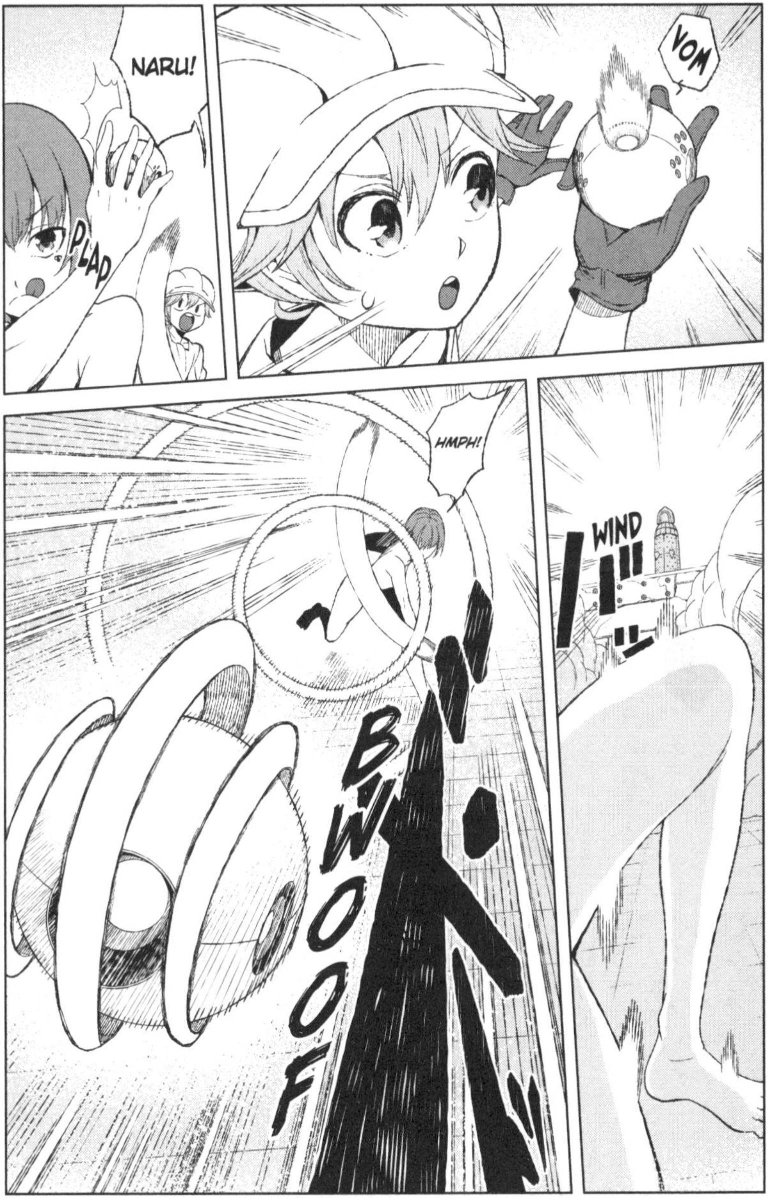
VOM
NARU!
PLAP
WIND
HMPH!
BWOOOF

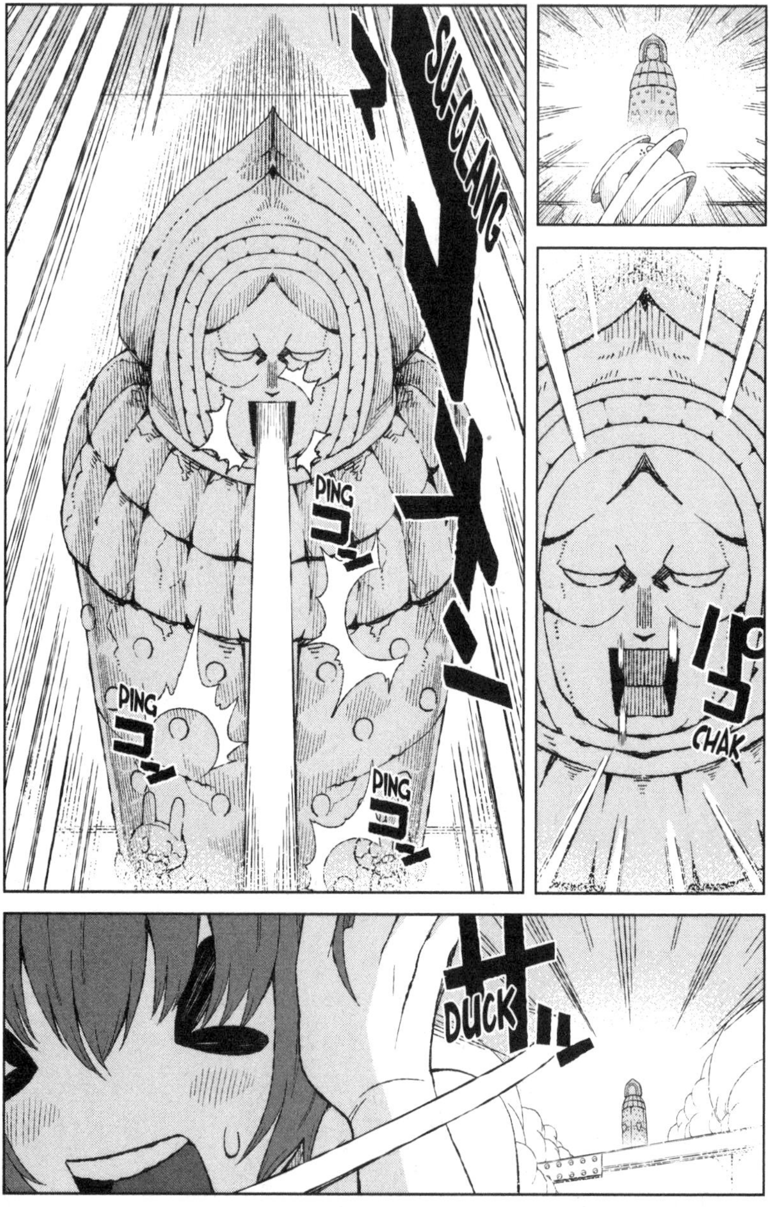
CHAK
SU-CLANG
PING
PING
PING
DUCK

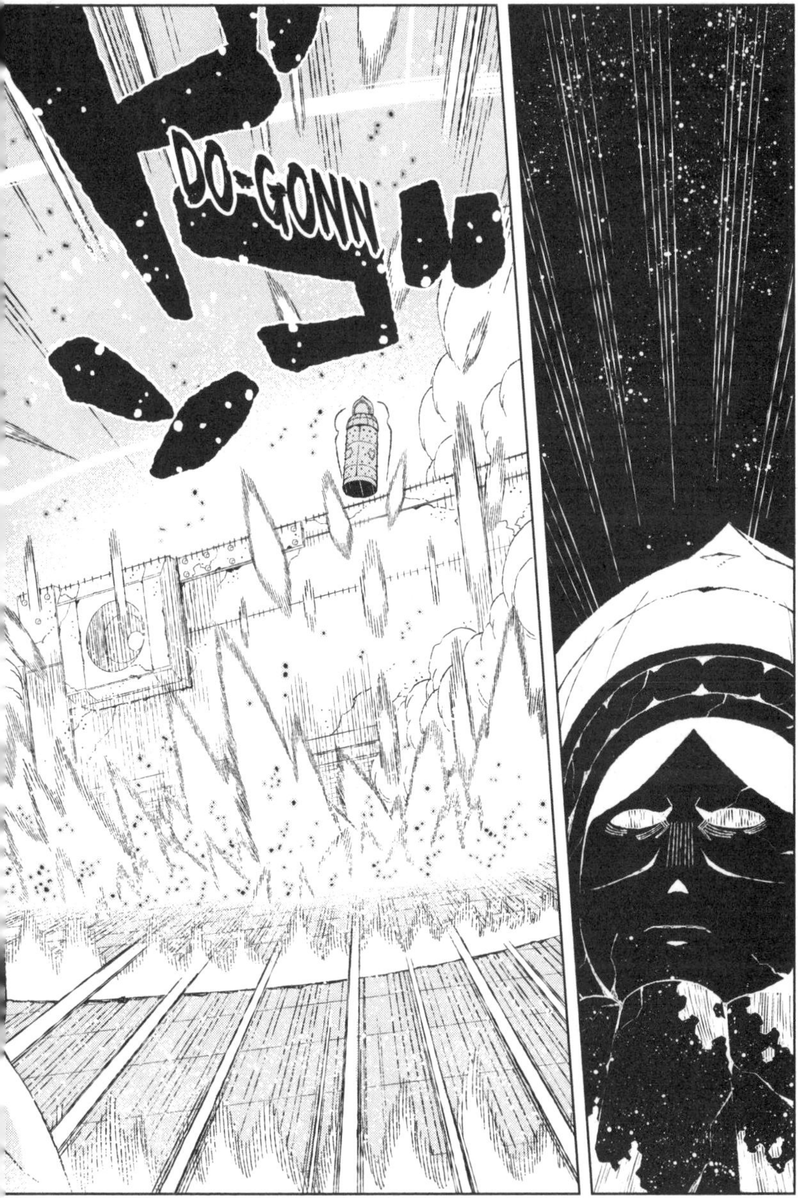
DO-GONN

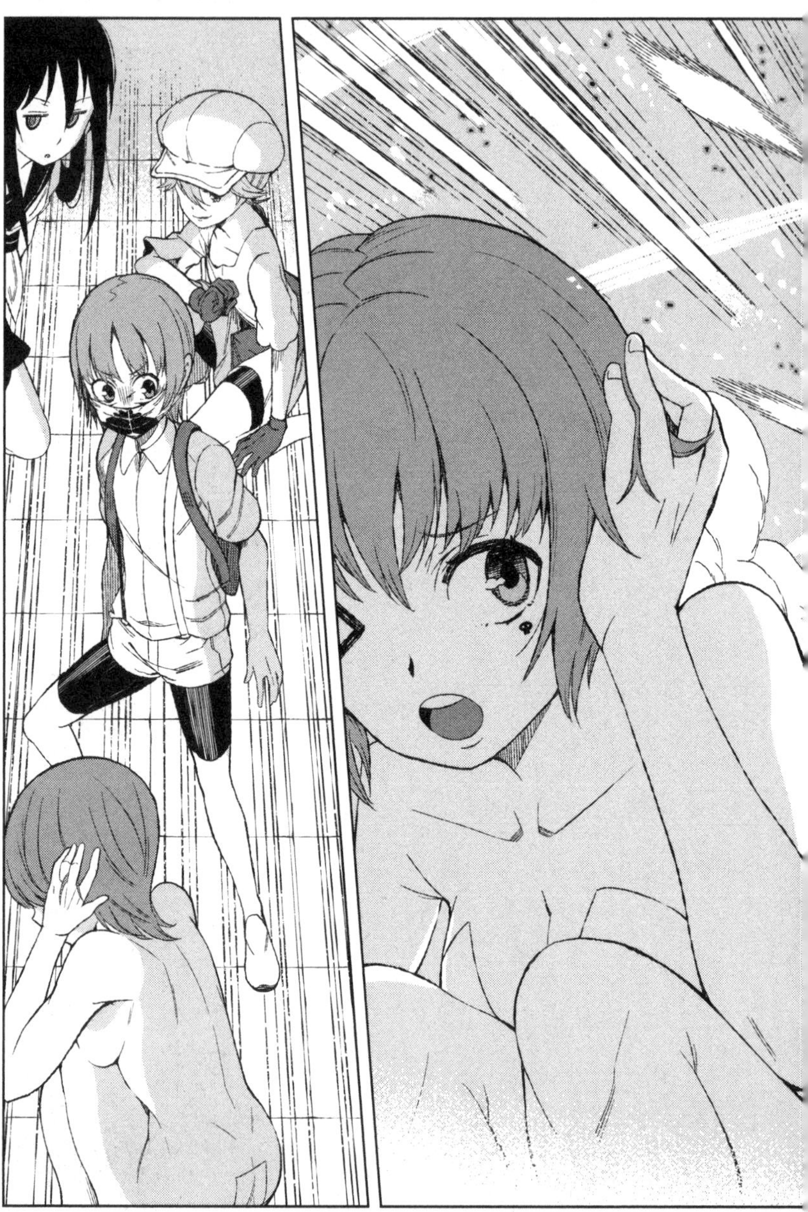

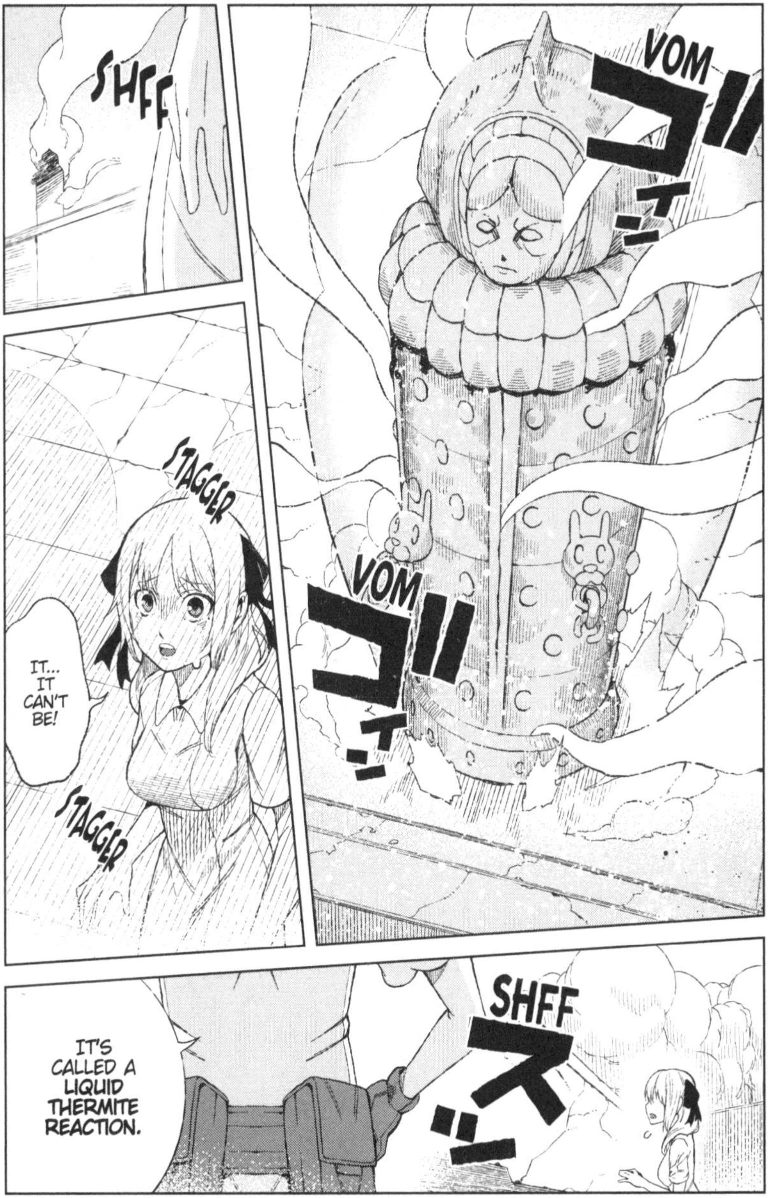
VOM
VOM
SHFF
STAGGER
IT... IT CAN'T BE!
STAGGER
SHFF
IT'S CALLED A LIQUID THERMITE REACTION.

WHEN ANTIMONY REACTS WITH POTASSIUM PERMANGANATE, **TONS** OF HEAT IS RELEASED.

THAT HEAT CAN HIT 4,000 DEGREES FAHRENHEIT. I DOUBT THERE'LL **BE BONES** LEFT.

PEEL ﾋﾟﾘ

PEEL ﾋﾟﾘ

I'M COLD, SO I'M TAKING THAT BACK. 'KAY-THANKS.

TWIRL

MOWAAHH
モ
わ
あ

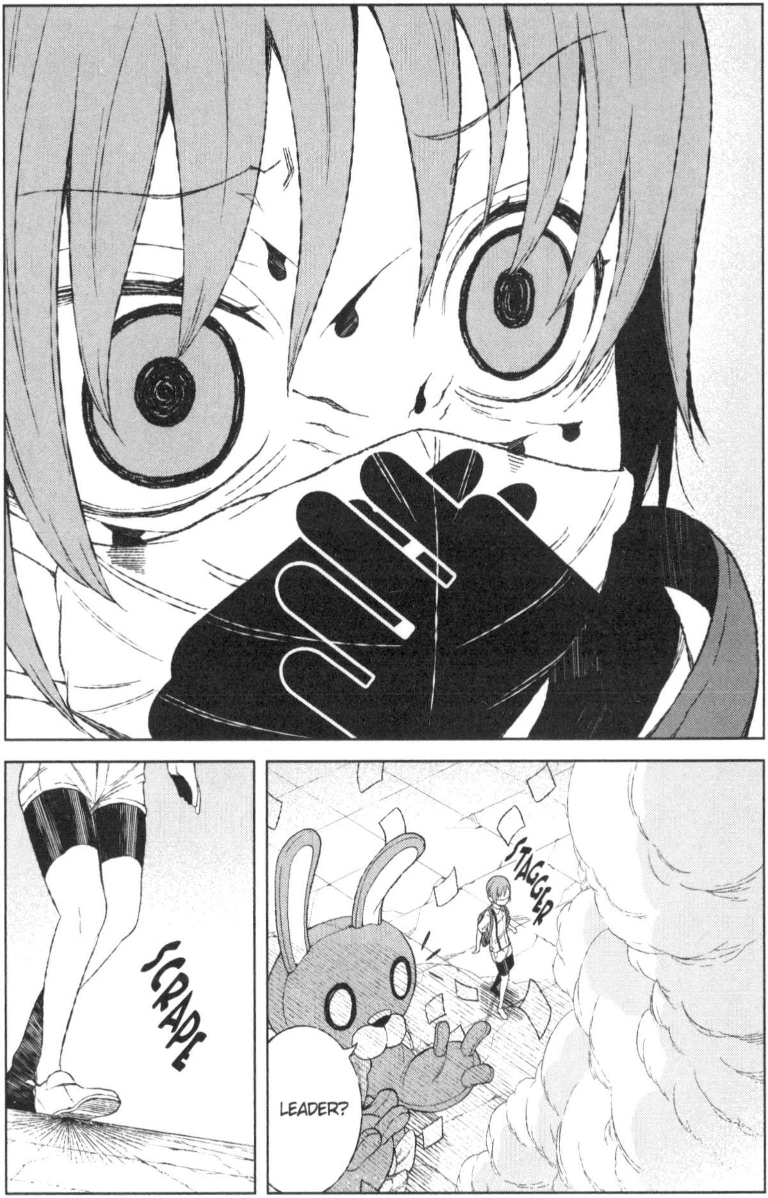
STAGGER
LEADER?
SCRAPE

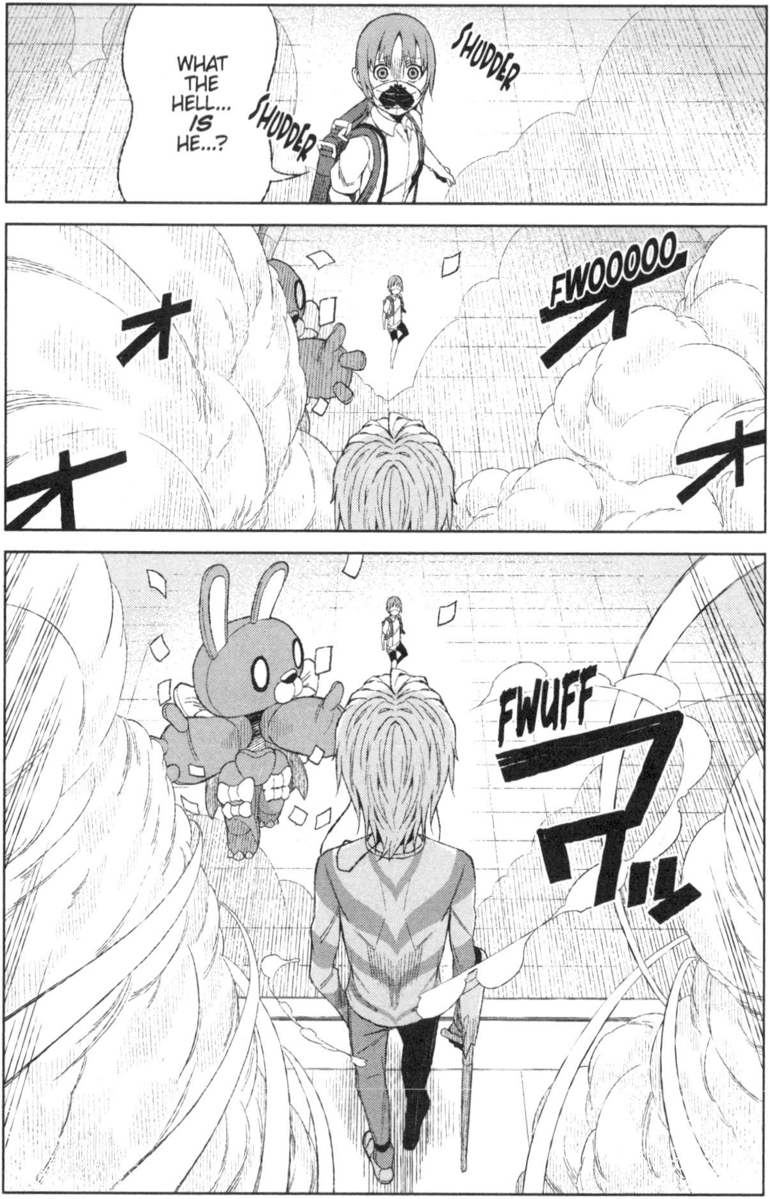
SHUDDER
SHUDDER
WHAT THE HELL... IS HE...?
FWOOOOO
オ
オ
オ
FWUFF
フワッ

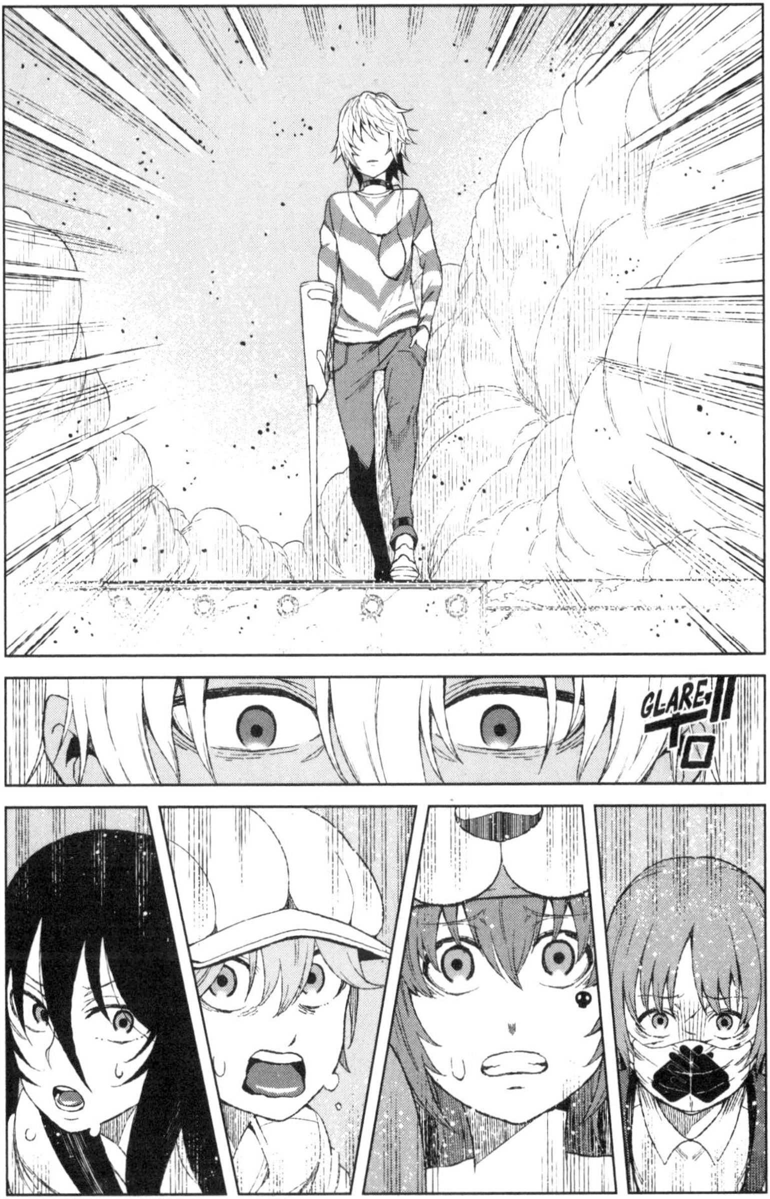
GLARE

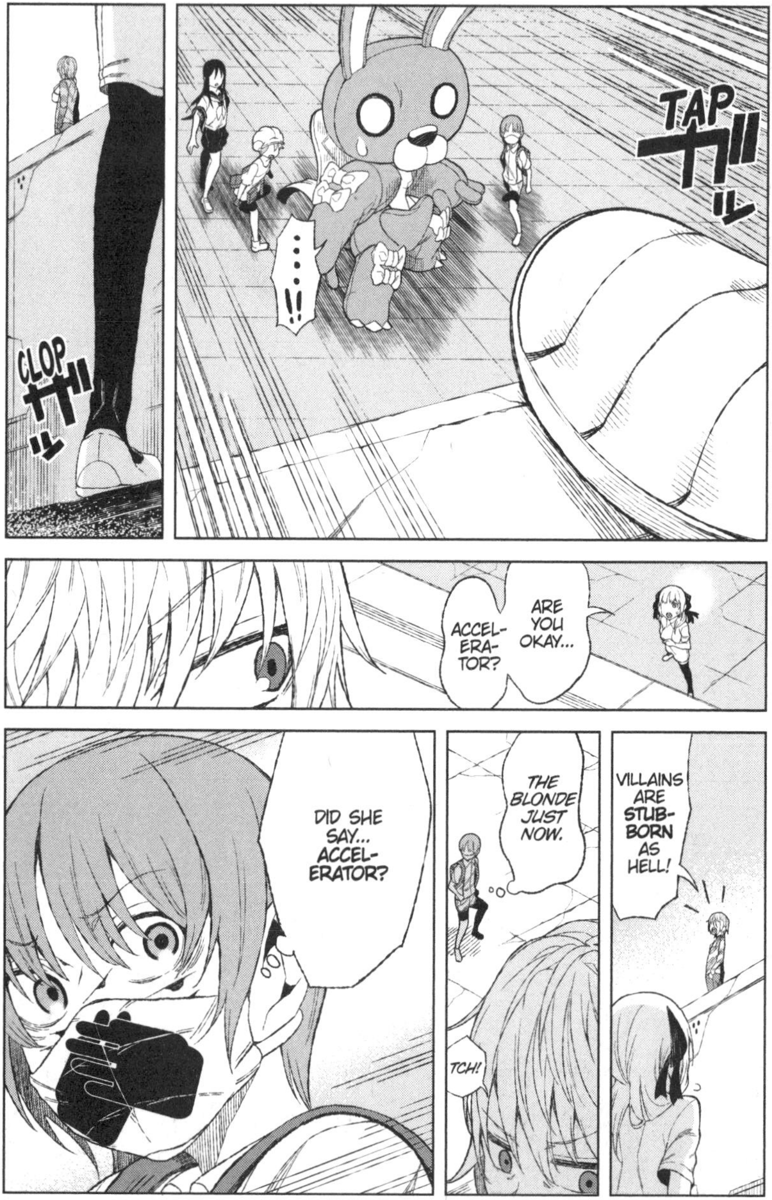
TAP
ガッ
......!!
CLOP
ザッ
ARE YOU OKAY...
ACCEL-ERA-TOR?
VILLAINS ARE STUB-BORN AS HELL!
THE BLONDE JUST NOW.
TCH!
DID SHE SAY... ACCEL-ERATOR?

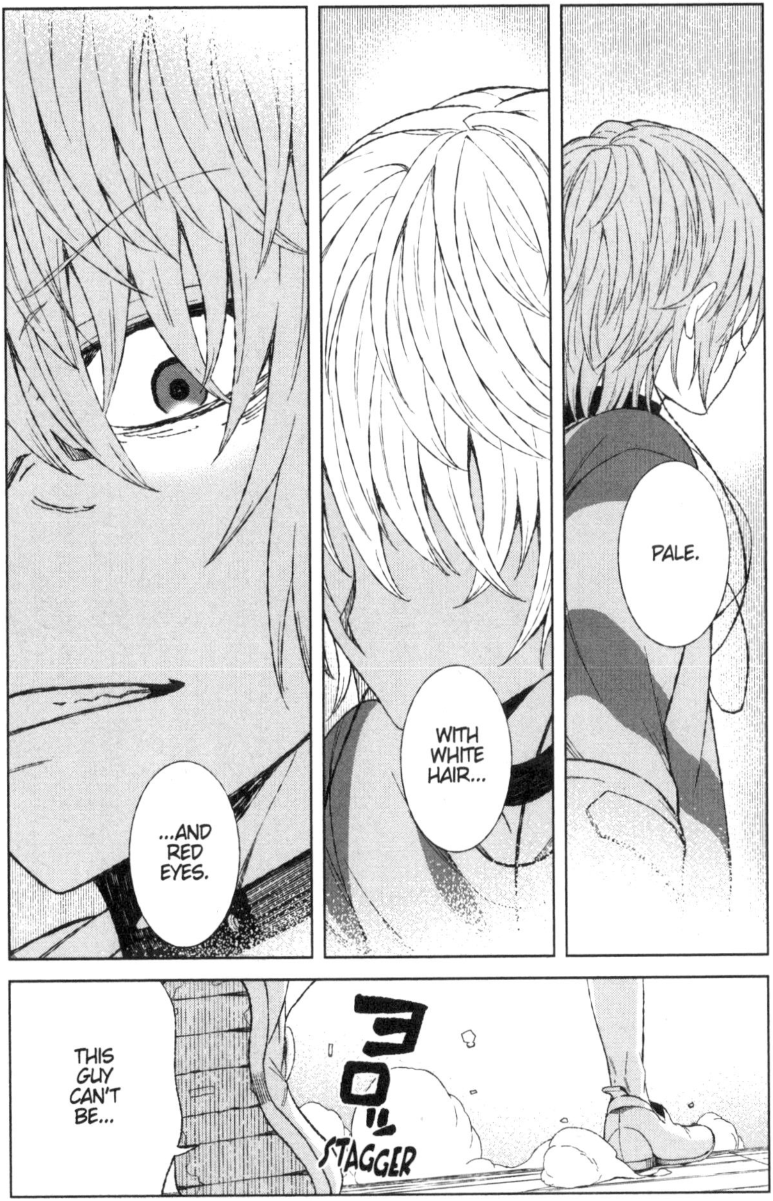
PALE.
WITH WHITE HAIR...
...AND RED EYES.
ヨロッ
STAGGER
THIS GUY CAN'T BE...

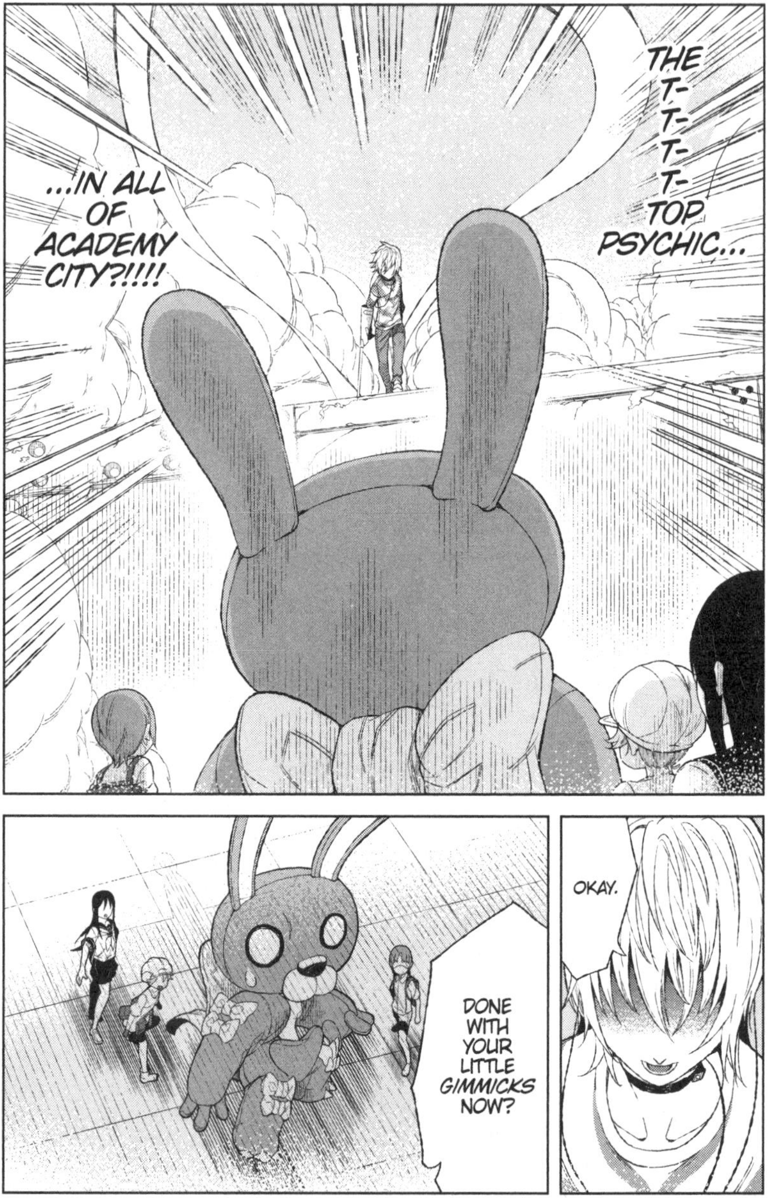
THE T-T-T-T-TOP PSYCHIC...
...IN ALL OF ACADEMY CITY?!!!!
OKAY.
DONE WITH YOUR LITTLE GIMMICKS NOW?

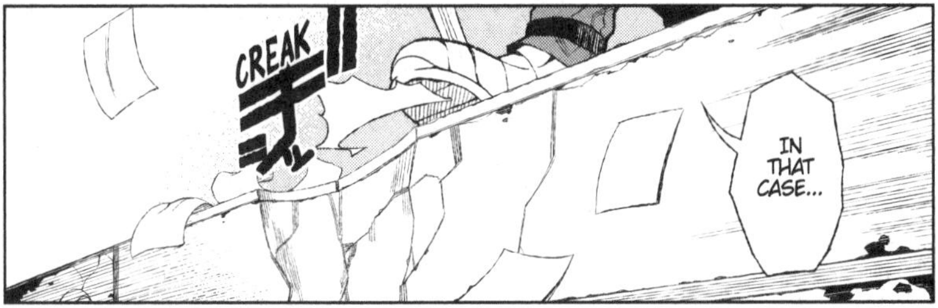
CREAK
IN THAT CASE...
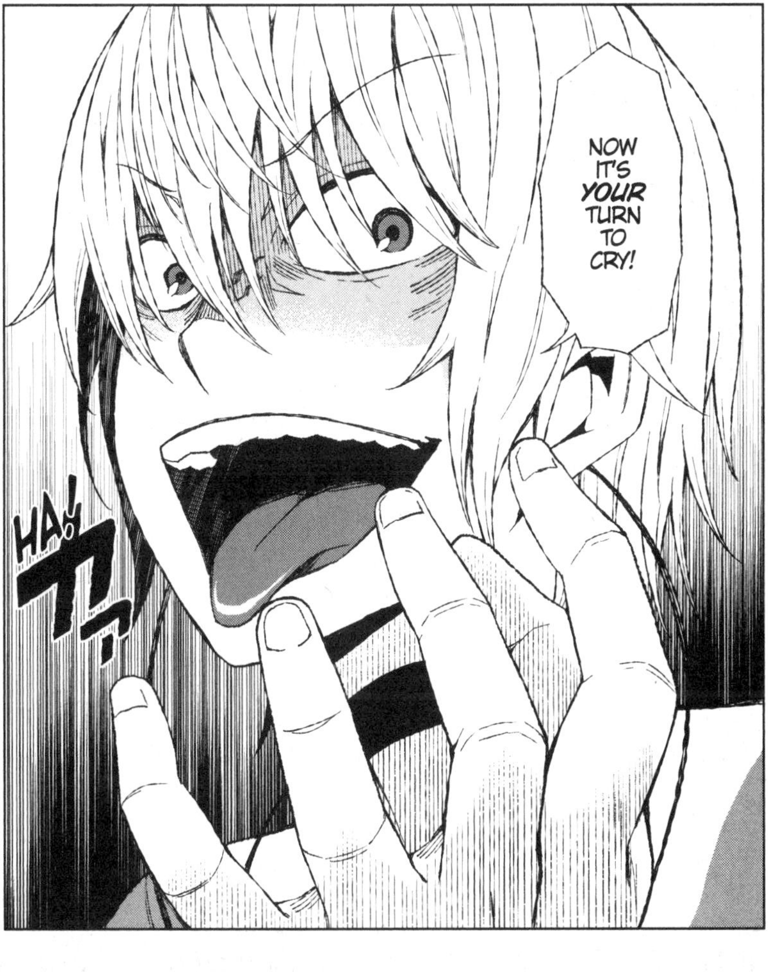
NOW IT'S *YOUR* TURN TO CRY!
HA!

a certain SCIENTIFIC ACCELERATOR

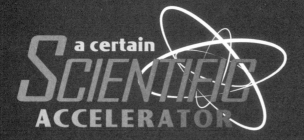

とある科学の一方通行

とある魔術の禁書目録外伝

CHAPTER 17

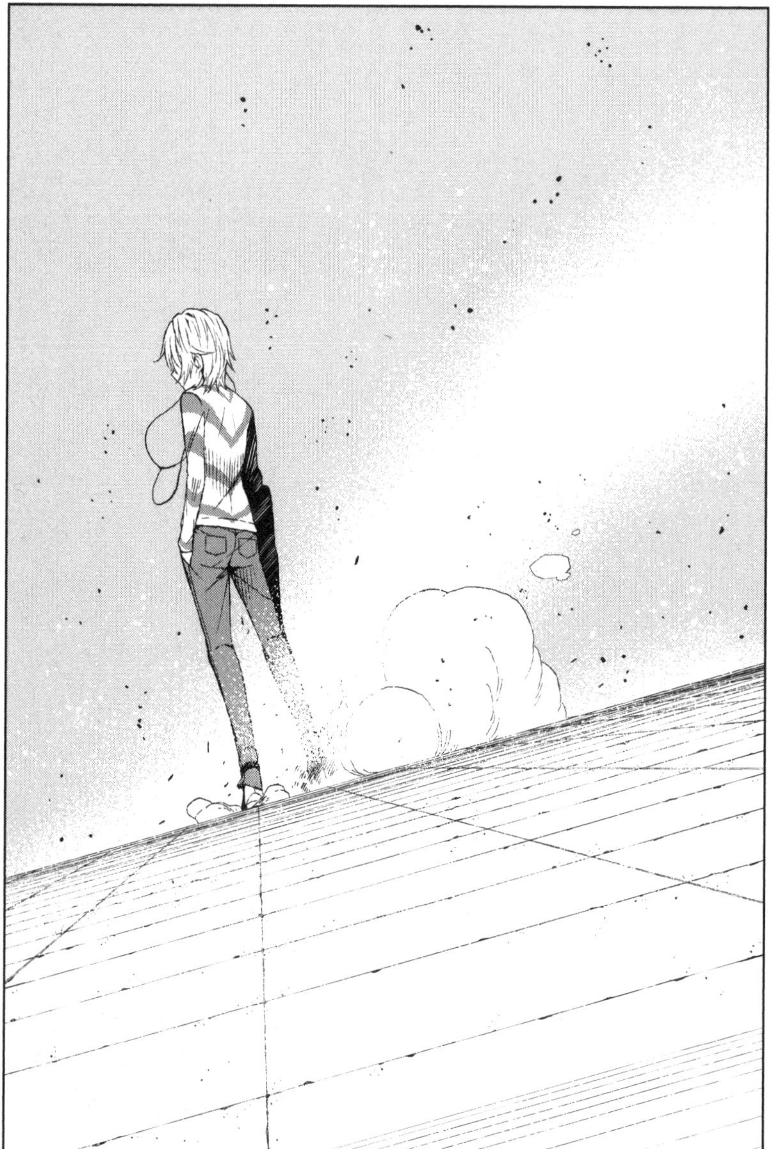

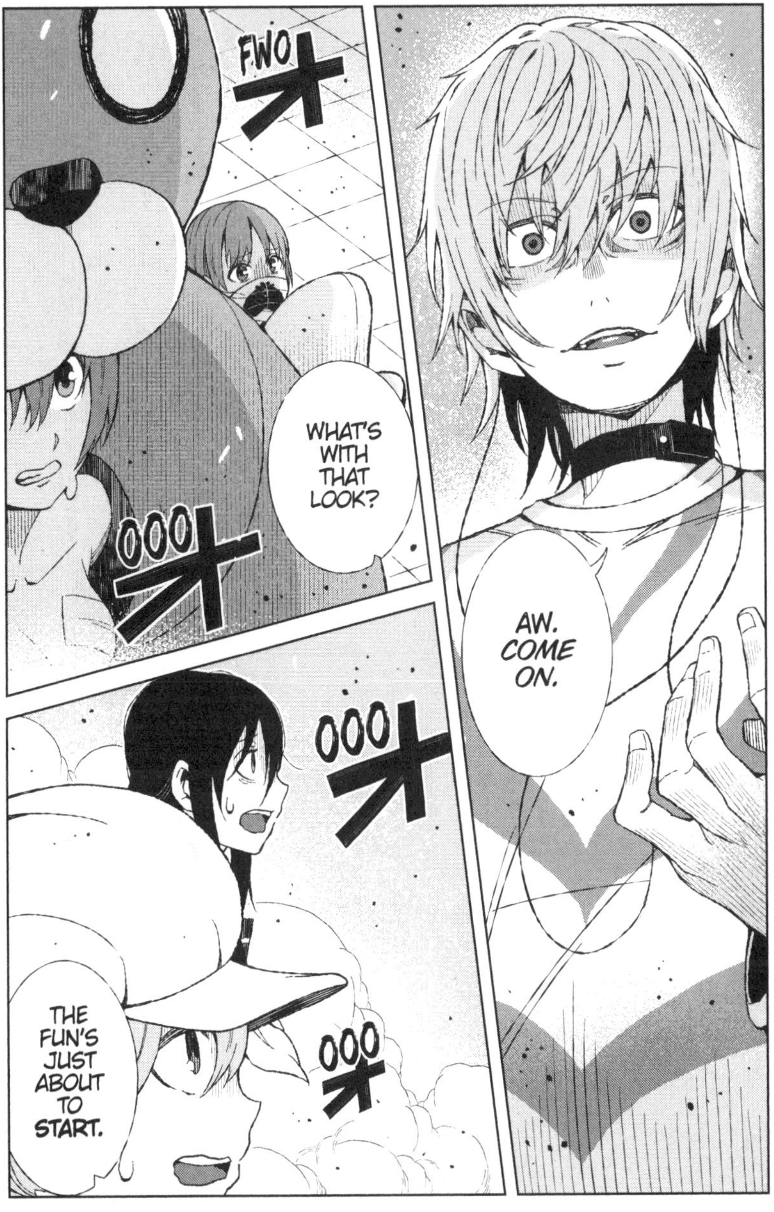
AW. COME ON.
FWO
WHAT'S WITH THAT LOOK?
OOO
OOO
THE FUN'S JUST ABOUT TO START.
OOO

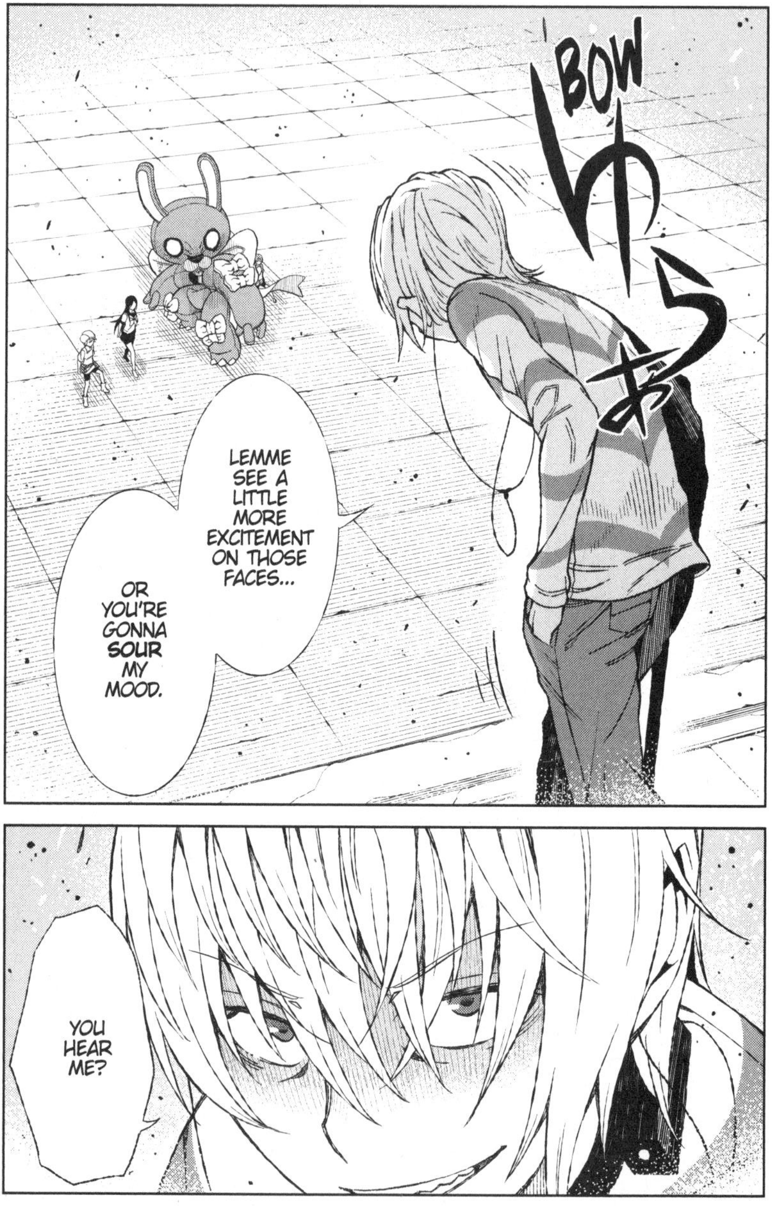
BOW
ゆらあ
LEMME SEE A LITTLE MORE EXCITEMENT ON THOSE FACES...
OR YOU'RE GONNA SOUR MY MOOD.
YOU HEAR ME?

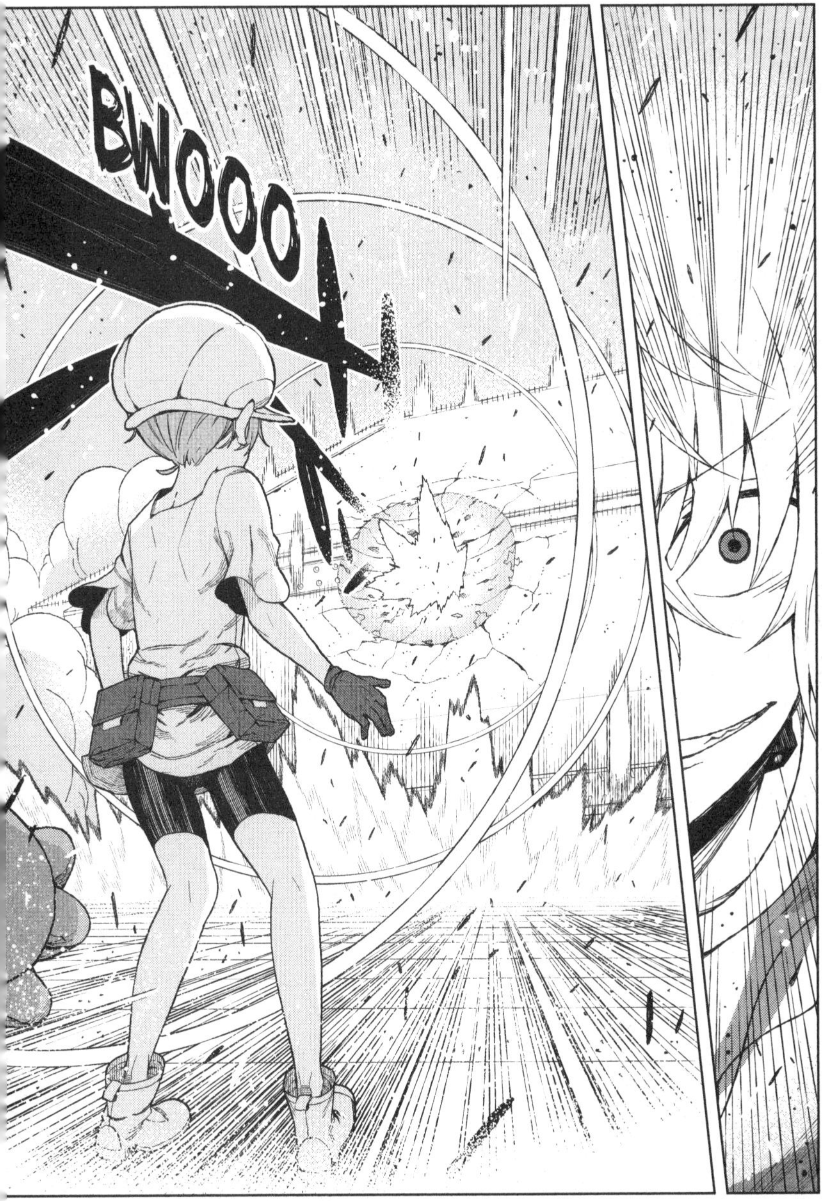
BWOOO

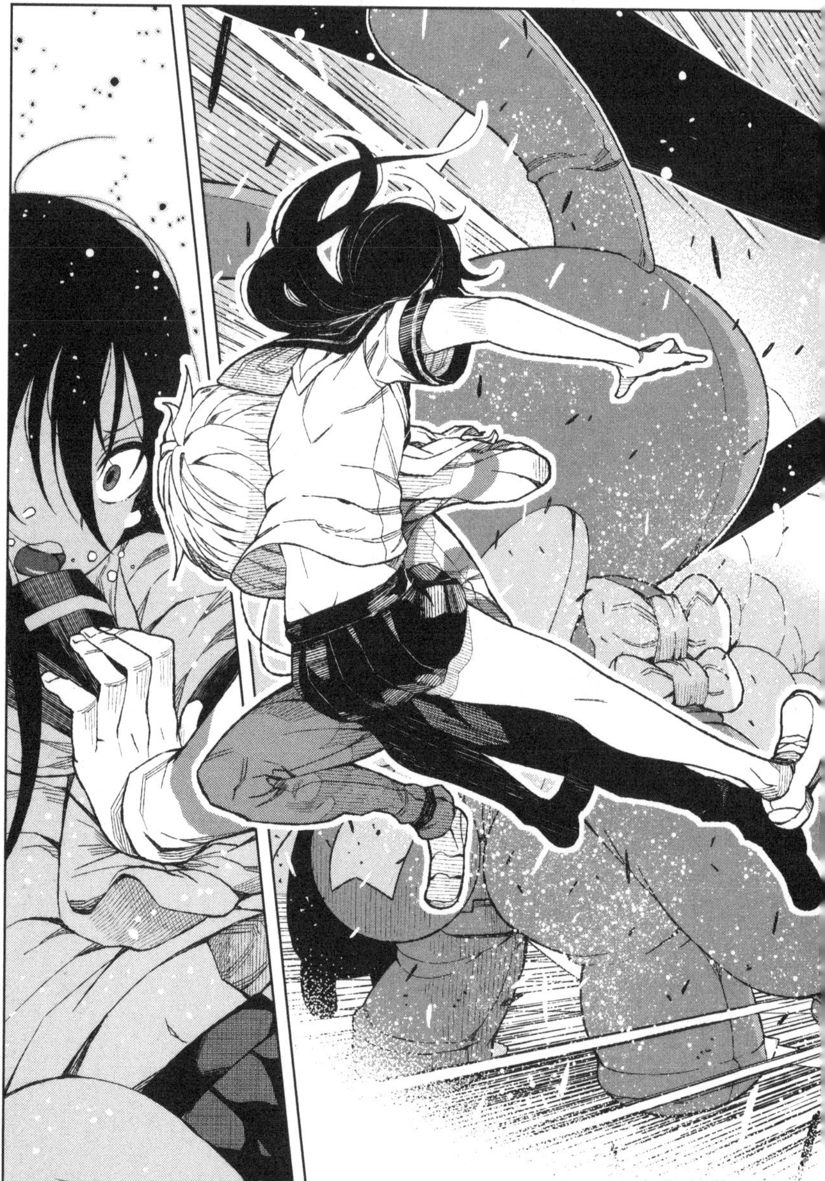

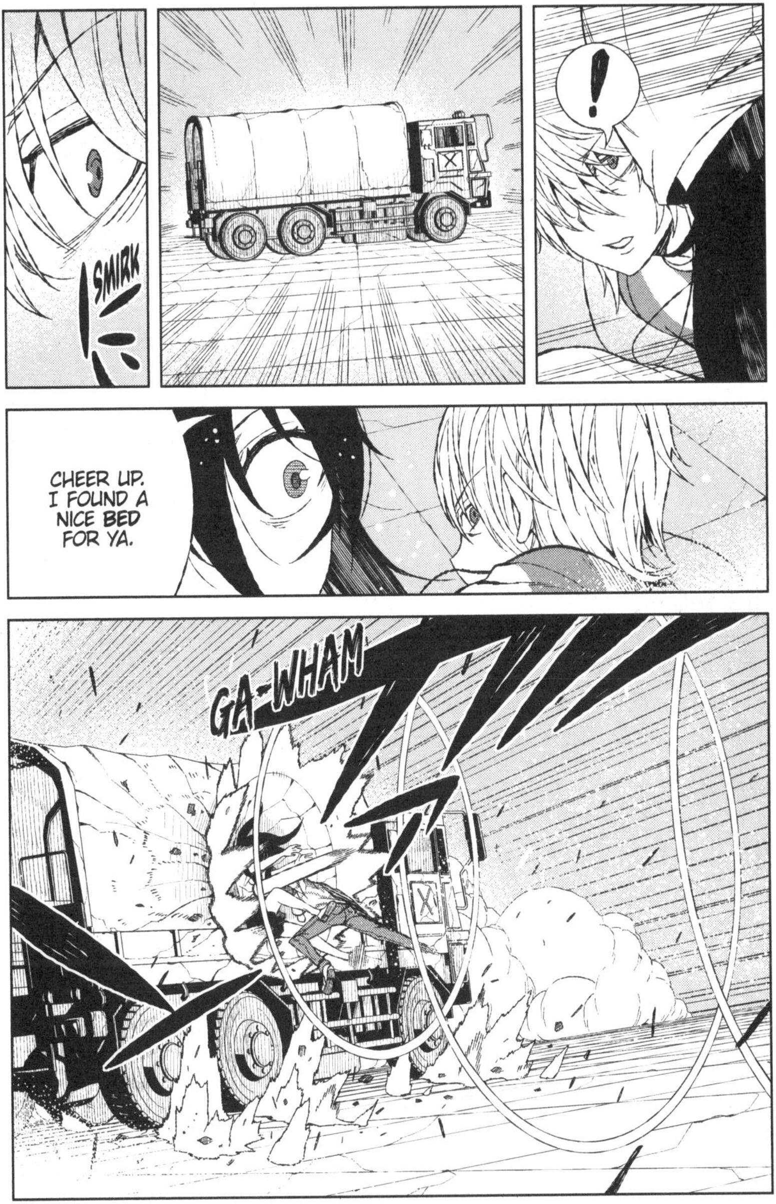
!
SMIRK
CHEER UP. I FOUND A NICE BED FOR YA.
GA-WHAM

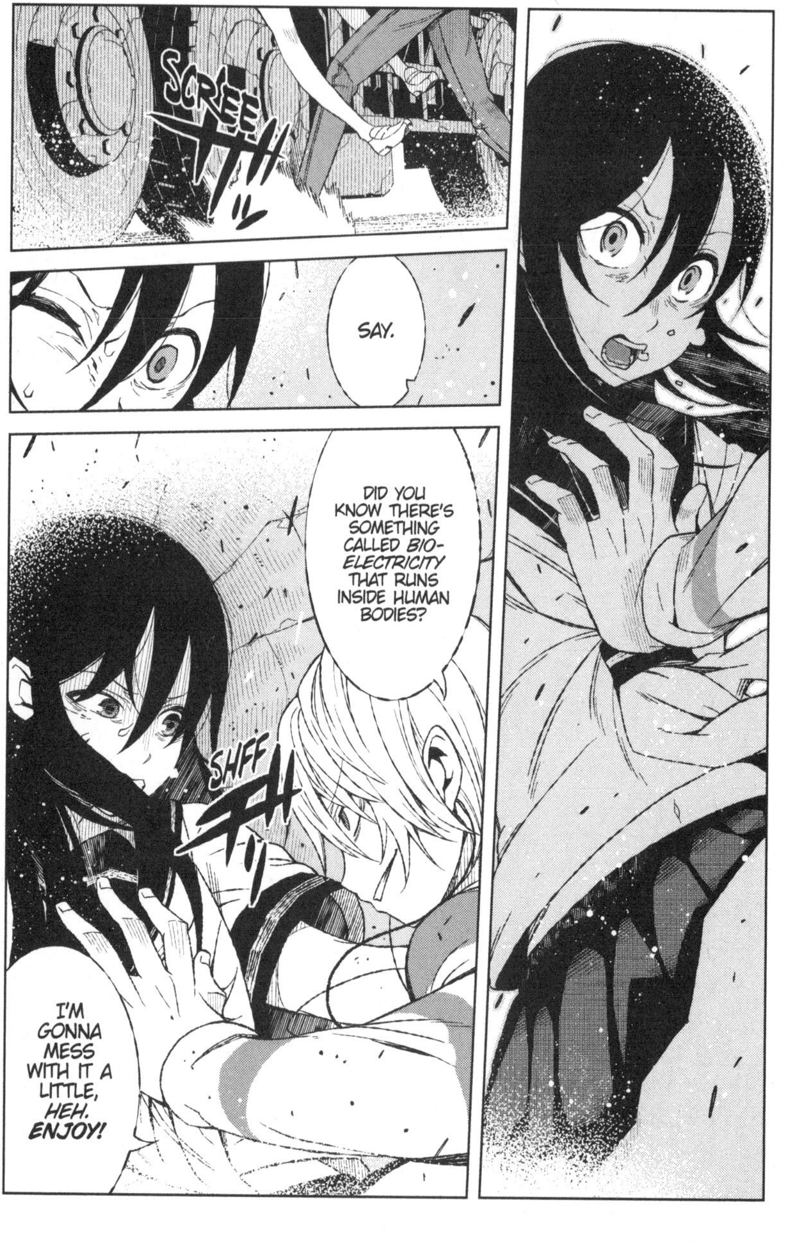
SCREEE
SAY.
DID YOU KNOW THERE'S SOMETHING CALLED *BIO-ELECTRICITY* THAT RUNS INSIDE HUMAN BODIES?
SHFF
I'M GONNA MESS WITH IT A LITTLE, **HEH. ENJOY!**

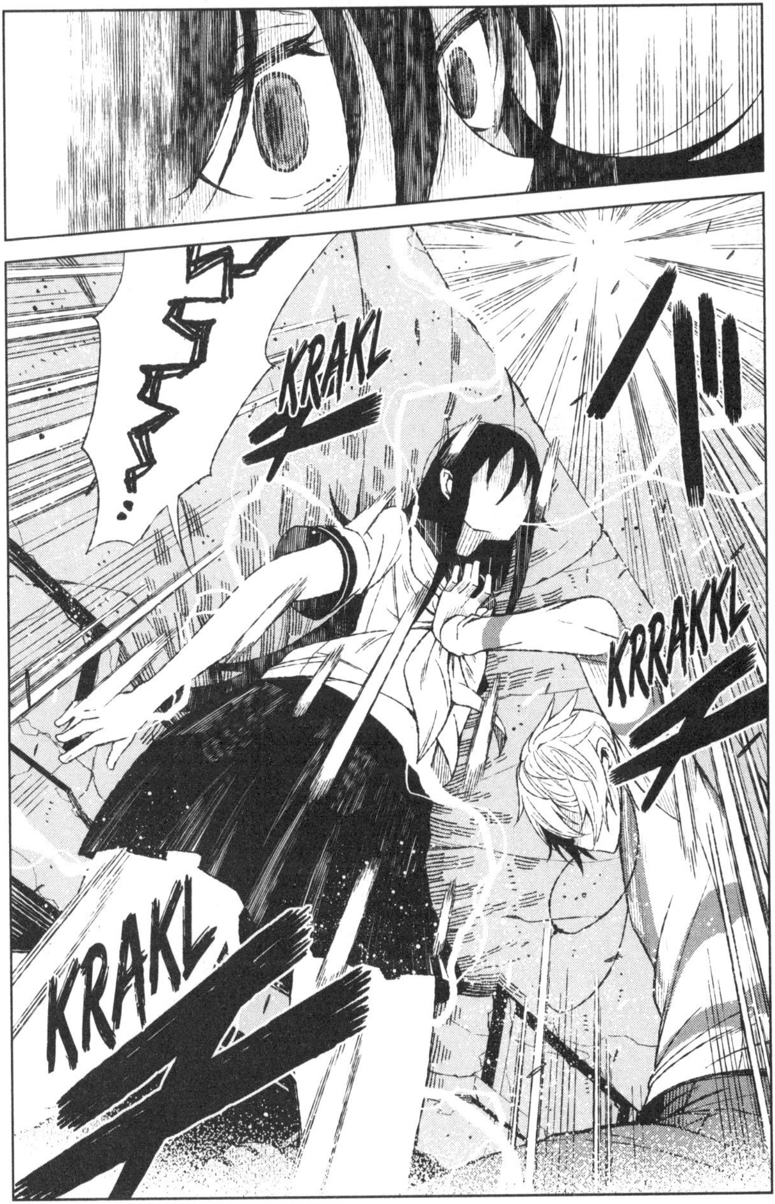
ド
KRAKL
KRRAKKL
KRAKL

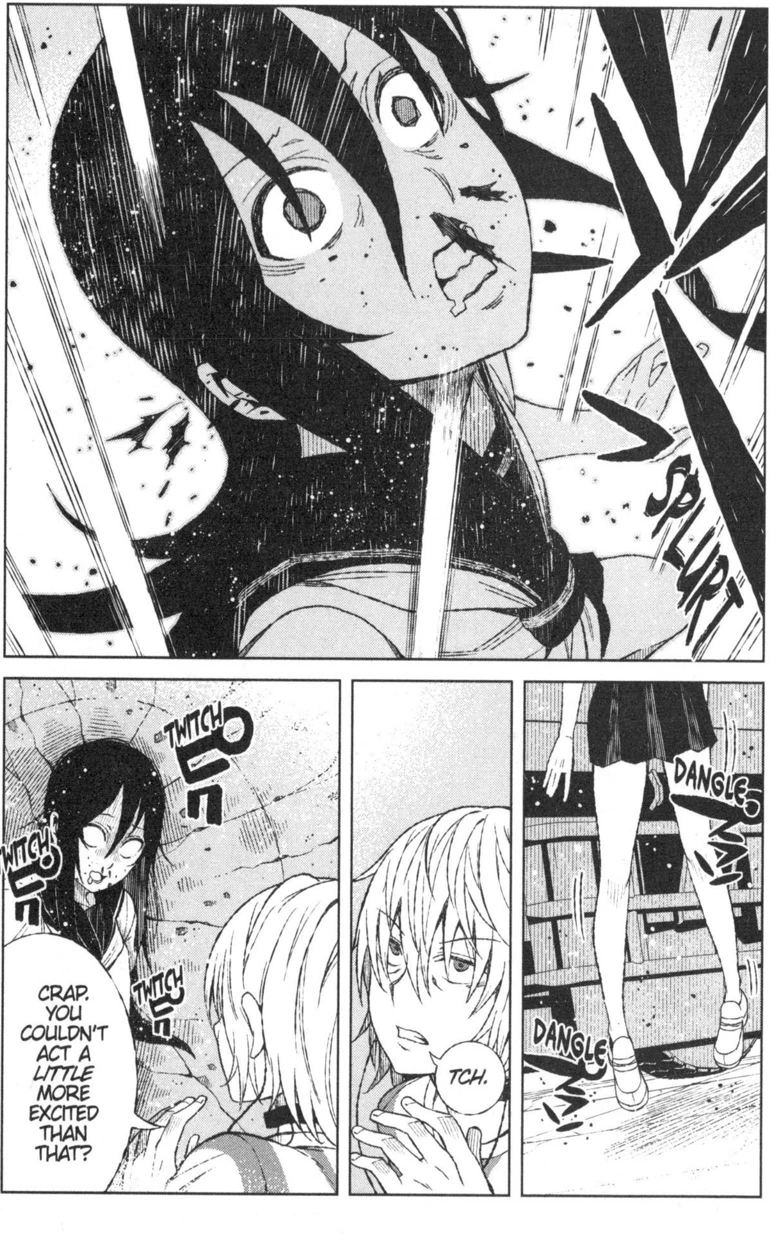
SPLURT
DANGLE
DANGLE
TCH.
TWITCH
TWITCH
TWITCH
CRAP. YOU COULDN'T ACT A *LITTLE* MORE EXCITED THAN THAT?

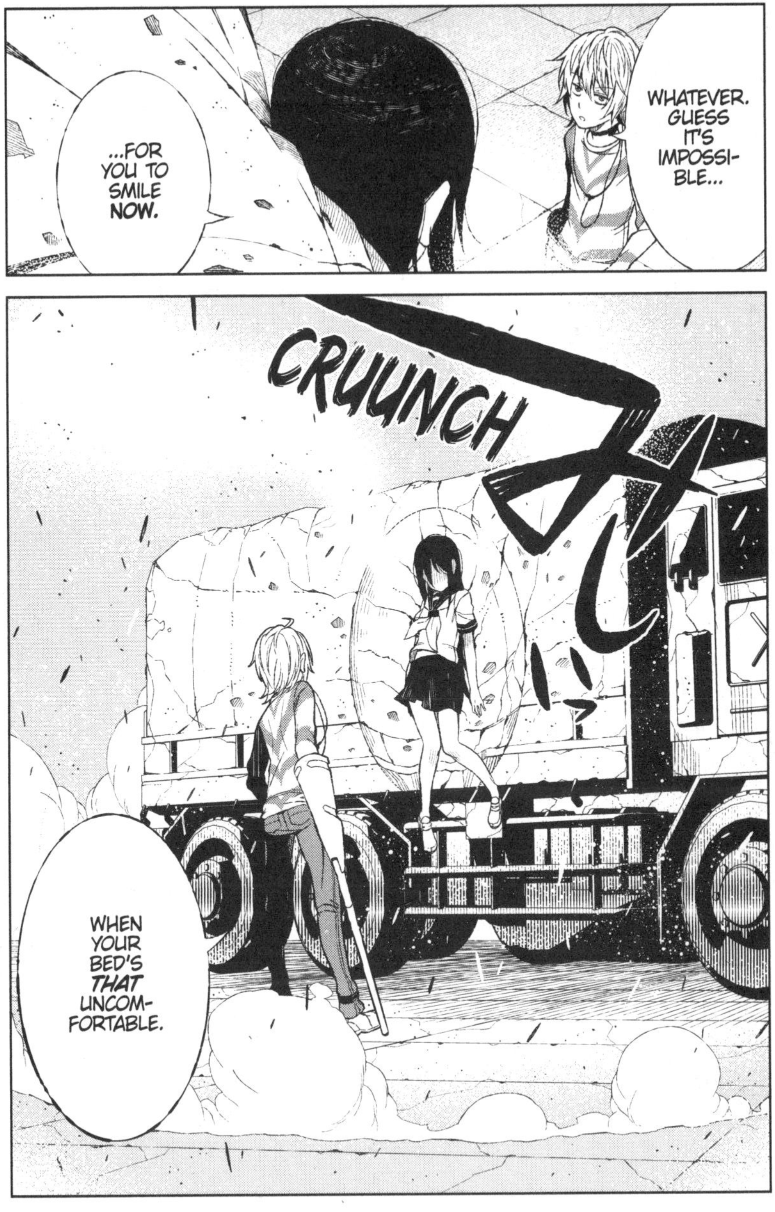
WHATEVER. GUESS IT'S IMPOSSI-BLE...
...FOR YOU TO SMILE NOW.
CRUUNCH
WHEN YOUR BED'S *THAT* UNCOM-FORTABLE.

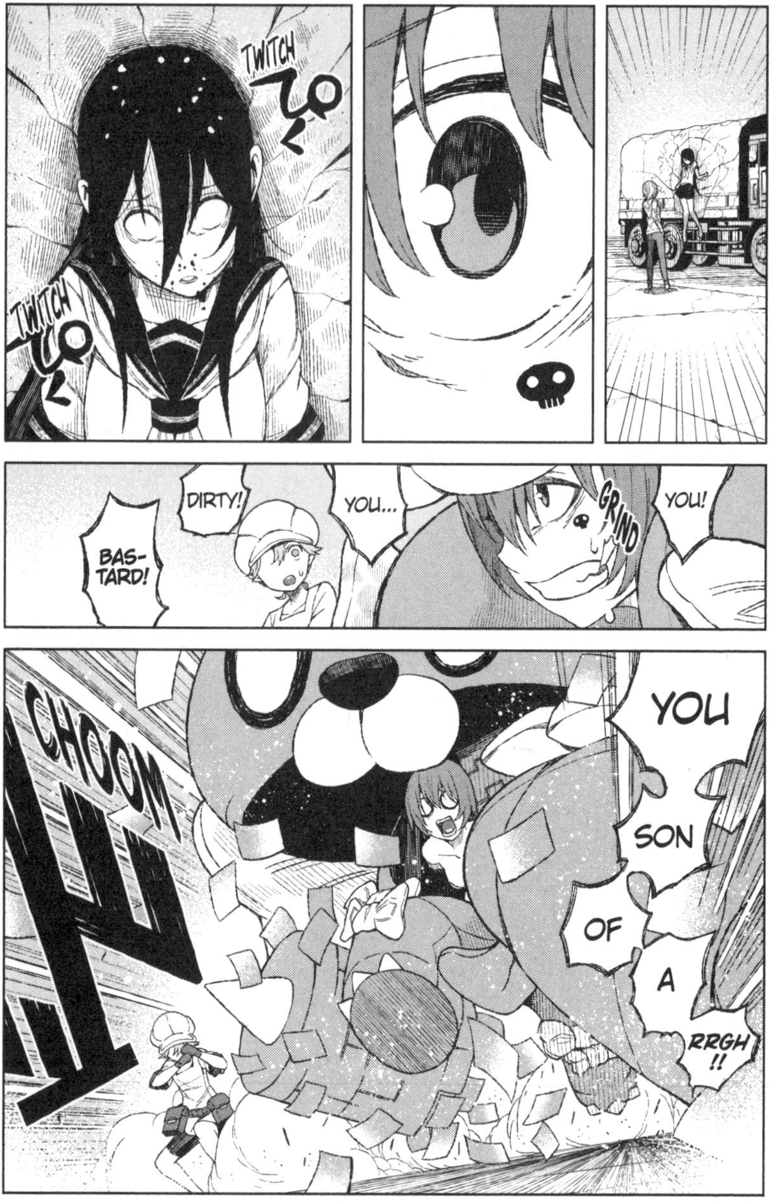
TWITCH
ぴく
TWITCH
ぴく
YOU!
GRIND
YOU...
DIRTY!
BAS-TARD!
YOU
SON
OF
A
RRGH !!
CHOOM

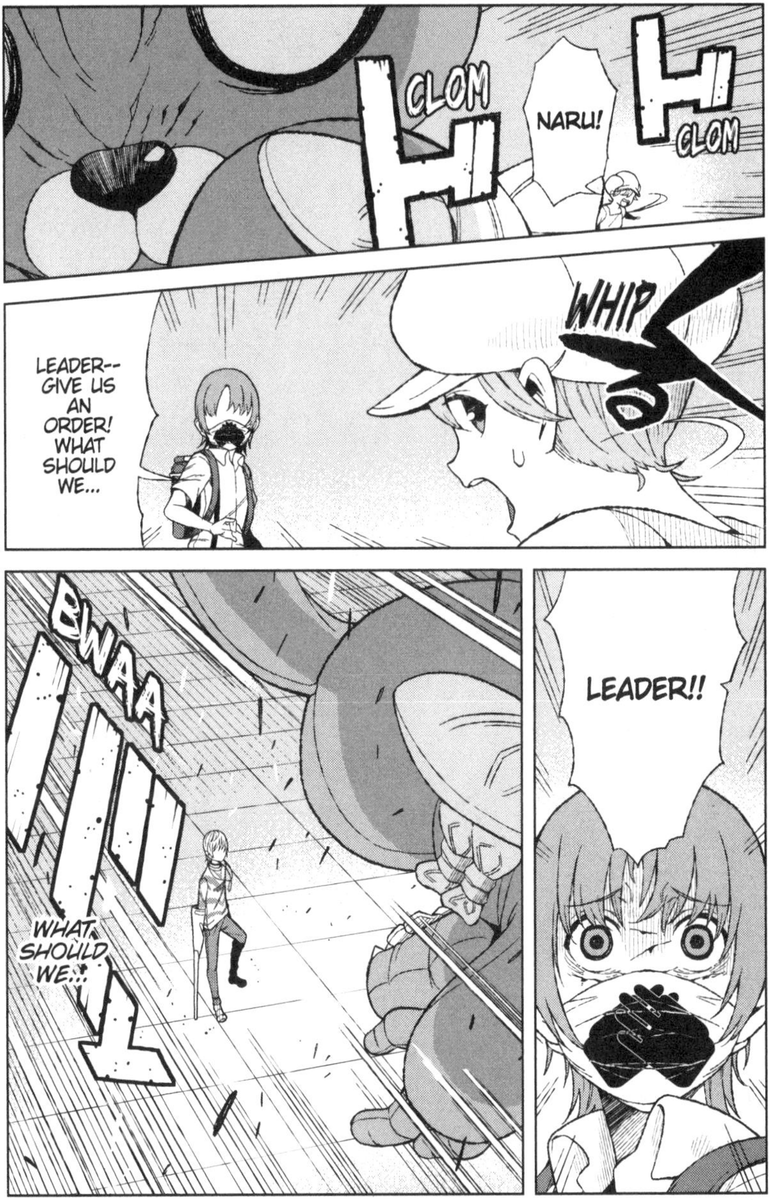
CLOM
NARU!
CLOM
WHIP
LEADER--
GIVE US
AN
ORDER!
WHAT
SHOULD
WE...
LEADER!!
BWAA
WHAT
SHOULD
WE...

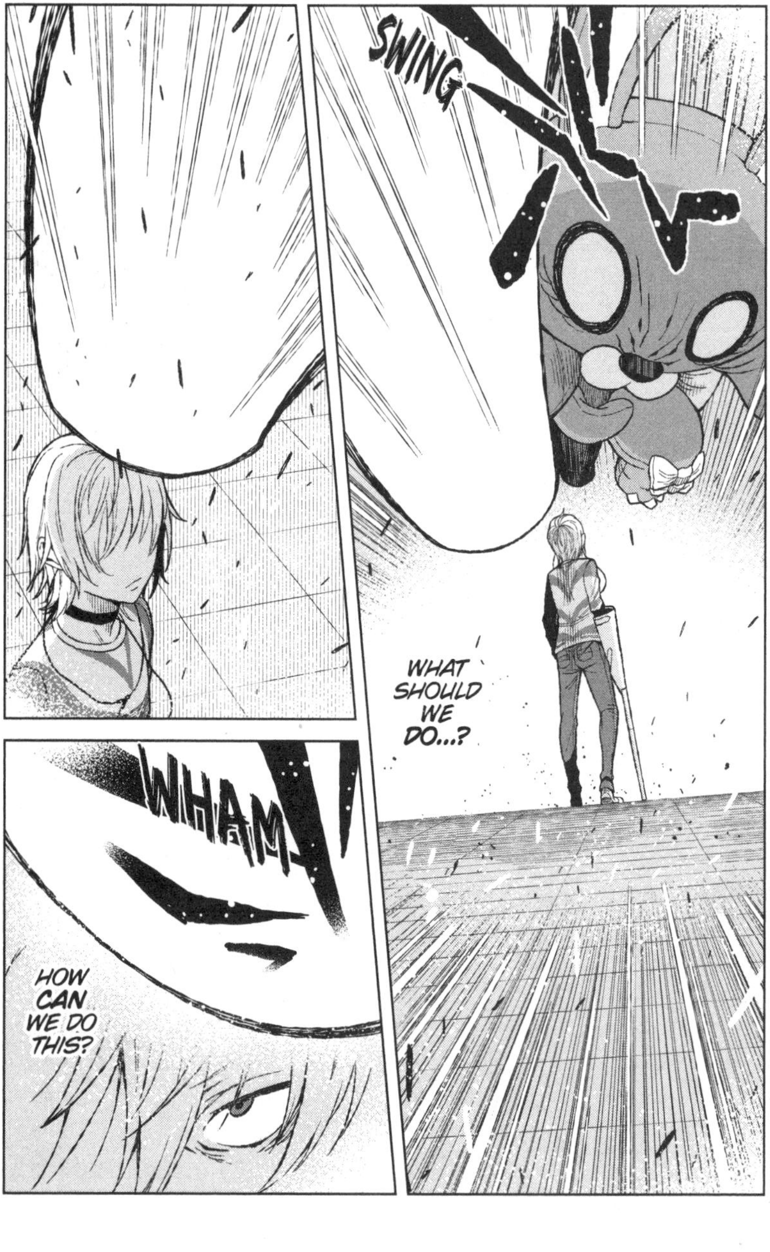
SWING
WHAT SHOULD WE DO...?
WHAM
HOW CAN WE DO THIS?

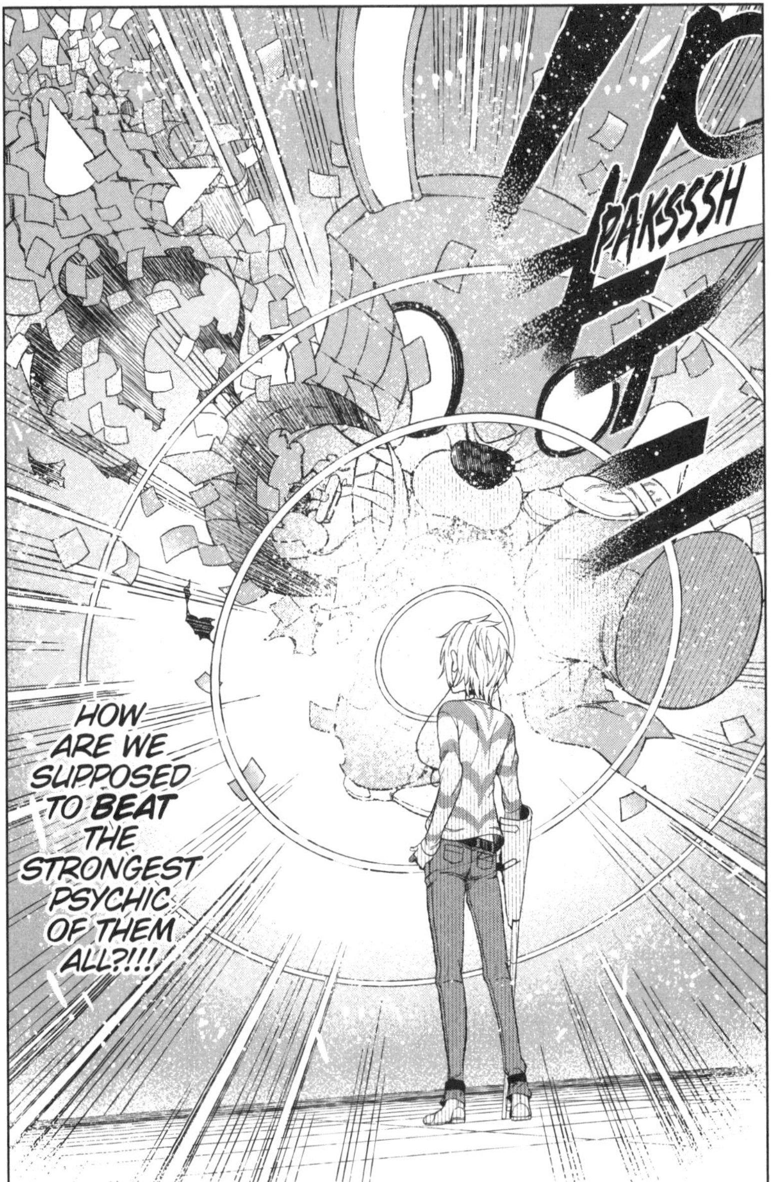
PAKSSSH
HOW ARE WE SUPPOSED TO BEAT THE STRONGEST PSYCHIC OF THEM ALL?!!!

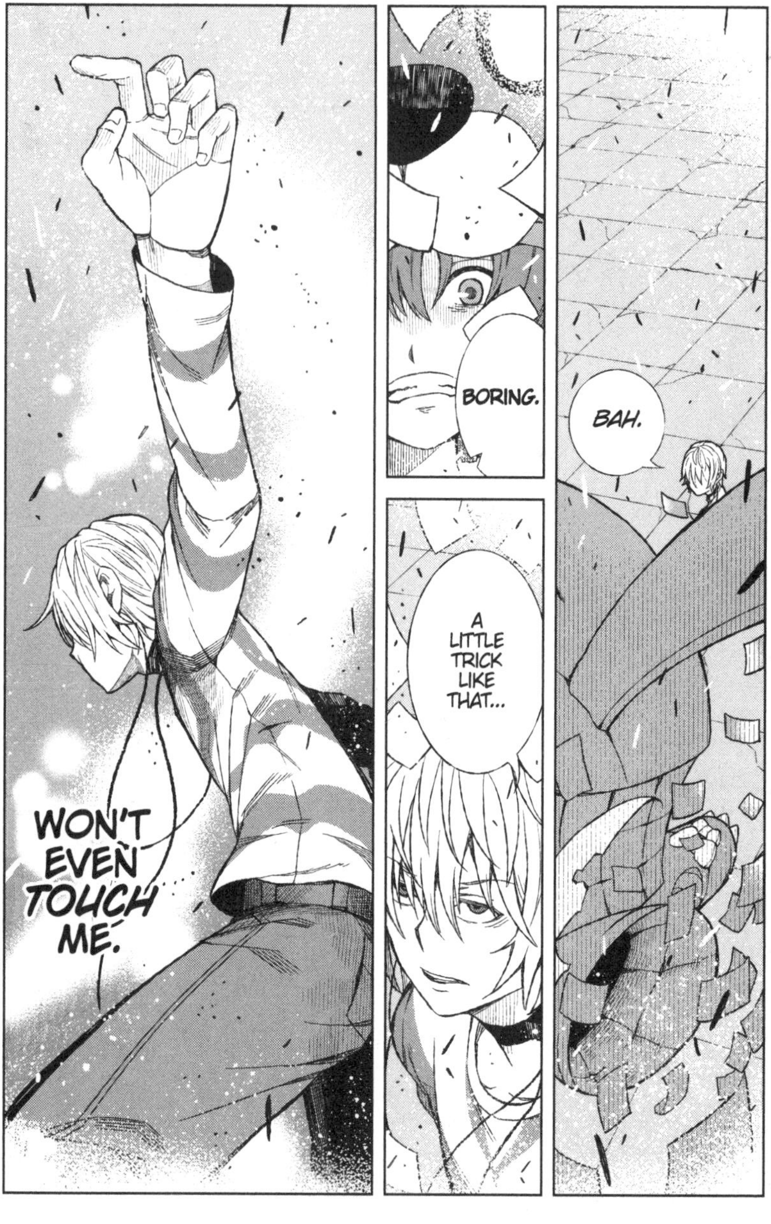
BAH.
BORING.
A LITTLE TRICK LIKE THAT...
WON'T EVEN TOUCH ME.

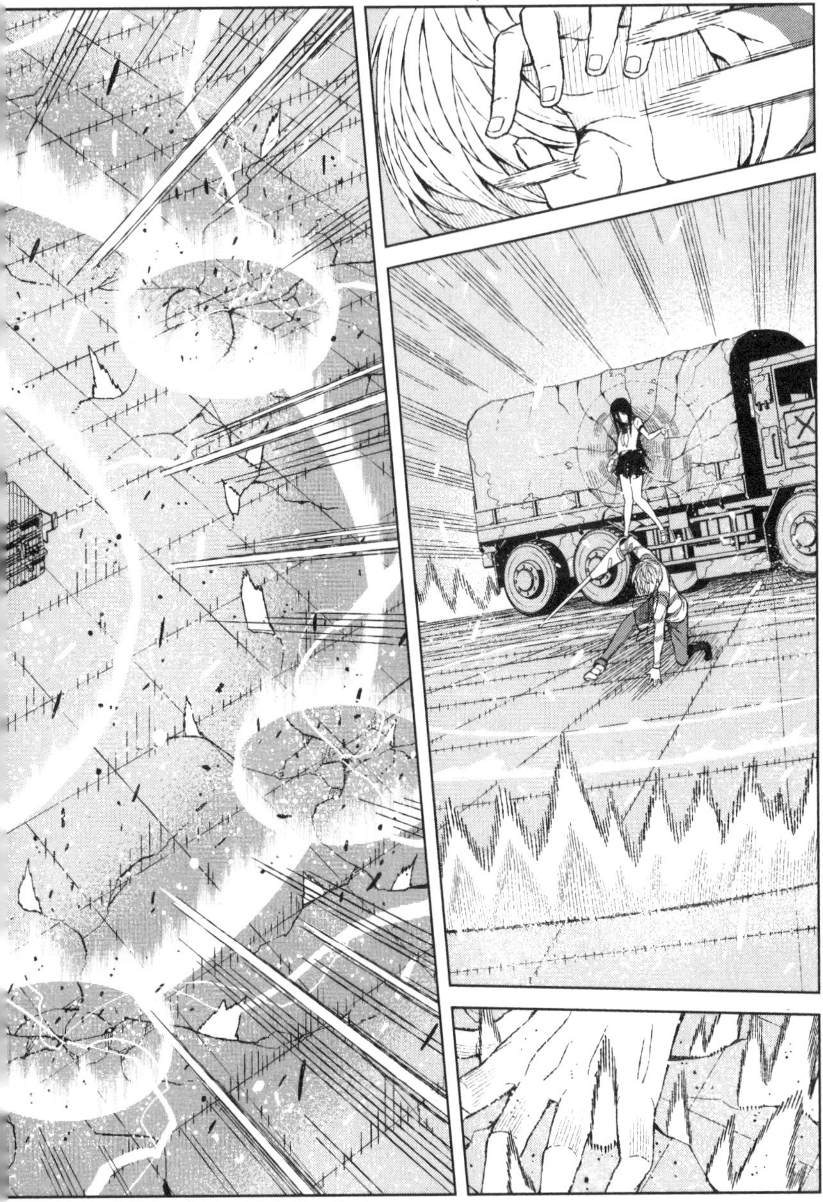

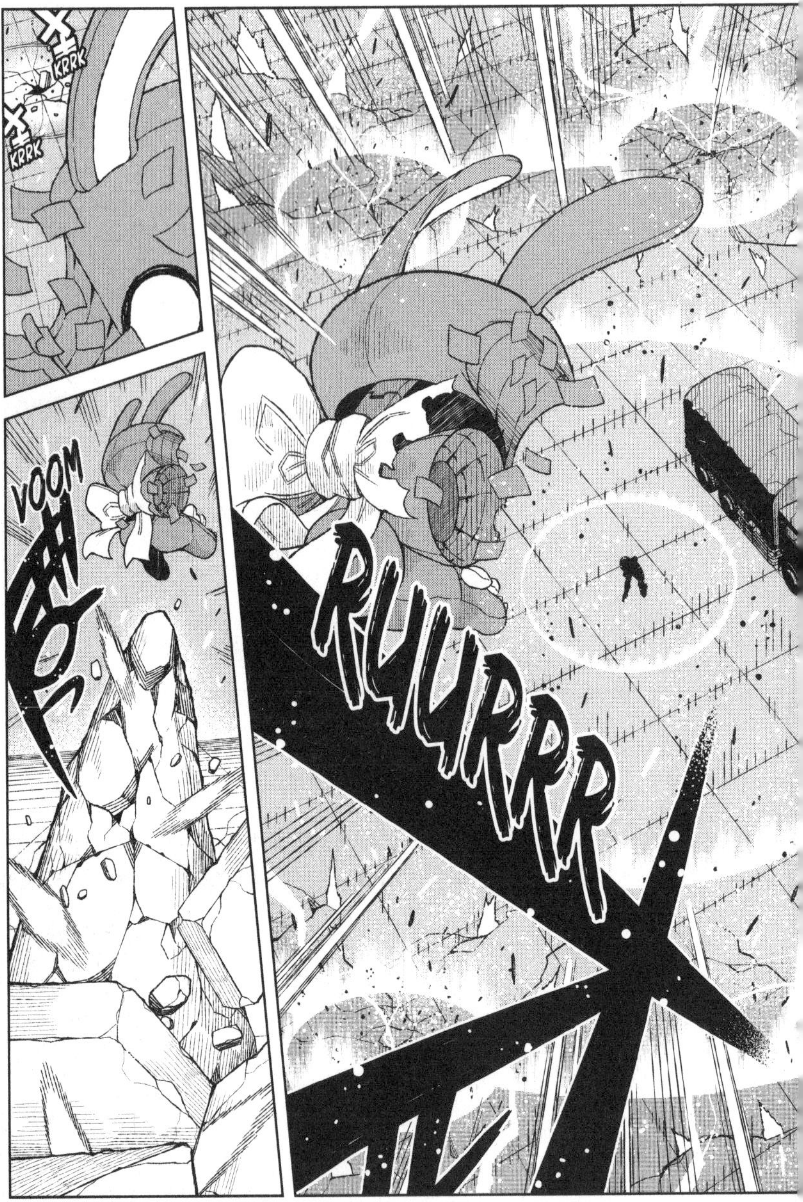
RUURRRR
KRRRK
KRRRK
VOOM

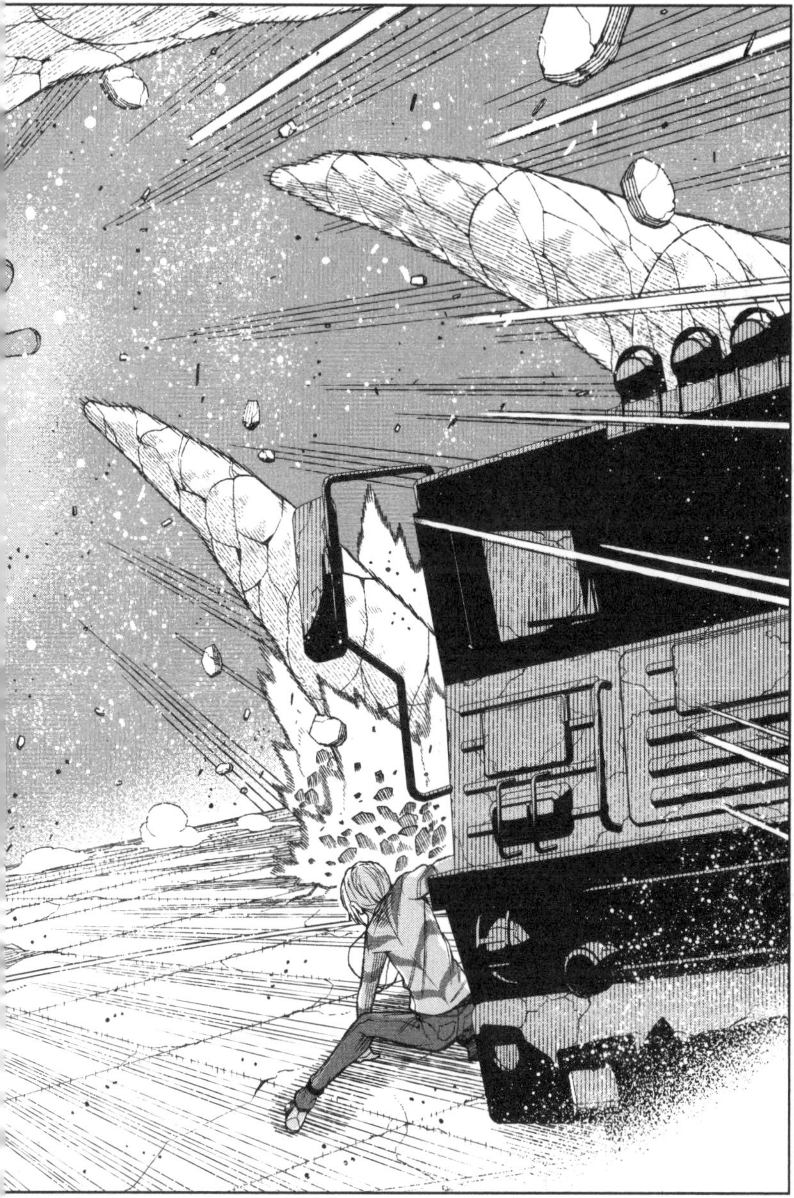

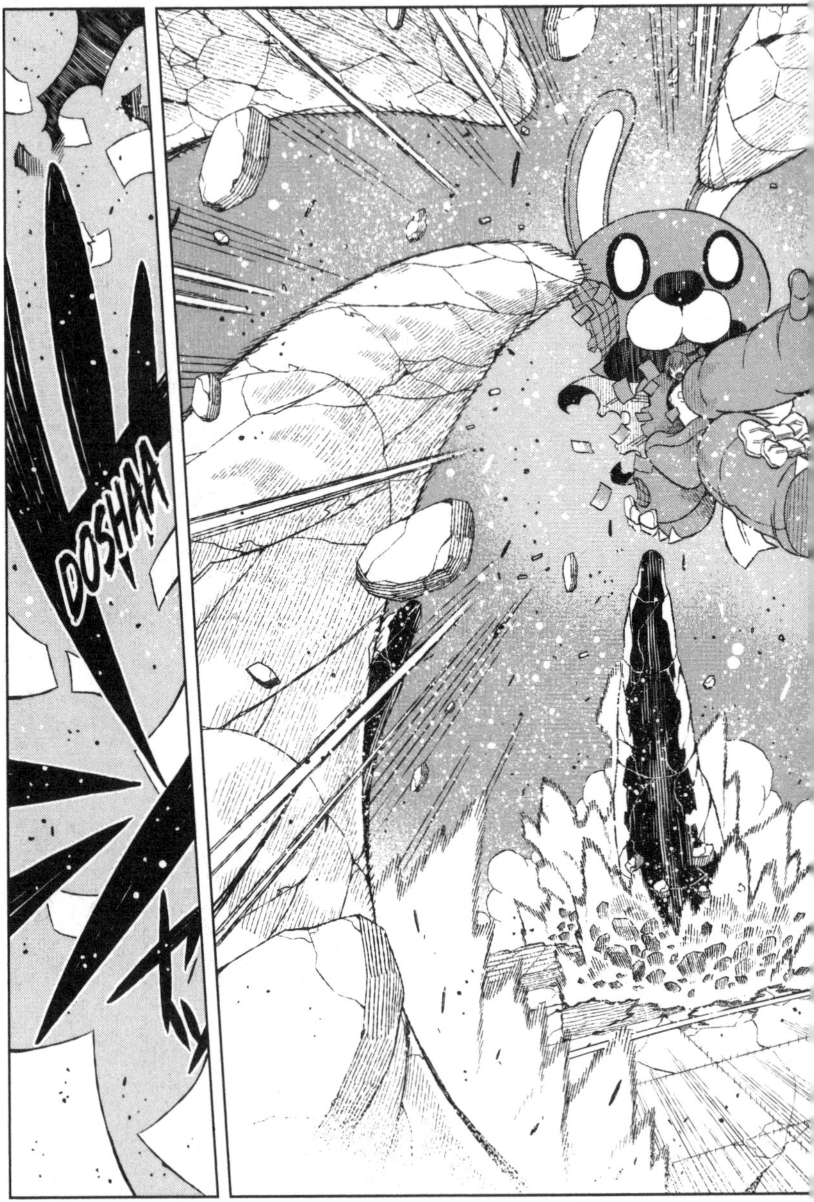
DOSHAA

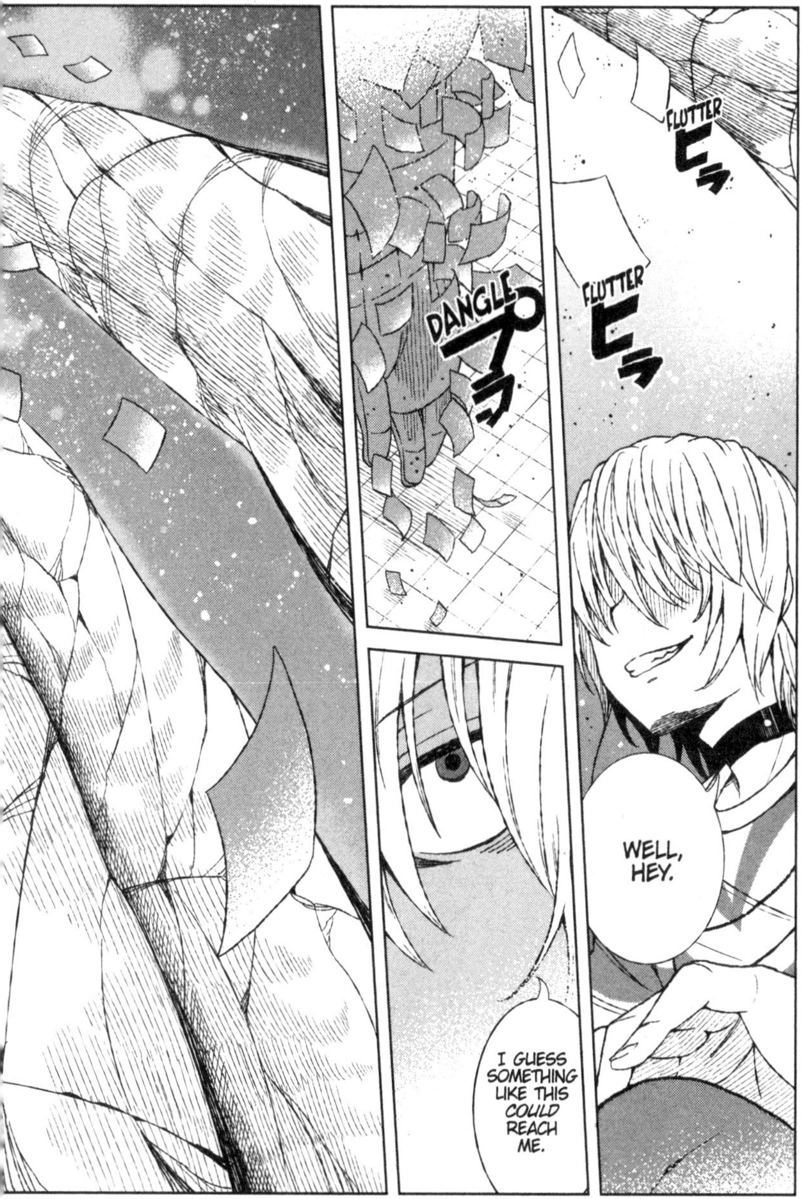
FLUTTER
ヒラ
FLUTTER
ヒラ
WELL, HEY.
DANGLE
プラ
I GUESS SOMETHING LIKE THIS COULD REACH ME.

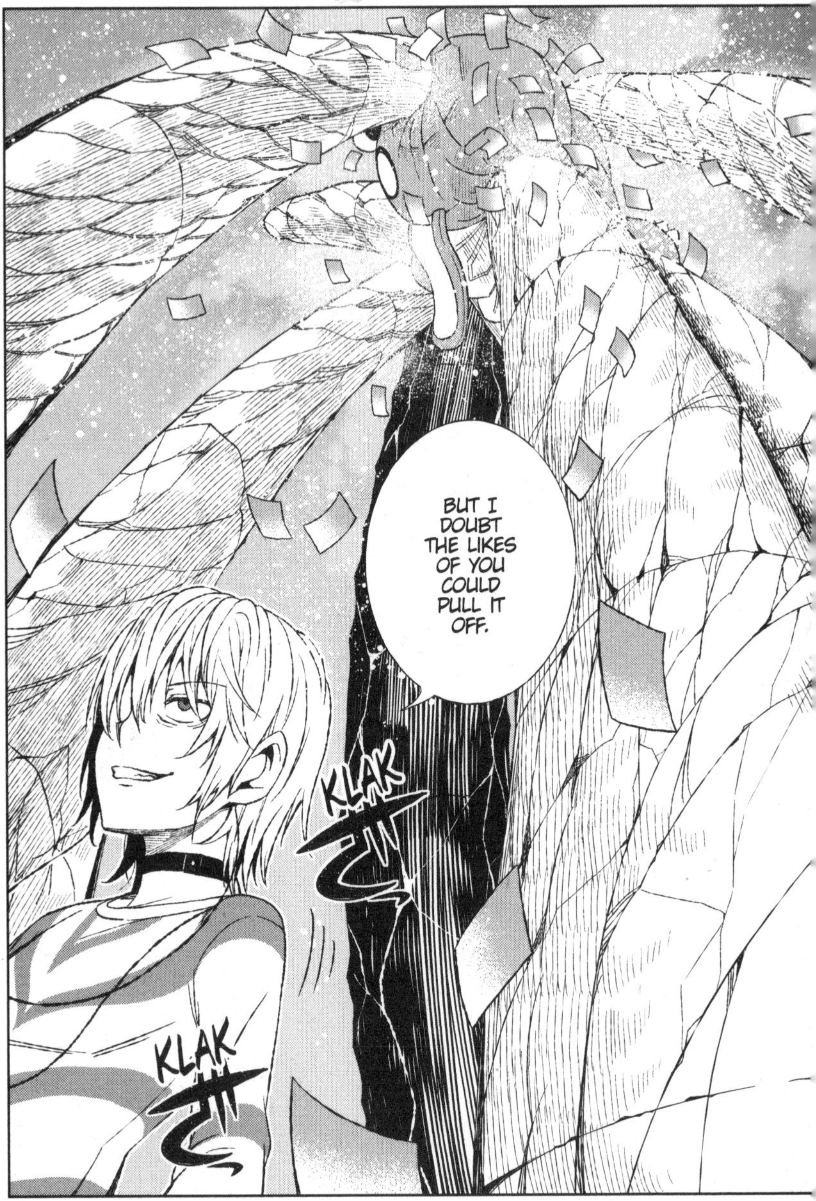
BUT I DOUBT THE LIKES OF YOU COULD PULL IT OFF.
KLAK
KLAK

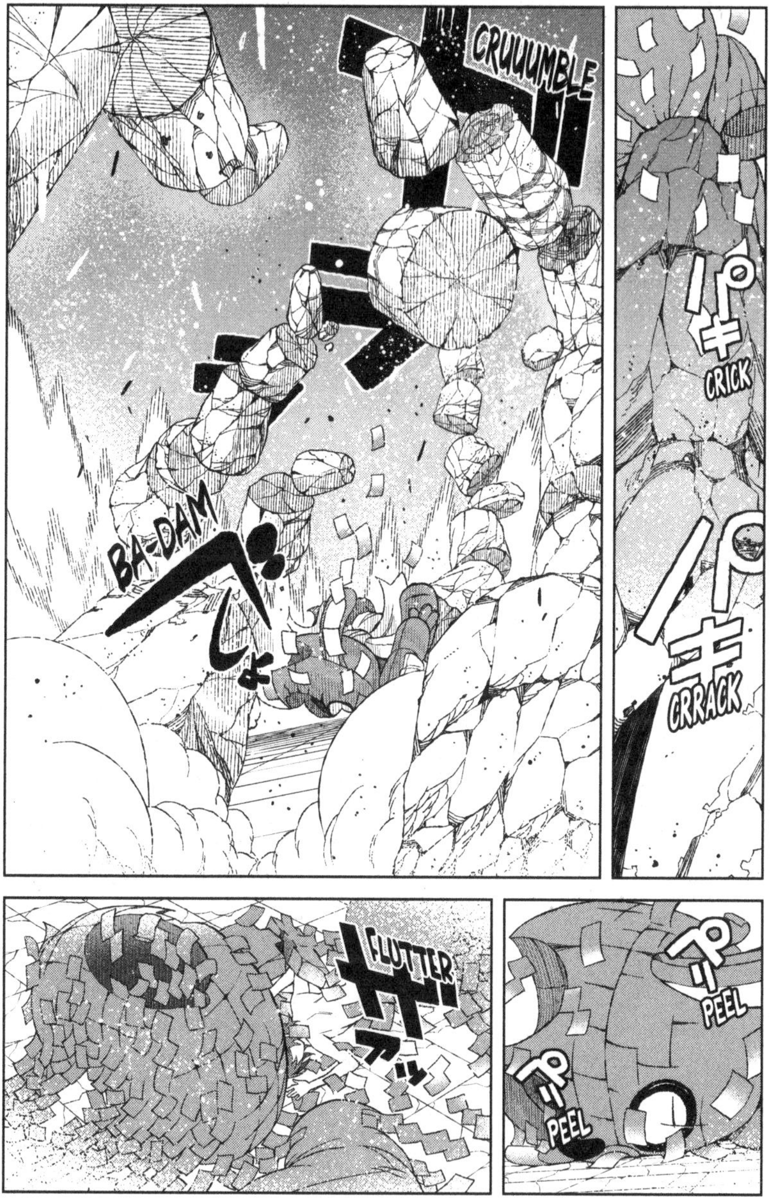
CRICK
CRRACK
CRUUUMBLE
BA-DAM
PEEL
PEEL
FLUTTER

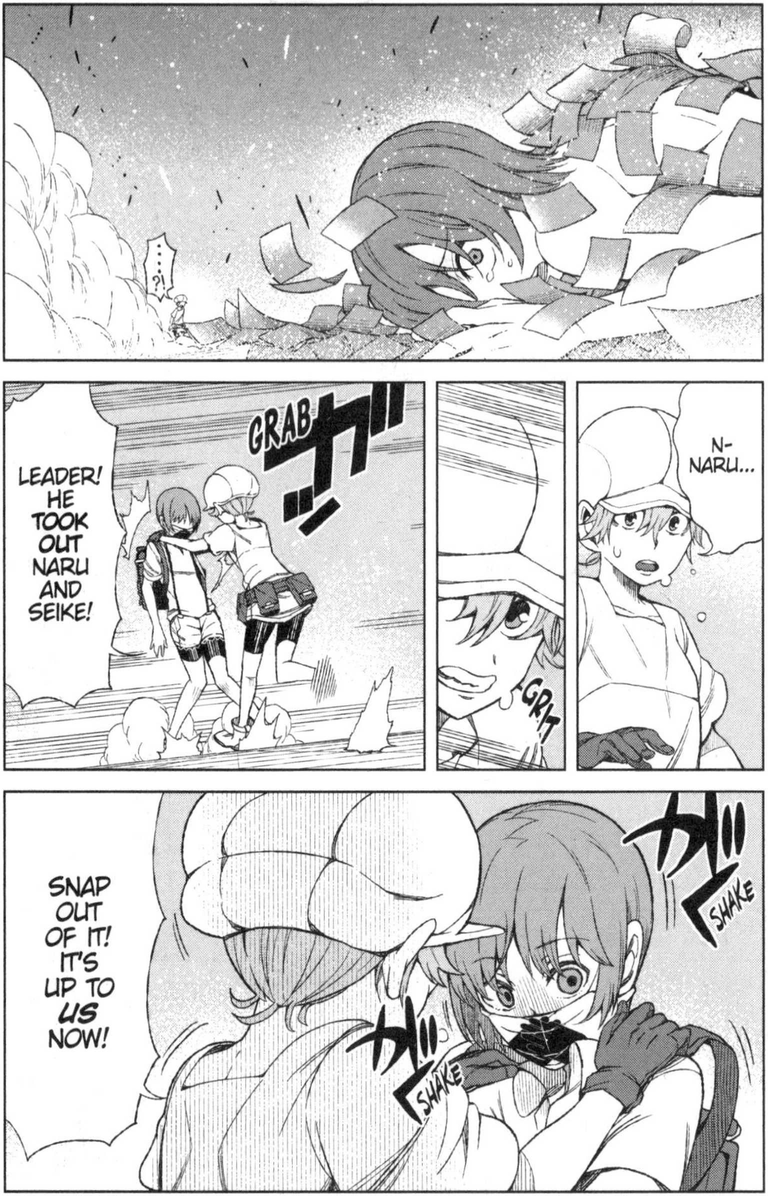
......?!
N-NARU...
GRIT
GRAB
LEADER! HE TOOK OUT NARU AND SEIKE!
SHAKE
SNAP OUT OF IT! IT'S UP TO US NOW!
SHAKE

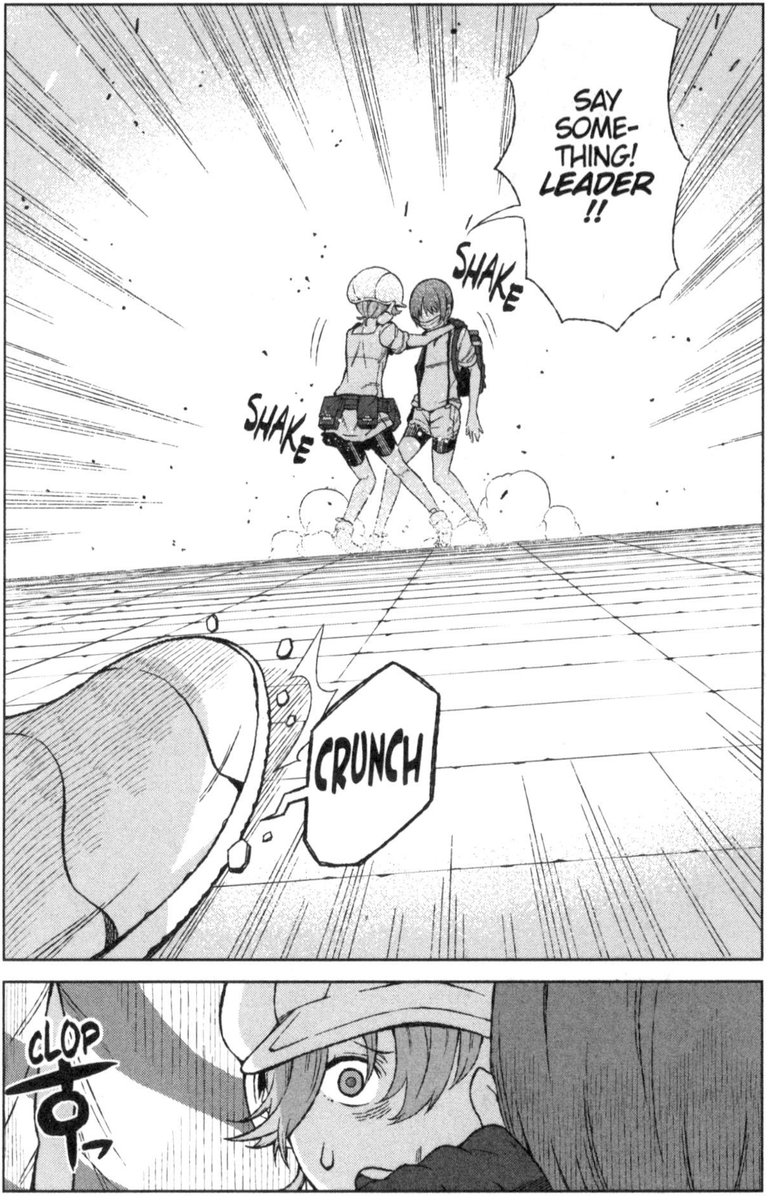
SAY SOME-THING! LEADER!!
SHAKE
SHAKE
CRUNCH
CLOP

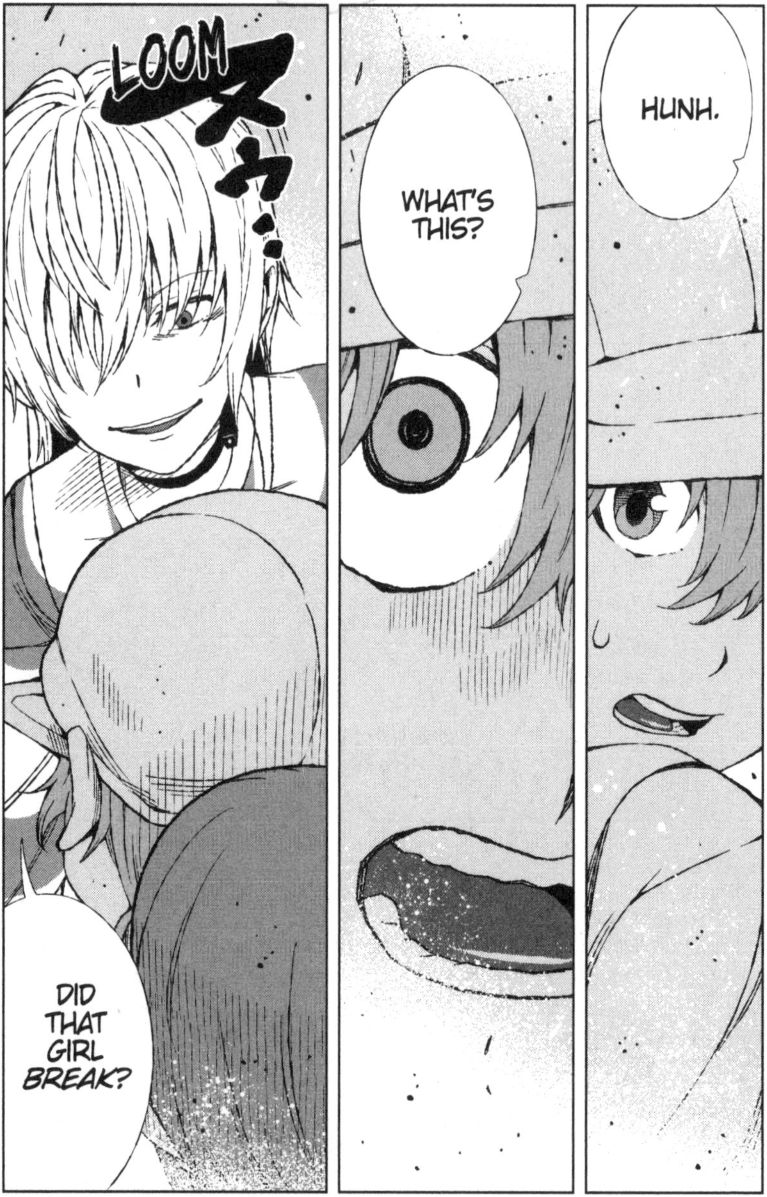
HUNH.
WHAT'S THIS?
LOOM
DID THAT GIRL BREAK?

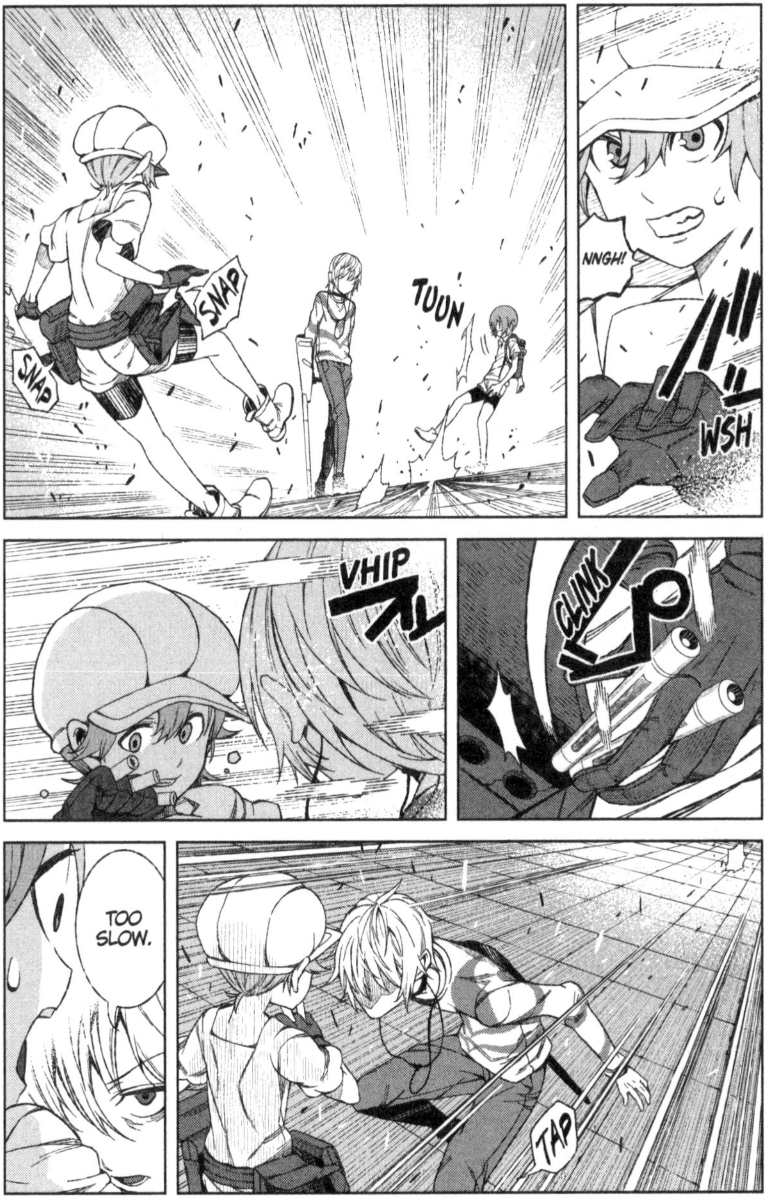
NNGH!
WSH
TUUN
SNAP
SNAP
CLINK
VHIP
TAP
TOO SLOW.

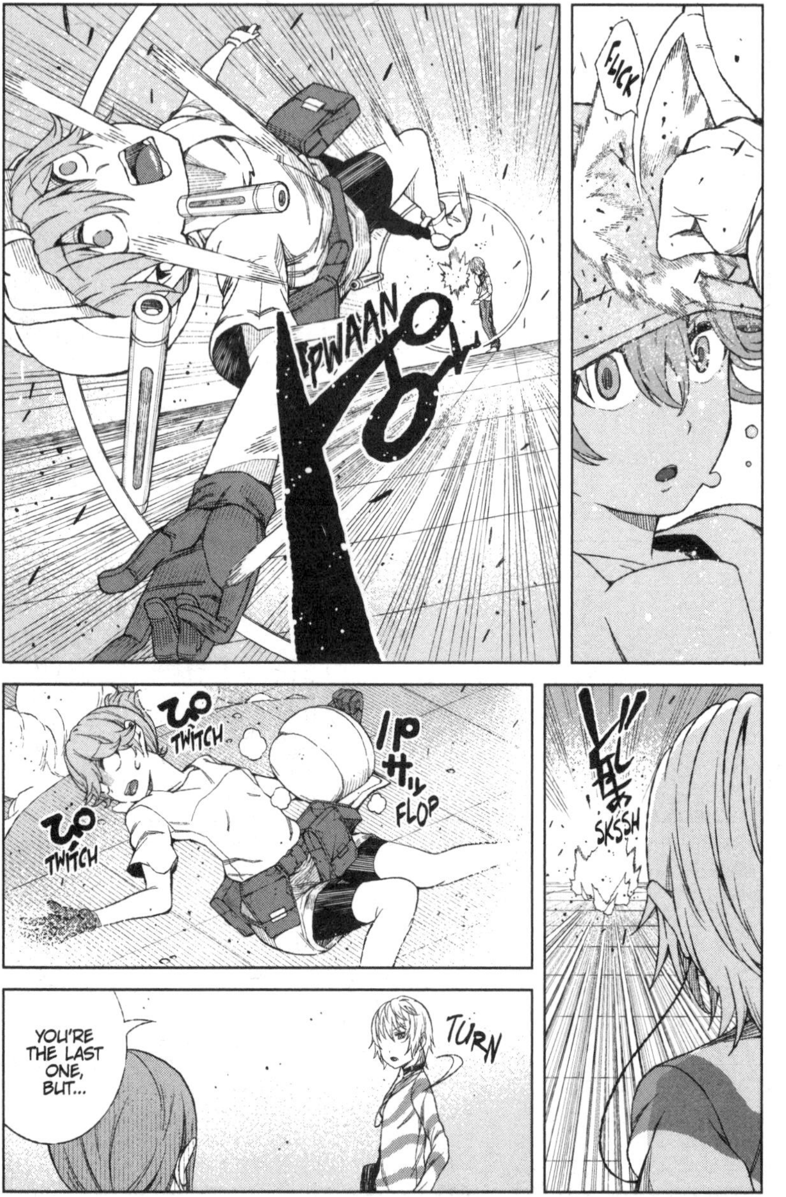
FLICK
PWAAN
SKSSH
TWITCH
FLOP
TWITCH
TURN
YOU'RE THE LAST ONE, BUT...

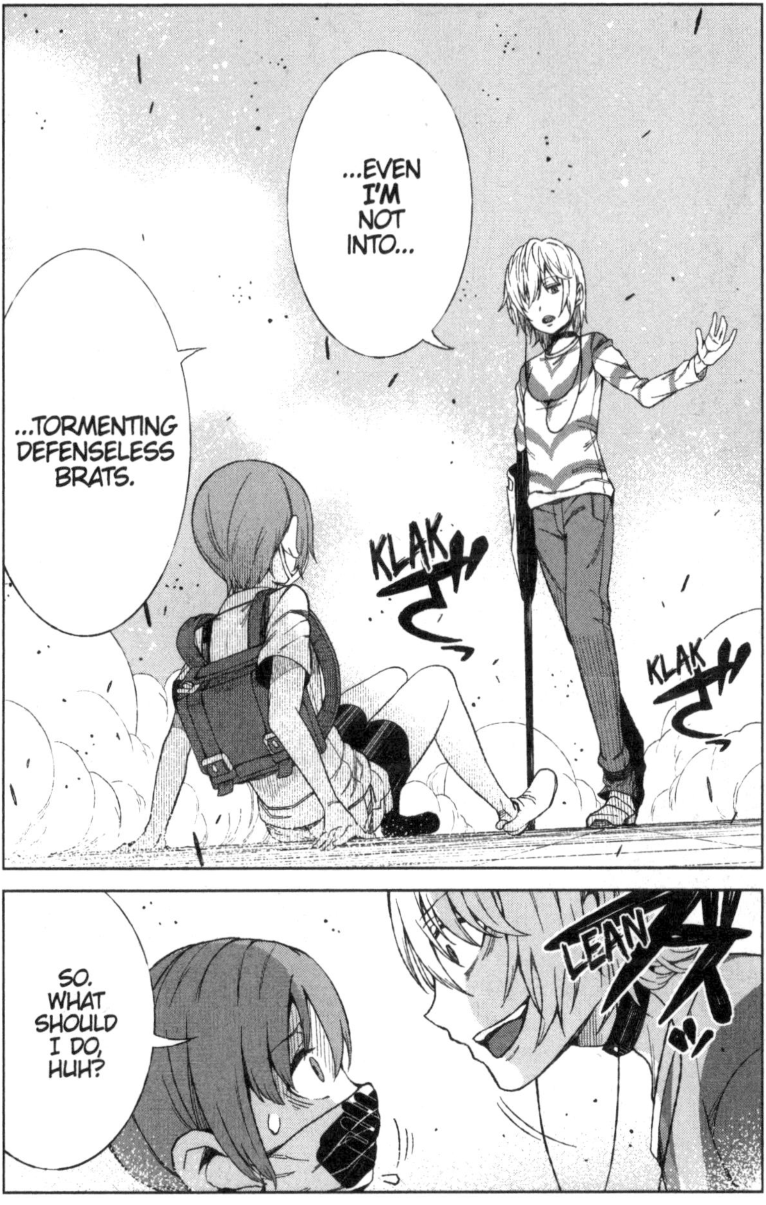
...EVEN I'M NOT INTO...
...TORMENTING DEFENSELESS BRATS.
KLAK
KLAK
LEAN
SO. WHAT SHOULD I DO, HUH?

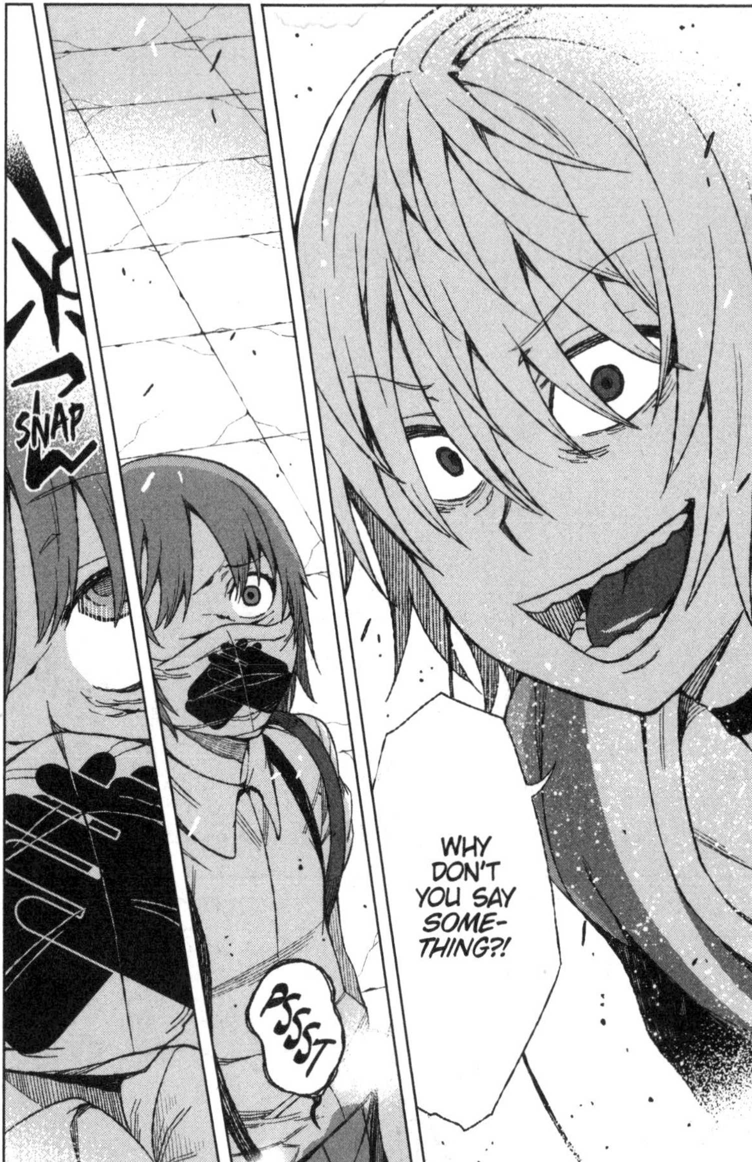
WHY DON'T YOU SAY SOME-THING?!
PSSST
SNAP

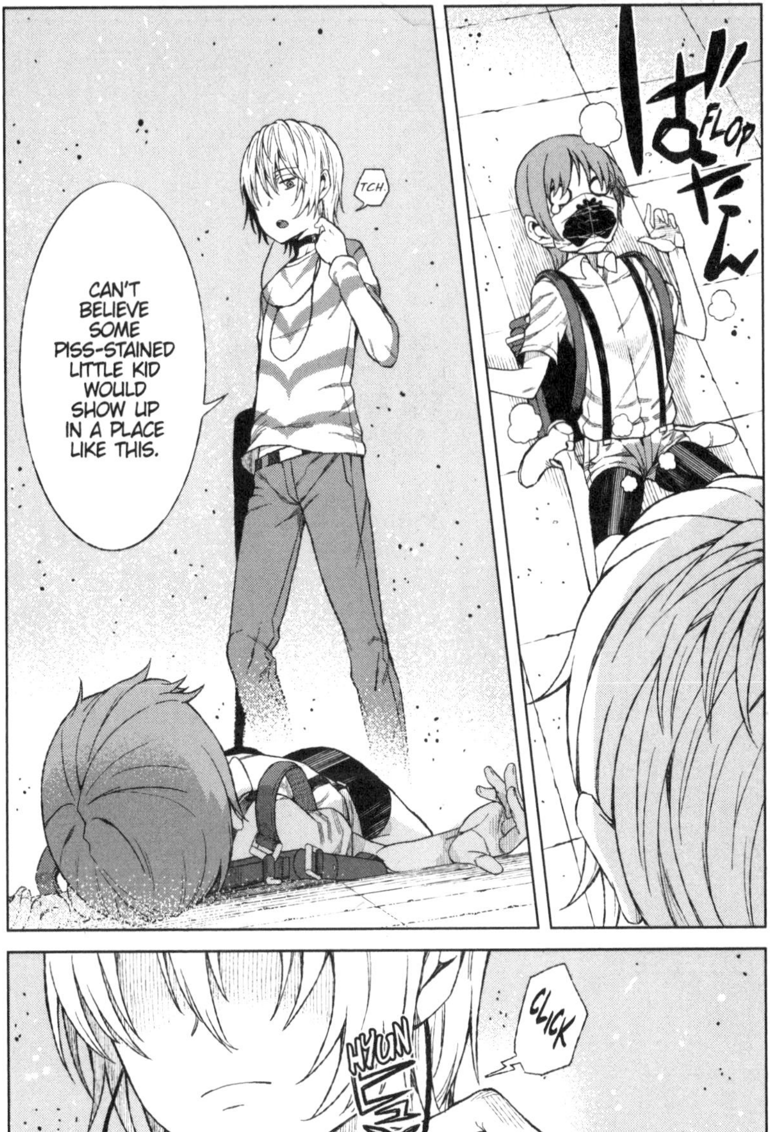
ばたん
FLOP
TCH.
CAN'T BELIEVE SOME PISS-STAINED LITTLE KID WOULD SHOW UP IN A PLACE LIKE THIS.
CLICK
HYUN

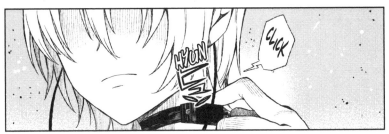

CHAPTER 18

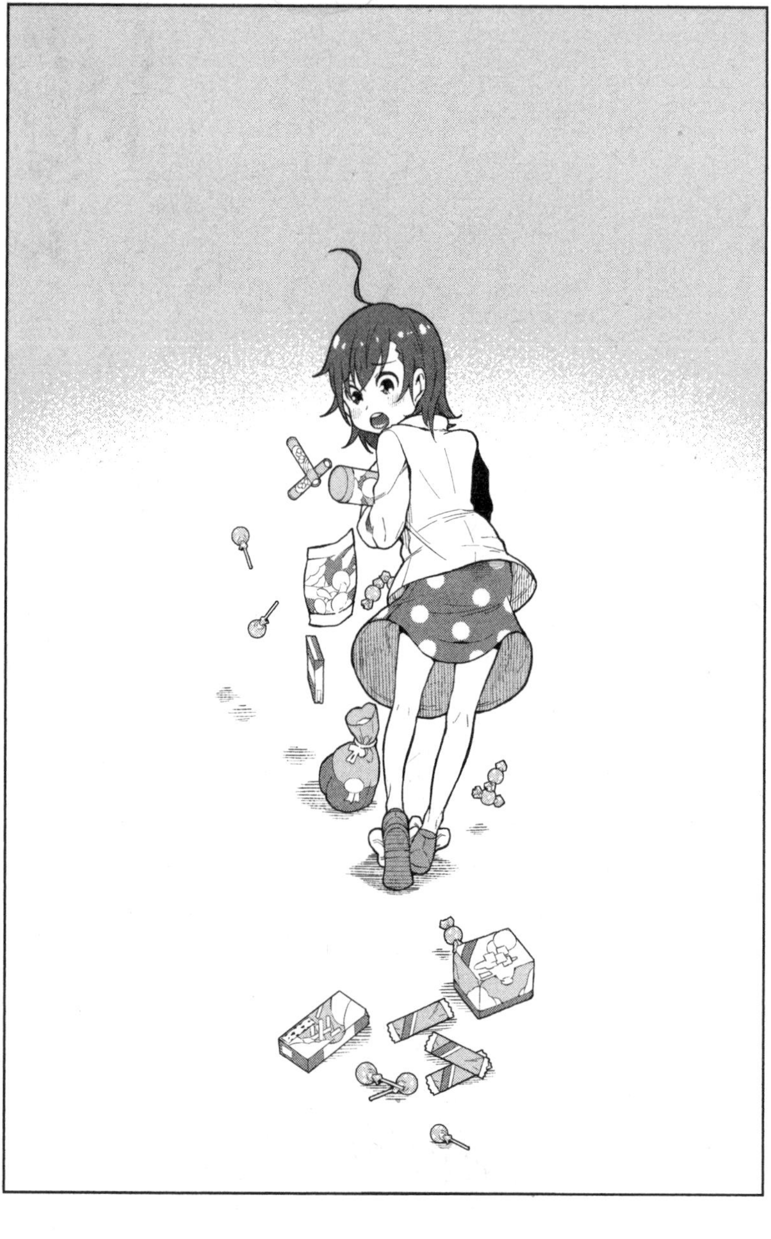

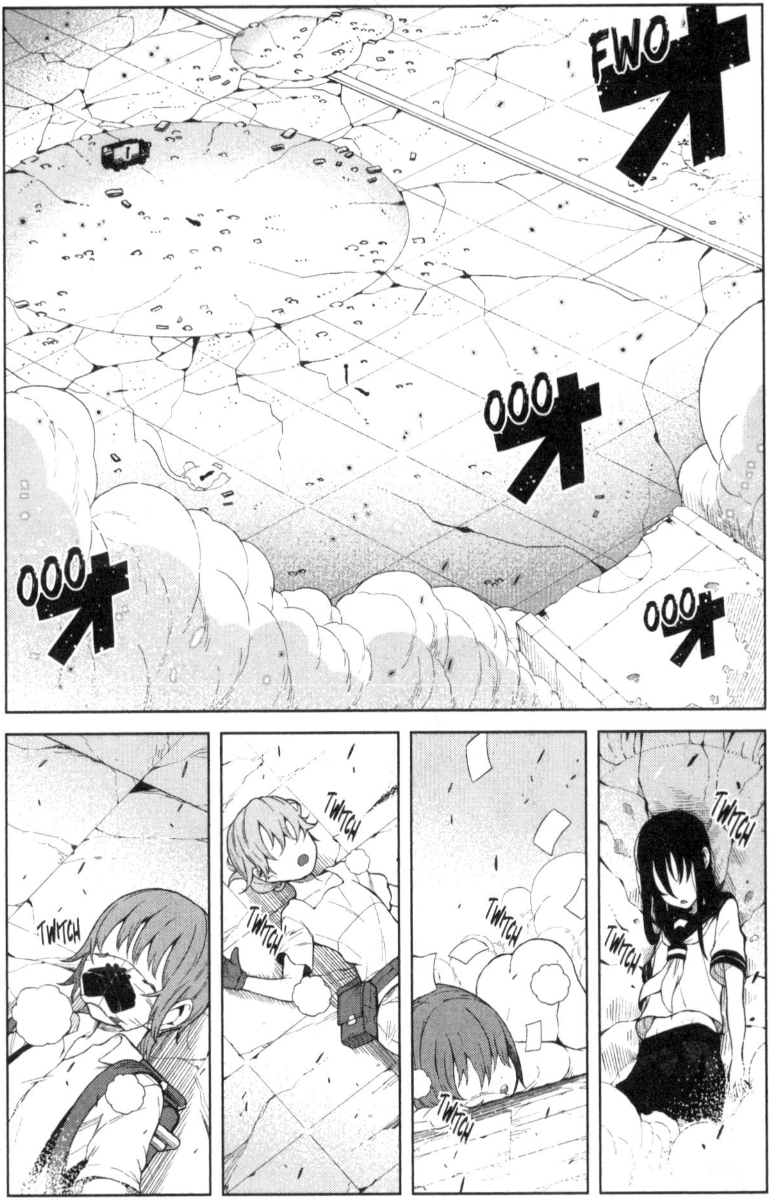
FWO
OOO
OOO
OOO
TWITCH
TWITCH
TWITCH
TWITCH
TWITCH
TWITCH
TWITCH

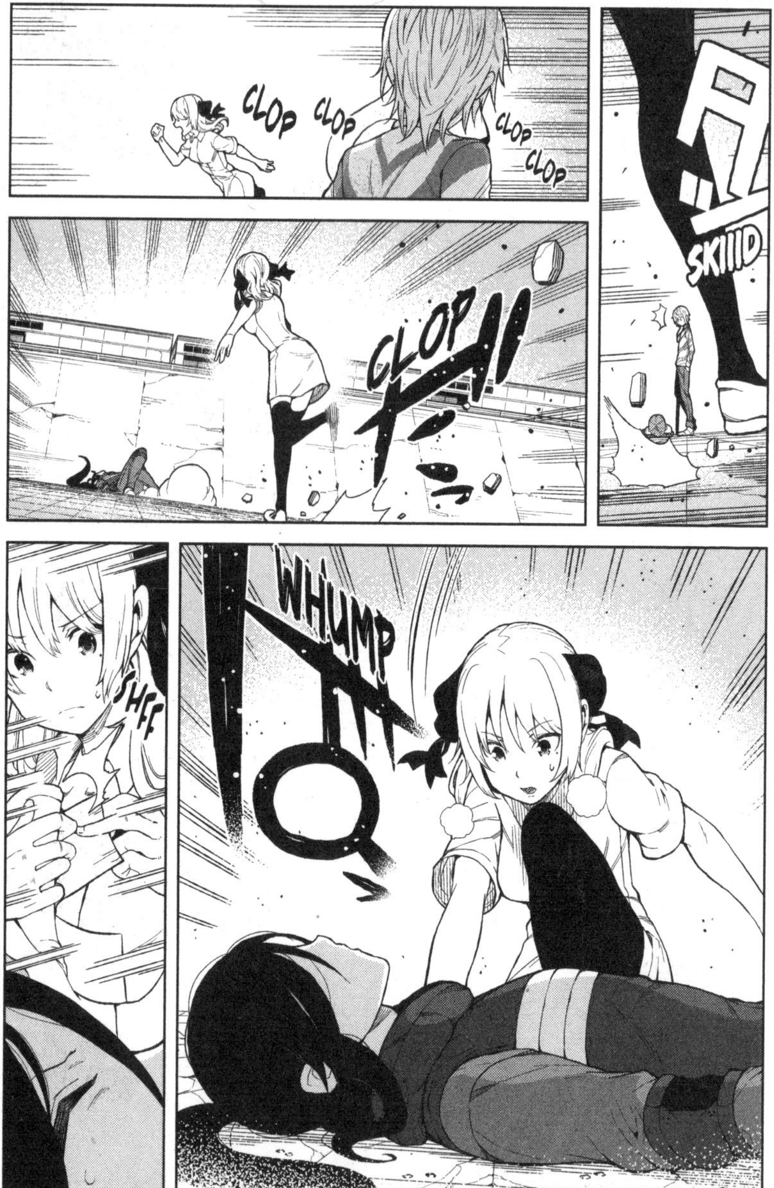
SKIIID
CLOP
CLOP
CLOP
CLOP
CLOP
WHUMP
SHFF

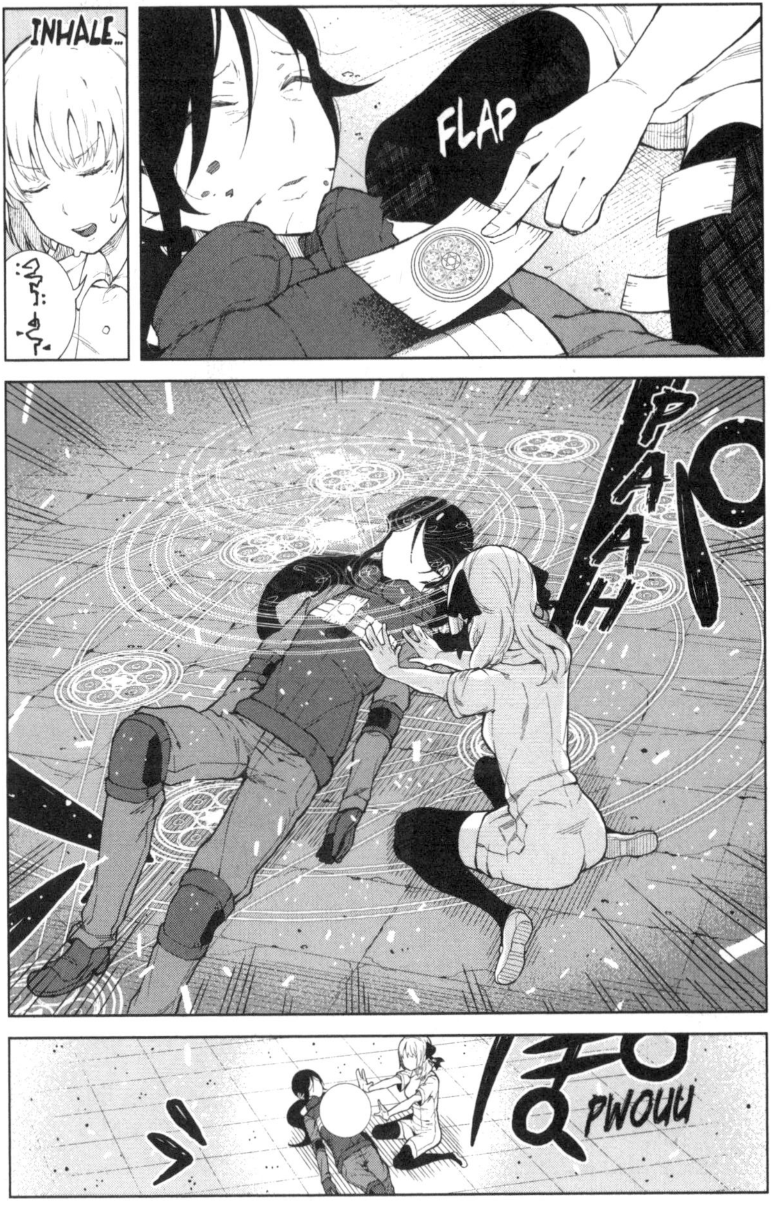
FLAP
INHALE...
PAAH
PWOUU

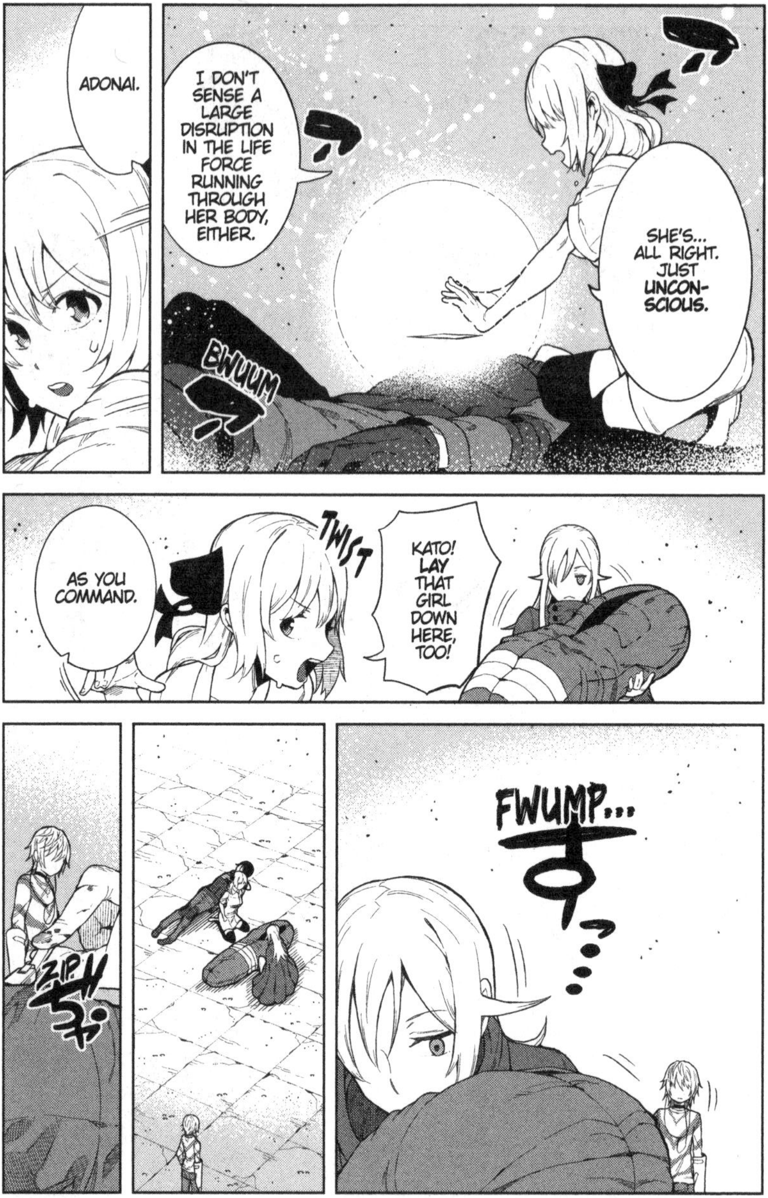
SHE'S... ALL RIGHT. JUST UNCON-SCIOUS.
I DON'T SENSE A LARGE DISRUPTION IN THE LIFE FORCE RUNNING THROUGH HER BODY, EITHER.
BWUUM
ADONAI.
KATO! LAY THAT GIRL DOWN HERE, TOO!
TWIST
AS YOU COMMAND.
FWUMP...
ZIP

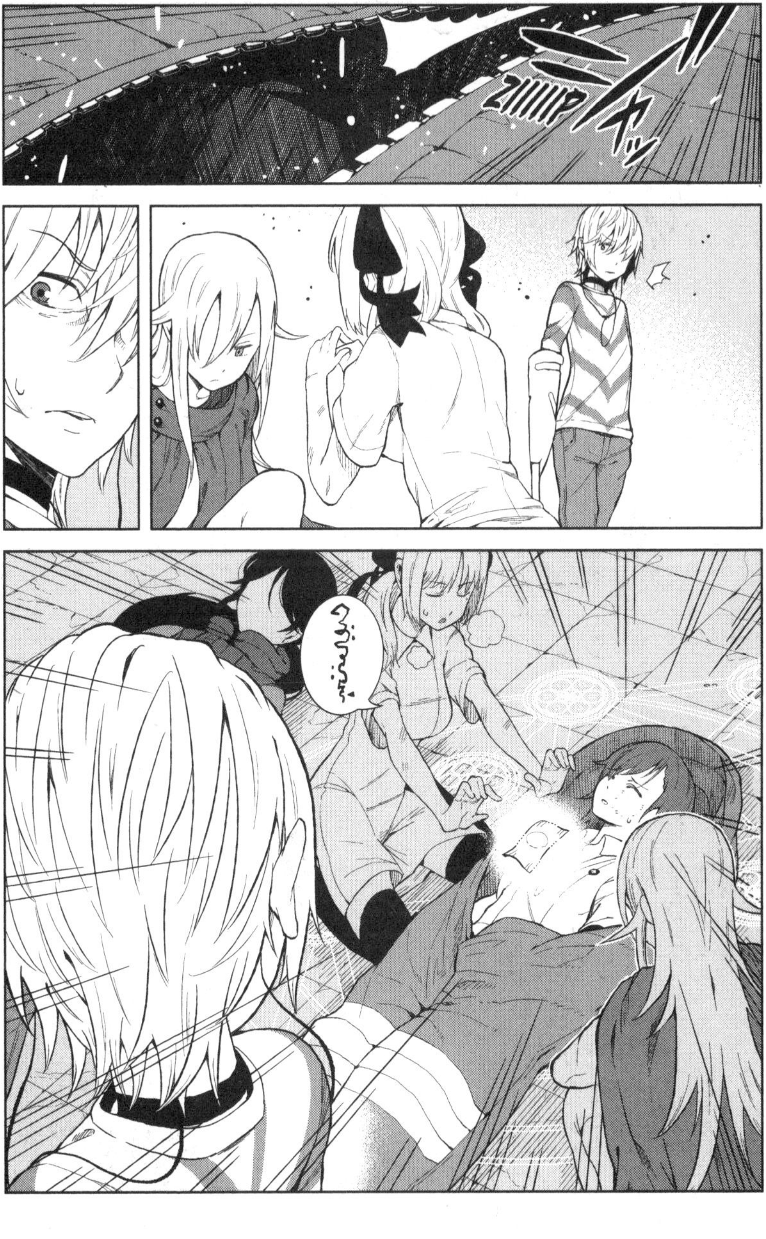
ジャッ
ZIIIIP

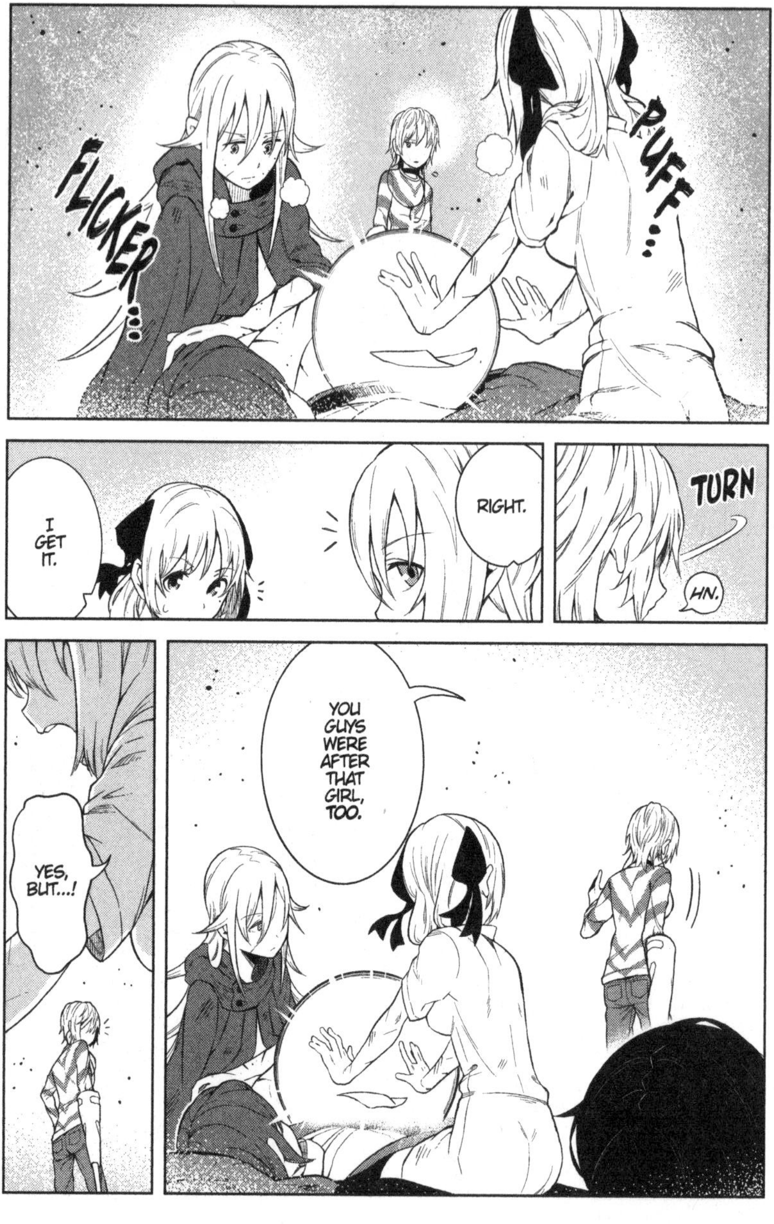
PUFF...
FLICKER...
TURN
HN.
RIGHT.
I GET IT.
YOU GUYS WERE AFTER THAT GIRL, TOO.
YES, BUT...!

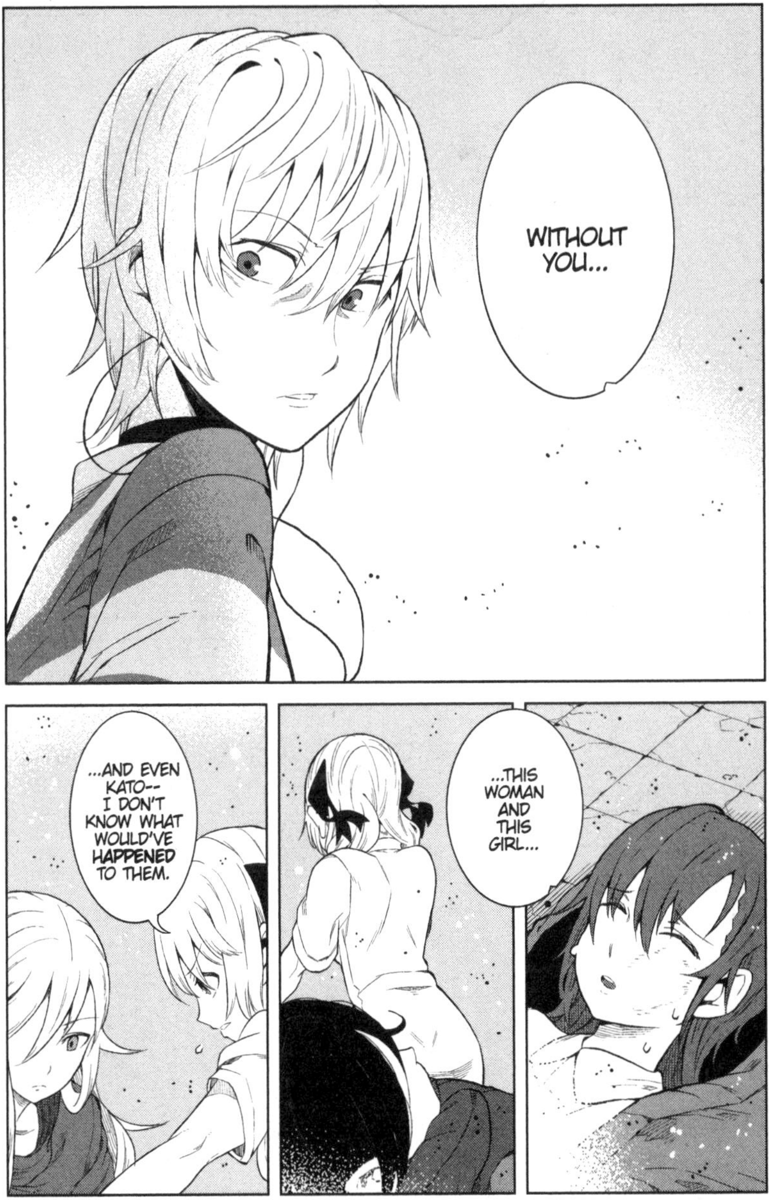
WITHOUT YOU...
...THIS WOMAN AND THIS GIRL...
...AND EVEN KATO-- I DON'T KNOW WHAT WOULD'VE **HAPPENED** TO THEM.

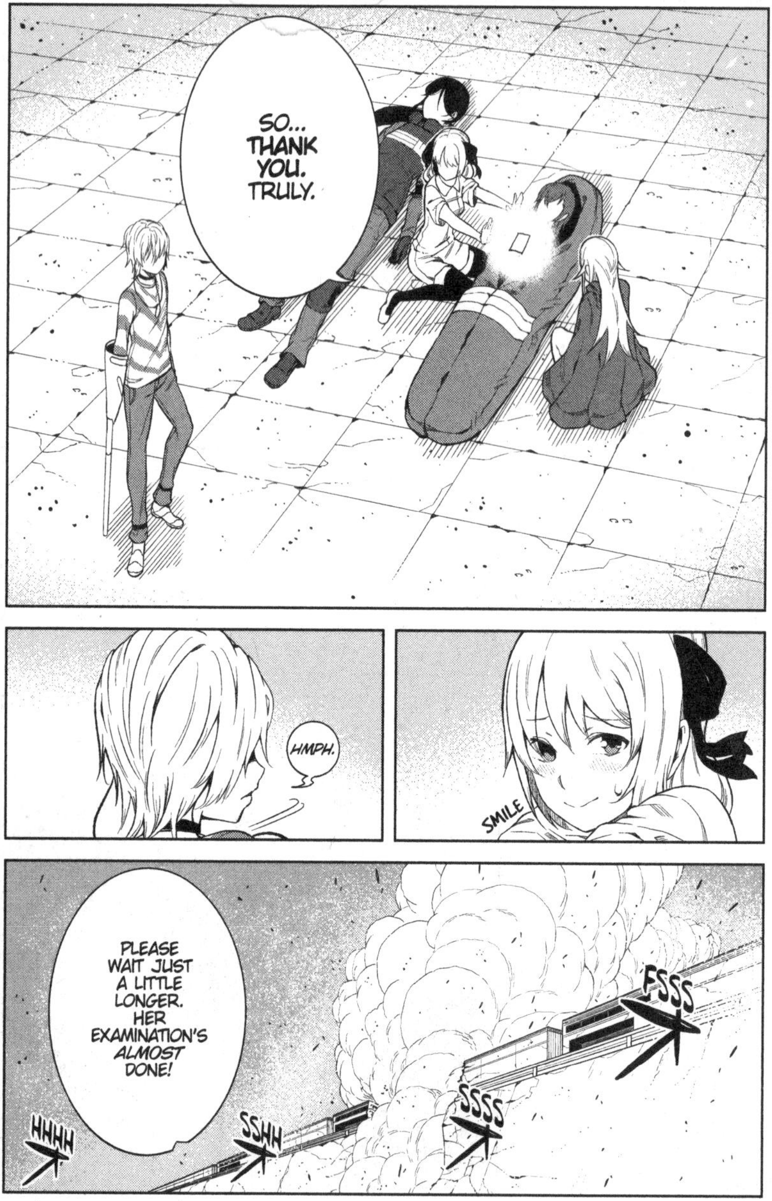
SO... THANK YOU. TRULY.
SMILE
HMPH.
PLEASE WAIT JUST A LITTLE LONGER. HER EXAMINATION'S *ALMOST* DONE!
FSSS
SSSS
SSHH
HHHH

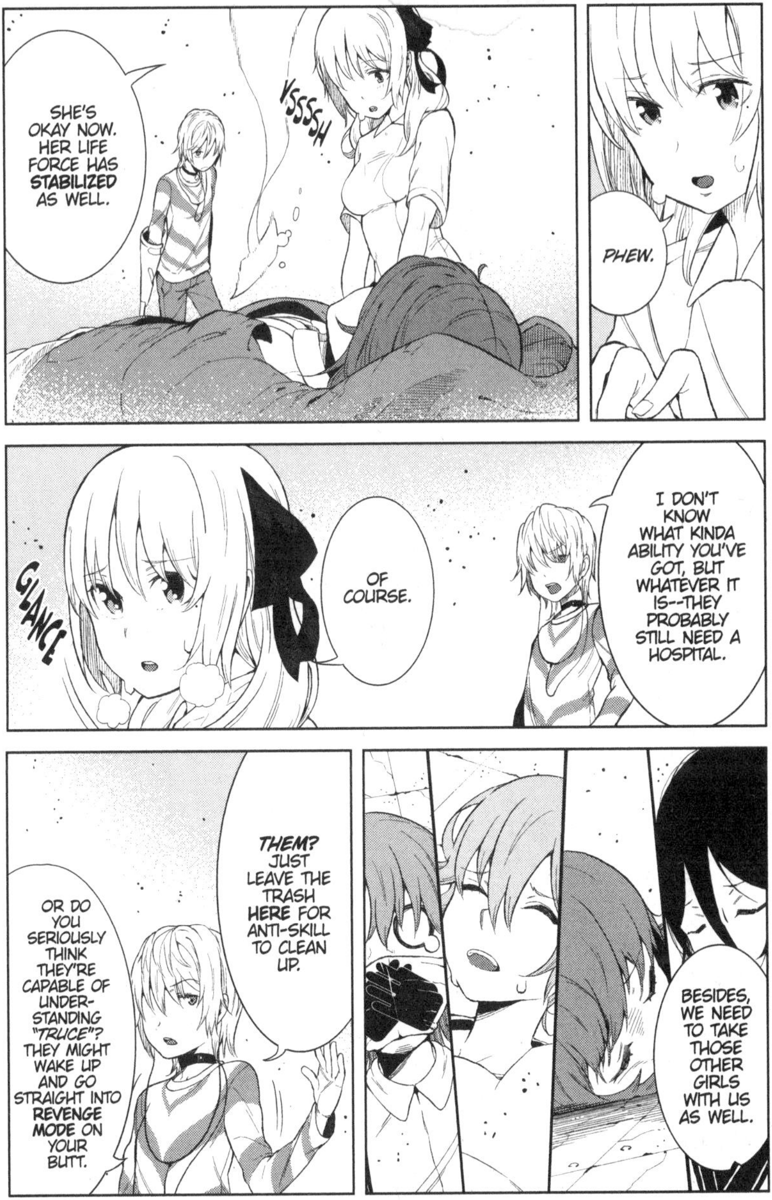
PHEW.
VSSSSH
SHE'S OKAY NOW. HER LIFE FORCE HAS **STABILIZED** AS WELL.
I DON'T KNOW WHAT KINDA ABILITY YOU'VE GOT, BUT WHATEVER IT IS--THEY PROBABLY STILL NEED A HOSPITAL.
OF COURSE.
GLANCE
BESIDES, WE NEED TO TAKE THOSE OTHER GIRLS WITH US AS WELL.
THEM? JUST LEAVE THE TRASH **HERE** FOR ANTI-SKILL TO CLEAN UP.
OR DO YOU SERIOUSLY THINK THEY'RE CAPABLE OF UNDER-STANDING "*TRUCE*"? THEY MIGHT WAKE UP AND GO STRAIGHT INTO **REVENGE MODE** ON YOUR BUTT.

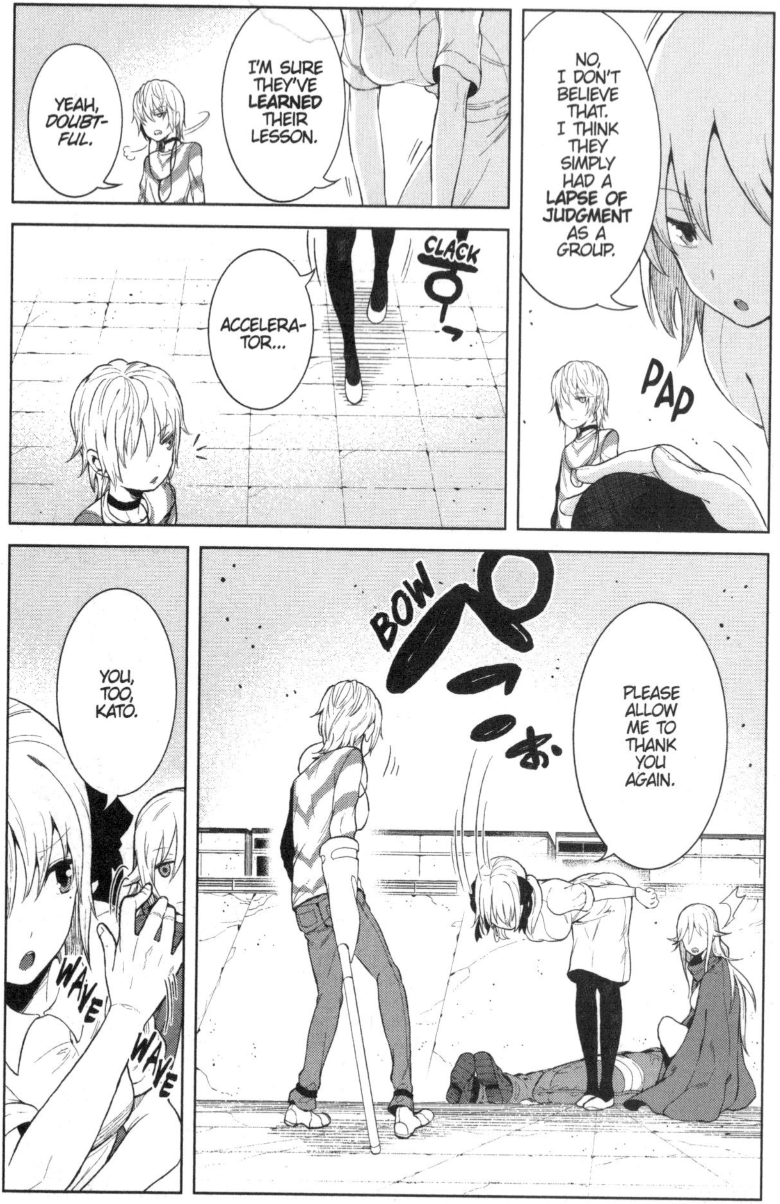
NO, I DON'T BELIEVE THAT. I THINK THEY SIMPLY HAD A **LAPSE OF JUDGMENT** AS A GROUP.
PAP
I'M SURE THEY'VE **LEARNED** THEIR LESSON.
YEAH, DOUBT-FUL.
CLACK
ACCELERA-TOR...
BOW
PLEASE ALLOW ME TO THANK YOU AGAIN.
YOU, TOO, KATO.
WAVE
WAVE

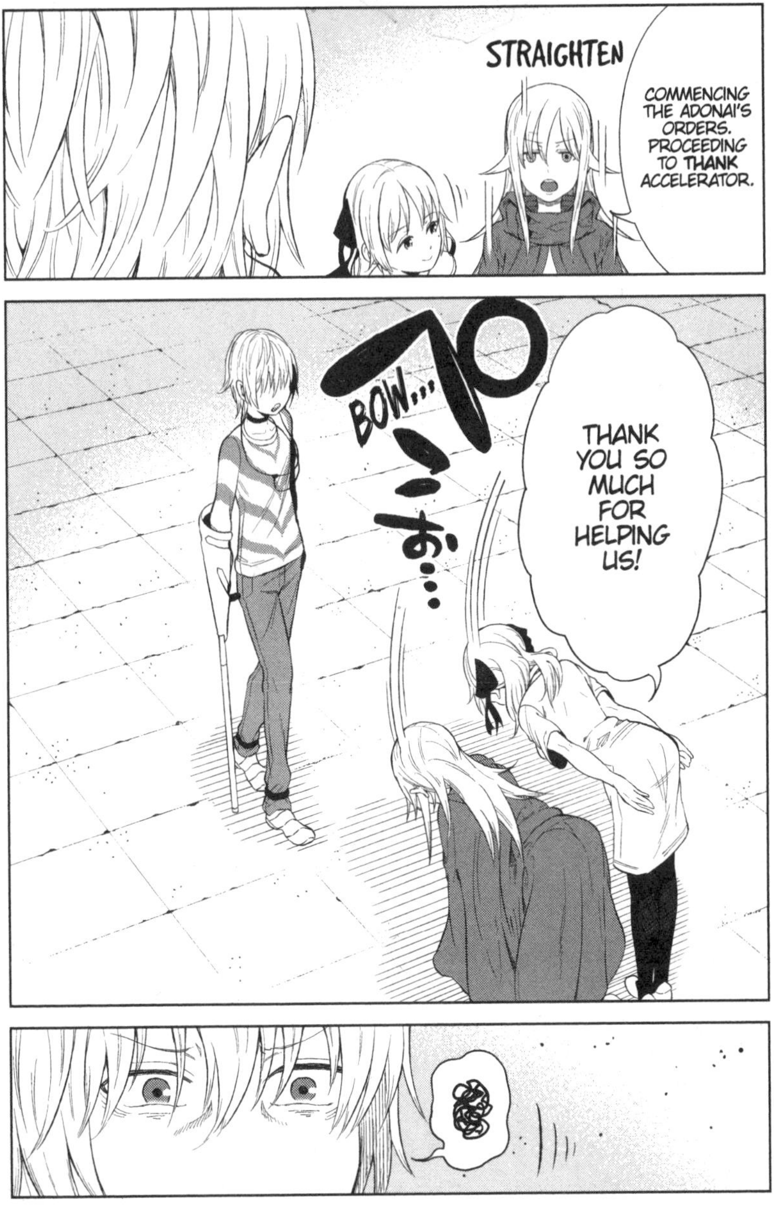
COMMENCING THE ADONAI'S ORDERS. PROCEEDING TO **THANK** ACCELERATOR.
STRAIGHTEN
THANK YOU SO MUCH FOR HELPING US!
ぺこお…
BOW...

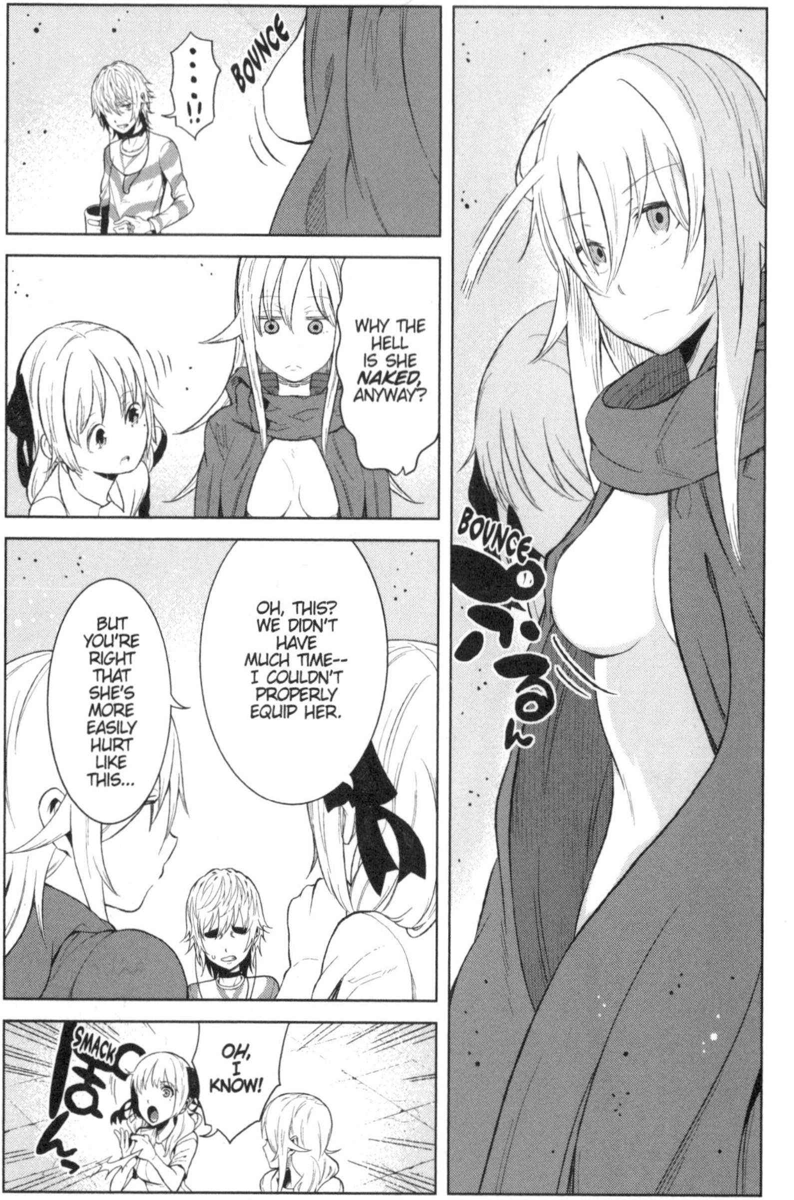
BOUNCE
ぷるん
BOUNCE
......!!
WHY THE HELL IS SHE *NAKED*, ANYWAY?
OH, THIS? WE DIDN'T HAVE MUCH TIME-- I COULDN'T PROPERLY EQUIP HER.
BUT YOU'RE RIGHT THAT SHE'S MORE EASILY HURT LIKE THIS...
OH, I KNOW!
SMACK
ぽん

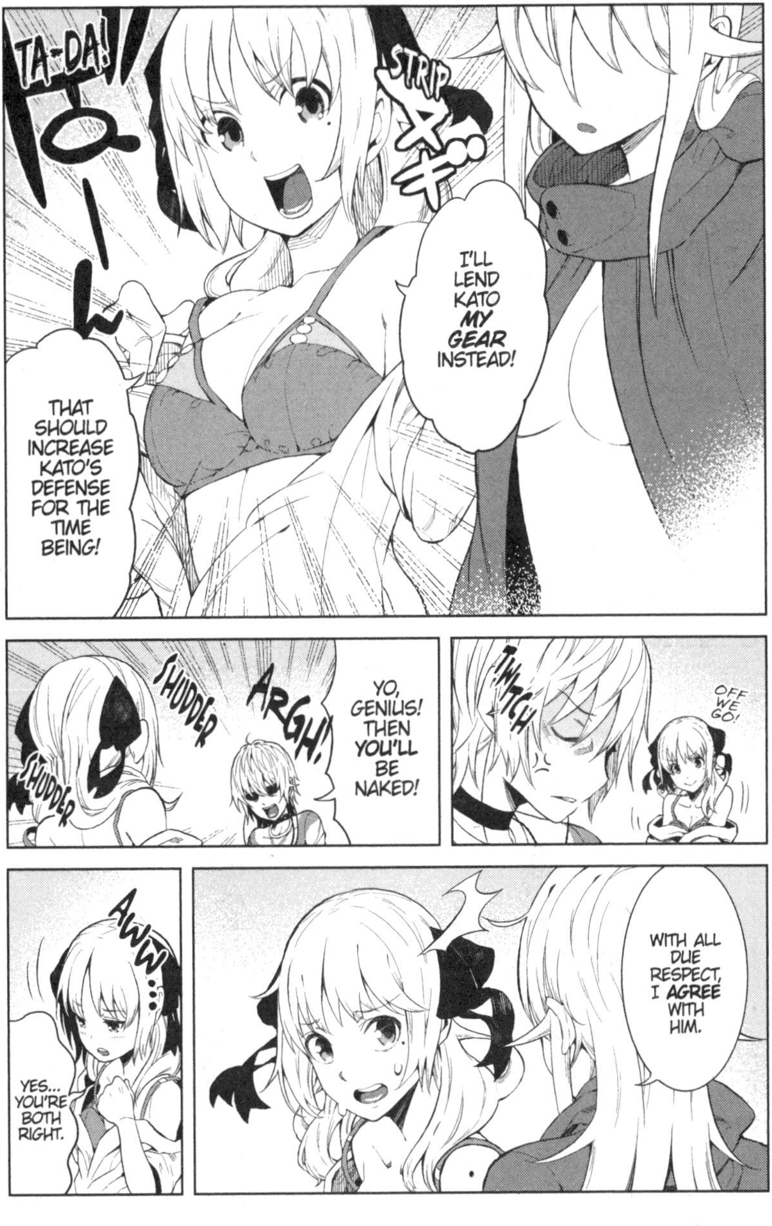
STRIP
I'LL LEND KATO MY GEAR INSTEAD!
TA-DA!
THAT SHOULD INCREASE KATO'S DEFENSE FOR THE TIME BEING!
TWITCH
OFF WE GO!
YO, GENIUS! THEN YOU'LL BE NAKED!
ARGH!
SHUDDER
SHUDDER
WITH ALL DUE RESPECT, I AGREE WITH HIM.
AWW...
YES... YOU'RE BOTH RIGHT.

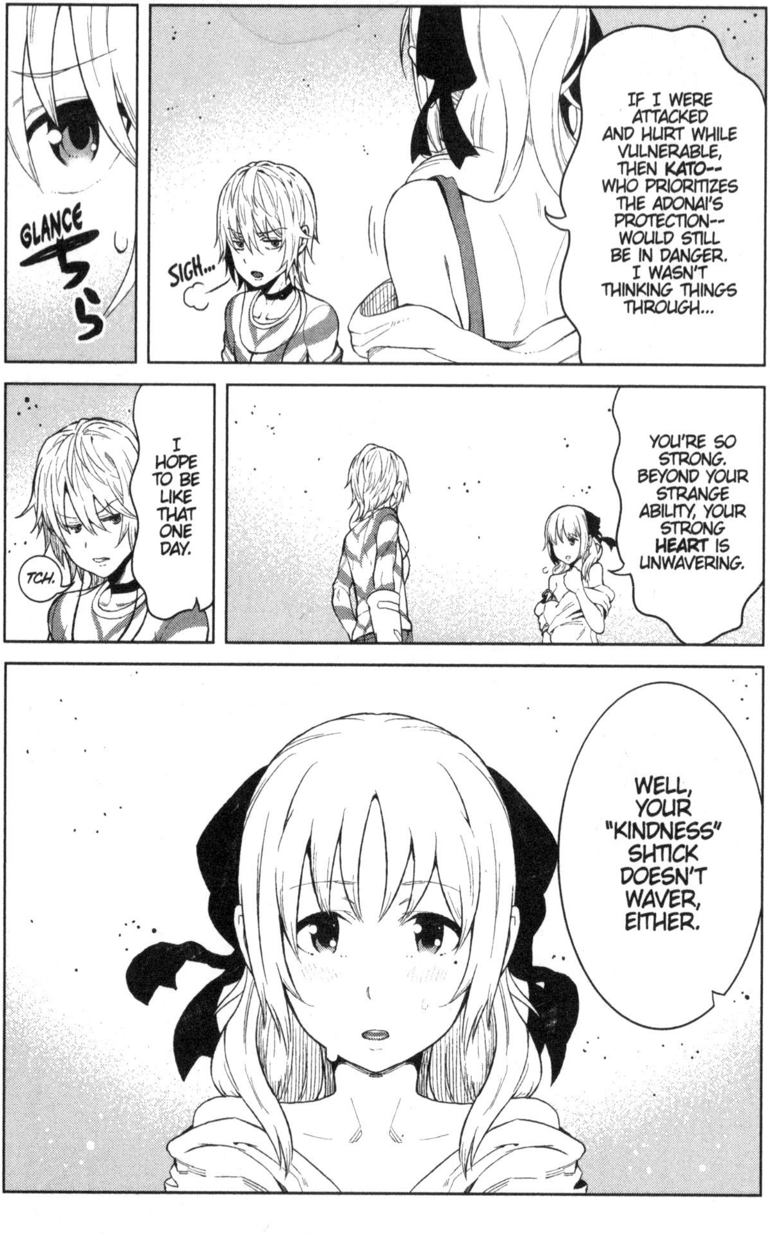
IF I WERE ATTACKED AND HURT WHILE VULNERABLE, THEN KATO-- WHO PRIORITIZES THE ADONAI'S PROTECTION-- WOULD STILL BE IN DANGER. I WASN'T THINKING THINGS THROUGH...
SIGH...
GLANCE
ちら
YOU'RE SO STRONG. BEYOND YOUR STRANGE ABILITY, YOUR STRONG HEART IS UNWAVERING.
I HOPE TO BE LIKE THAT ONE DAY.
TCH.
WELL, YOUR "KINDNESS" SHTICK DOESN'T WAVER, EITHER.

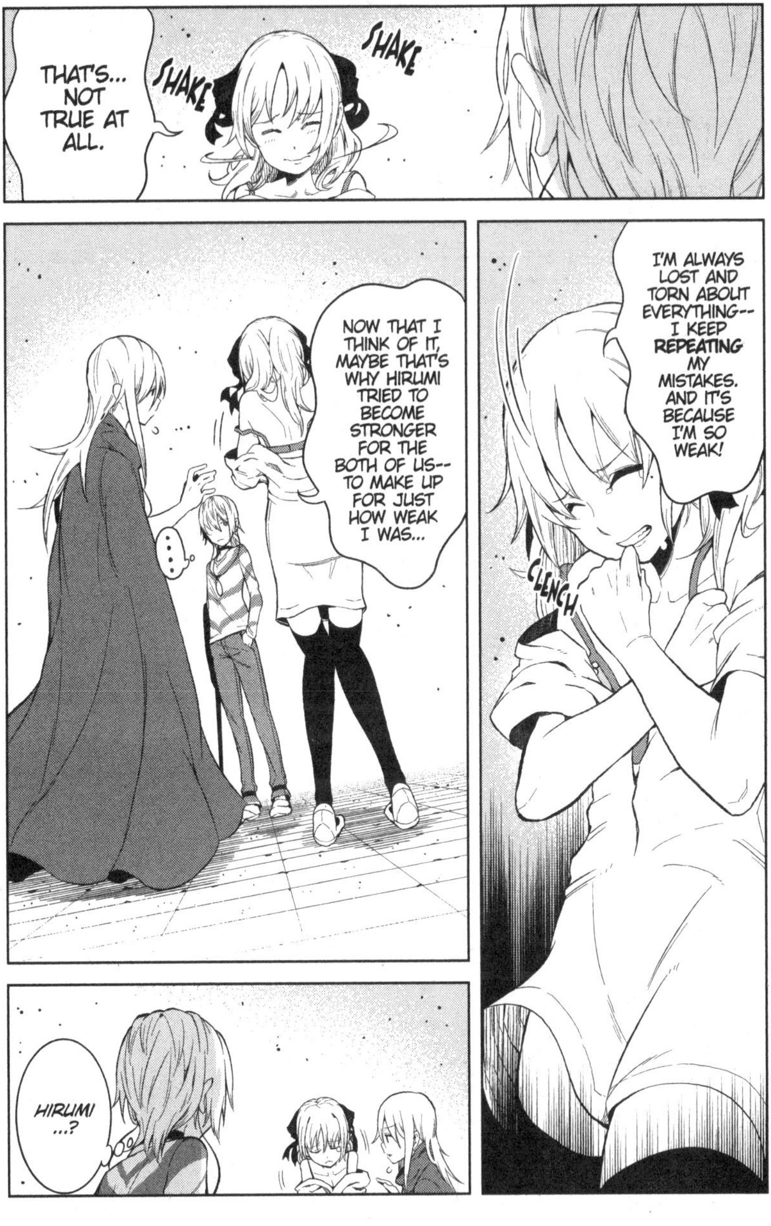
SHAKE
SHAKE
THAT'S... NOT TRUE AT ALL.
I'M ALWAYS LOST AND TORN ABOUT EVERYTHING-- I KEEP **REPEATING** MY MISTAKES. AND IT'S BECAUSE I'M SO WEAK!
CLENCH
NOW THAT I THINK OF IT, MAYBE THAT'S WHY HIRUMI TRIED TO BECOME STRONGER FOR THE BOTH OF US-- TO MAKE UP FOR JUST HOW WEAK I WAS...
...
...
HIRUMI ...?

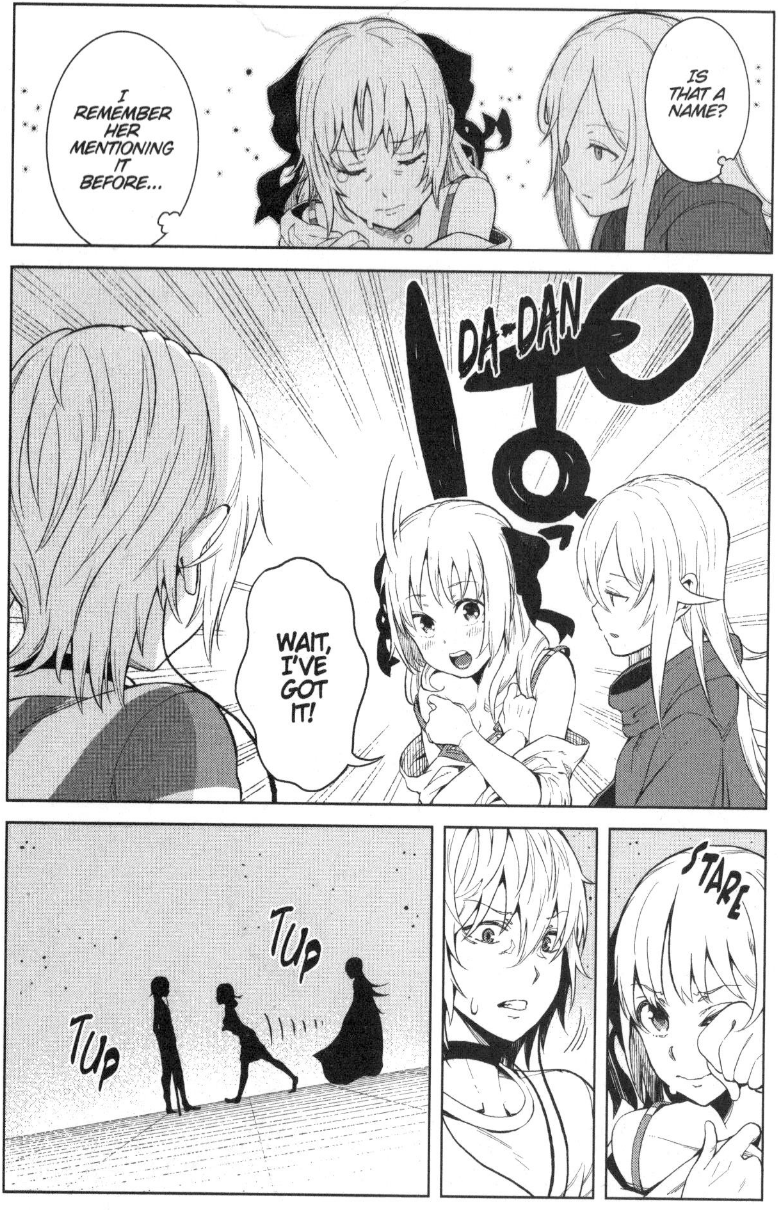
IS THAT A NAME?
I REMEMBER HER MENTIONING IT BEFORE...
DA-DAN
WAIT, I'VE GOT IT!
STARE
TUP
TUP

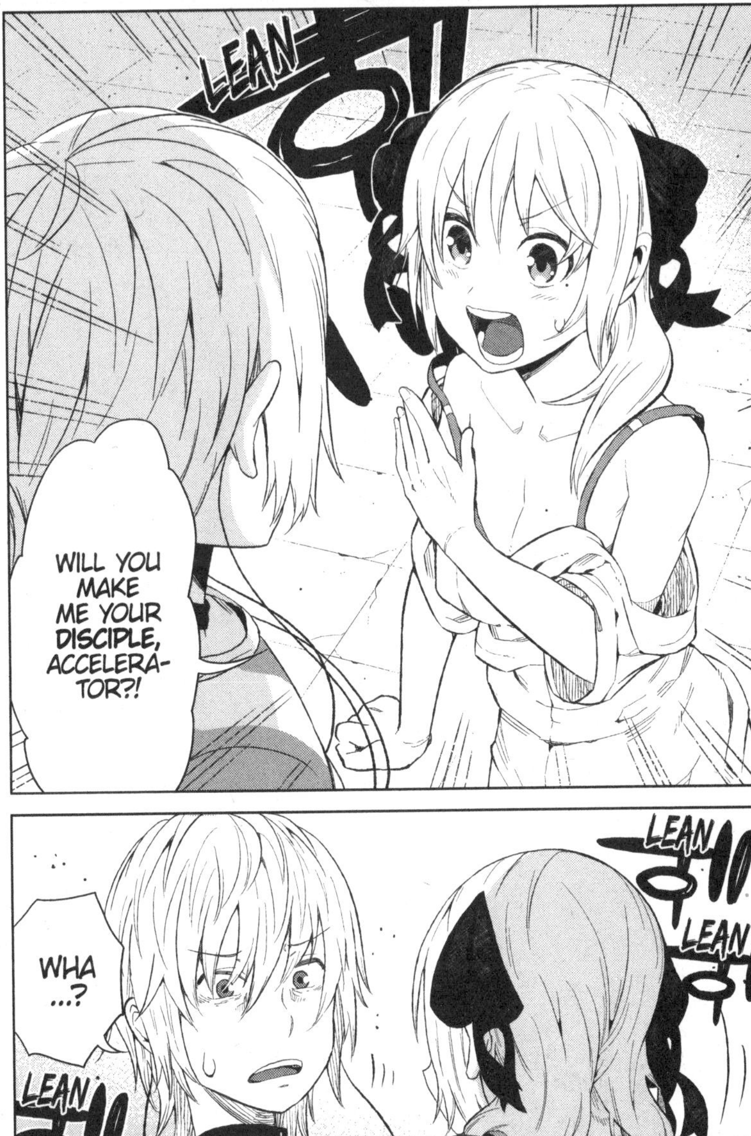
LEAN
WILL YOU MAKE ME YOUR DISCIPLE, ACCELERATOR?!
LEAN
LEAN
WHA ...?
LEAN

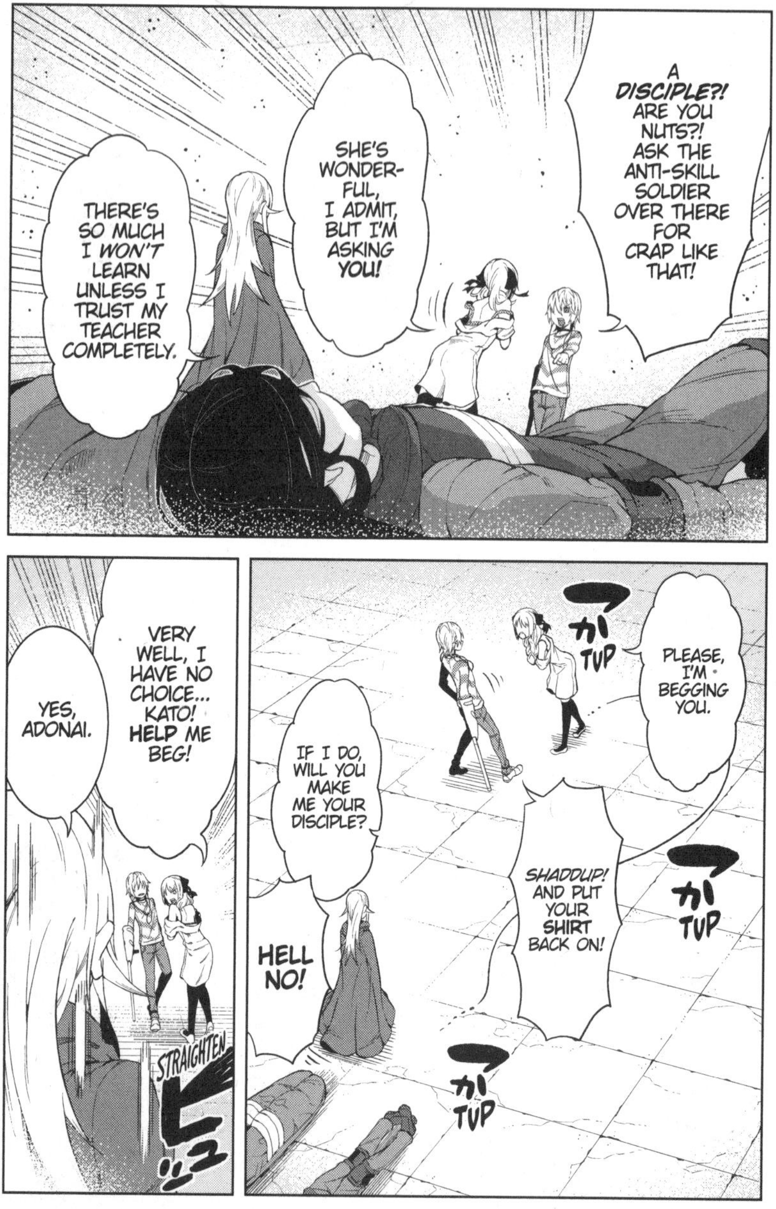
A DISCIPLE?! ARE YOU NUTS?! ASK THE ANTI-SKILL SOLDIER OVER THERE FOR CRAP LIKE THAT!
SHE'S WONDERFUL, I ADMIT, BUT I'M ASKING YOU!
THERE'S SO MUCH I WON'T LEARN UNLESS I TRUST MY TEACHER COMPLETELY.
TUP
PLEASE, I'M BEGGING YOU.
SHADDUP! AND PUT YOUR SHIRT BACK ON!
TUP
IF I DO, WILL YOU MAKE ME YOUR DISCIPLE?
HELL NO!
TUP
VERY WELL, I HAVE NO CHOICE... KATO! HELP ME BEG!
YES, ADONAI.
STRAIGHTEN

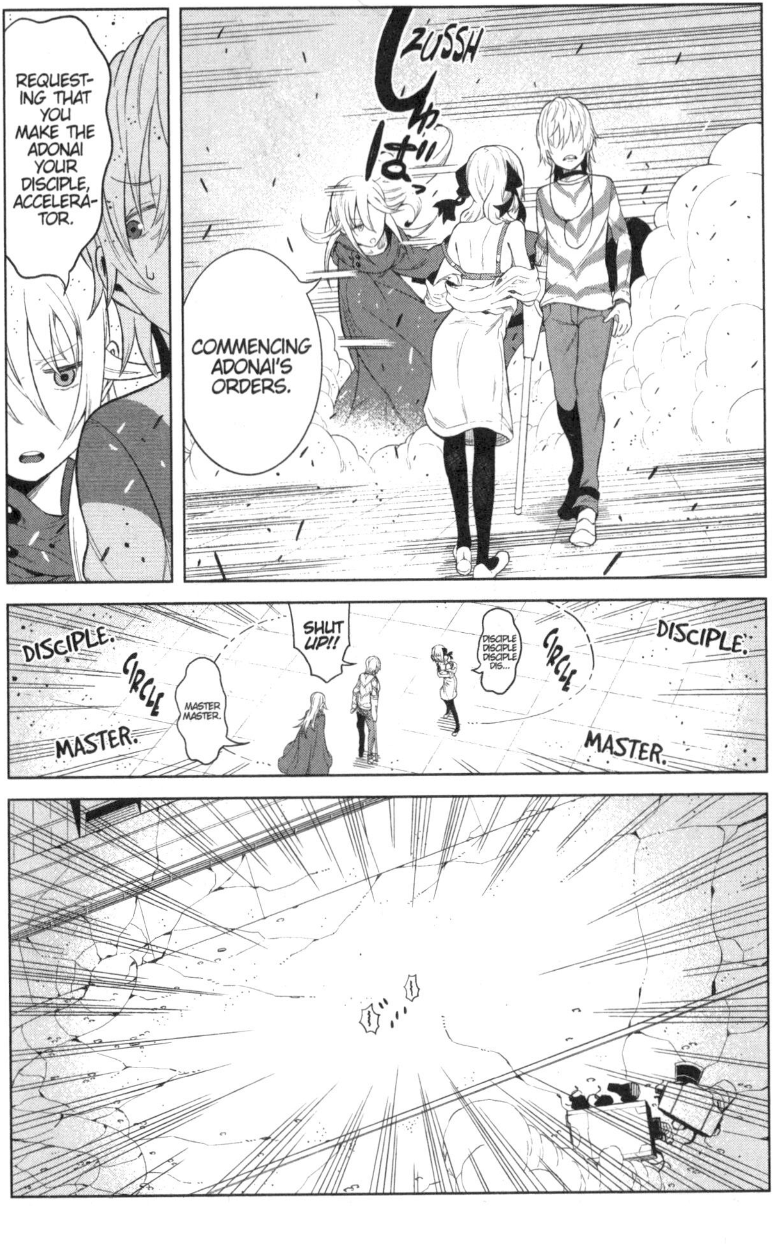
ZUSSH
COMMENCING ADONAI'S ORDERS.
REQUESTING THAT YOU MAKE THE ADONAI YOUR DISCIPLE, ACCELERATOR.
DISCIPLE.
CIRCLE
MASTER.
DISCIPLE DISCIPLE DISCIPLE DIS...
SHUT UP!!
MASTER MASTER.
DISCIPLE.
CIRCLE
MASTER.

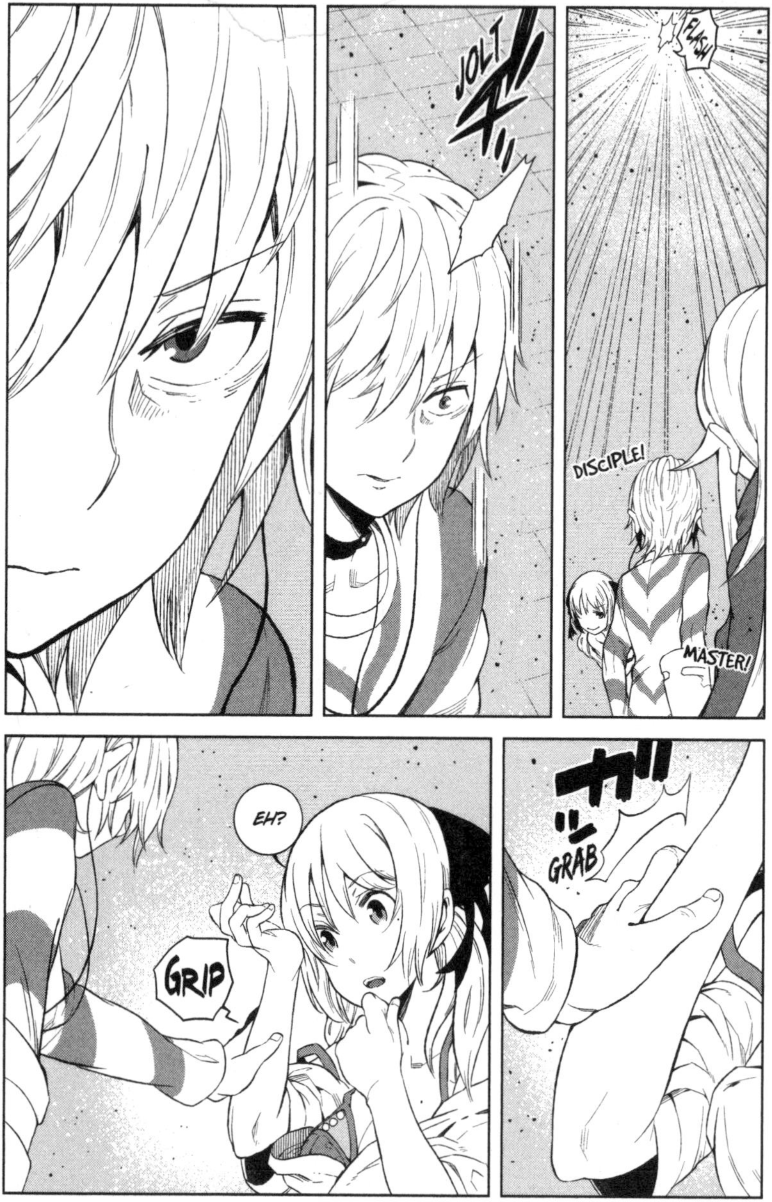
FLASH
DISCIPLE!
MASTER!
JOLT
GRAB
EH?
GRIP

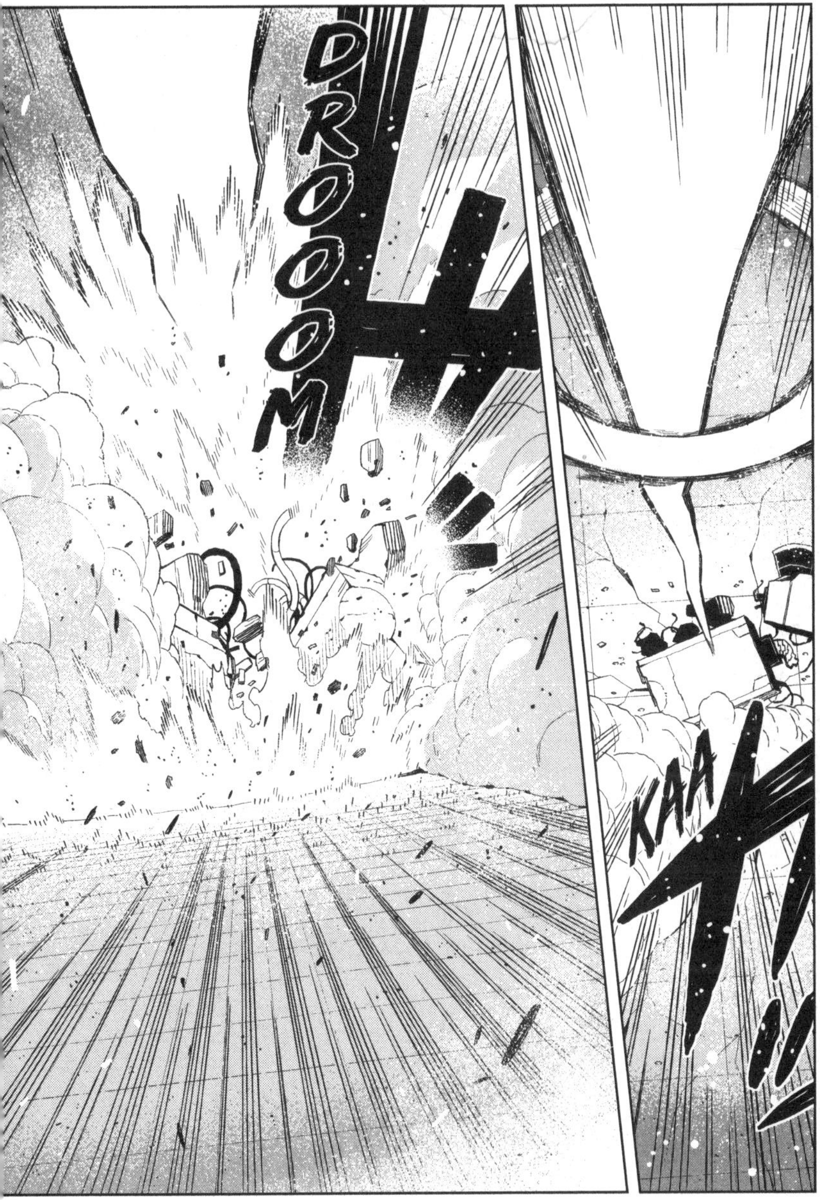
KAA
DROOOM

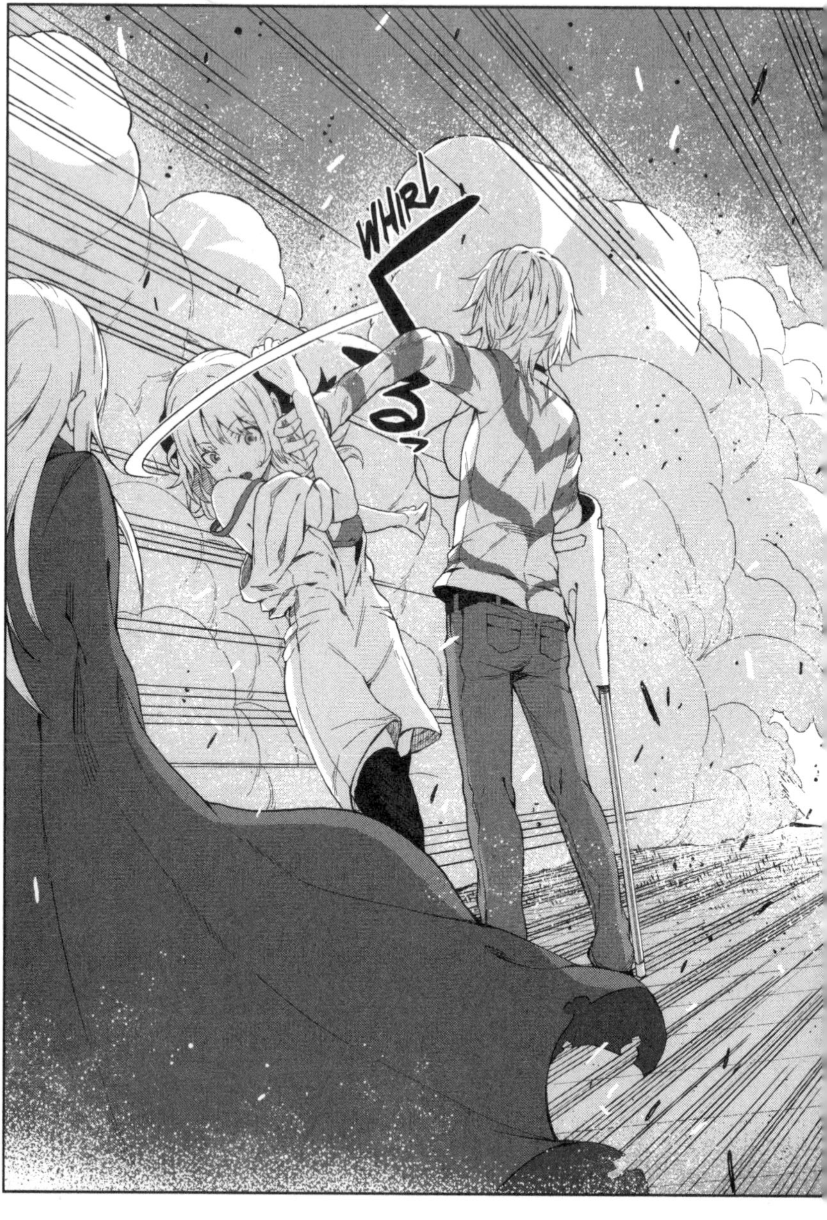
WHIRL

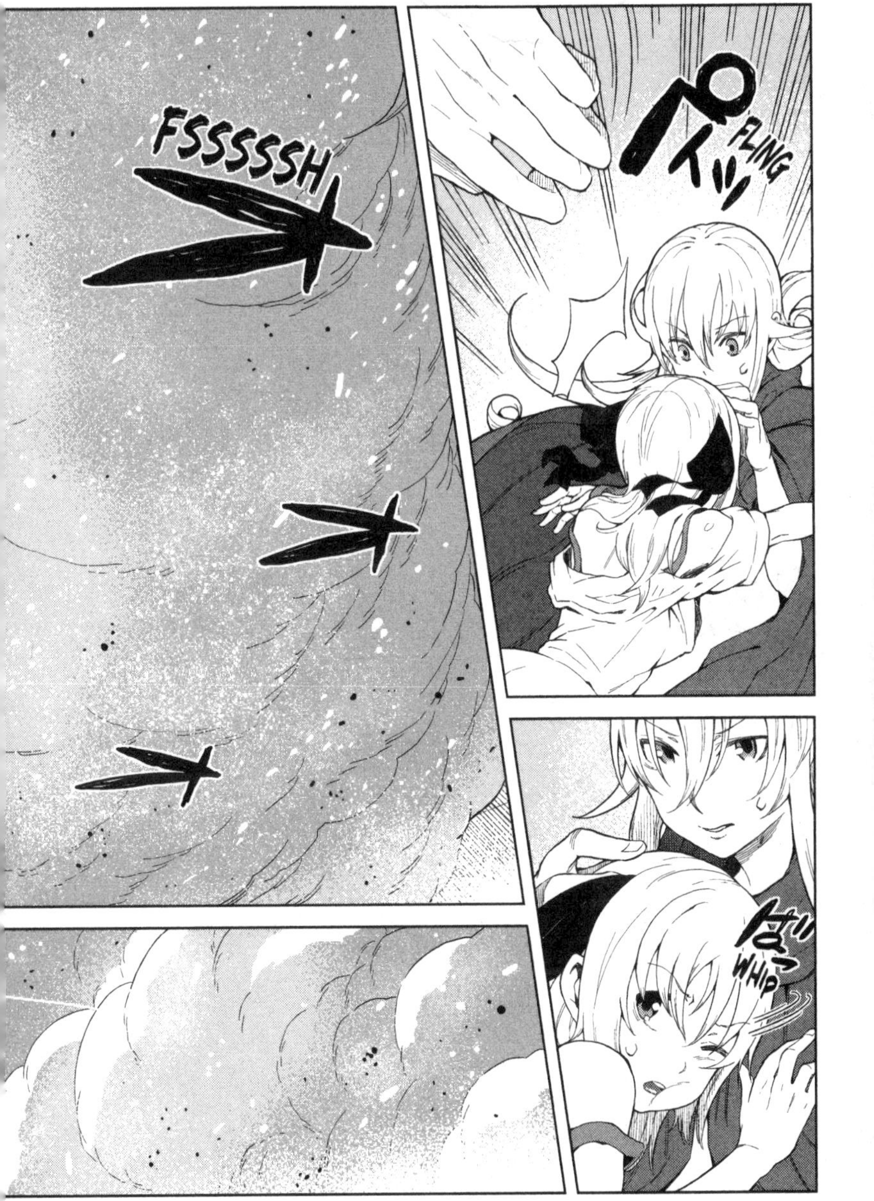
パイッ
FLING
FSSSSSH
WHIP

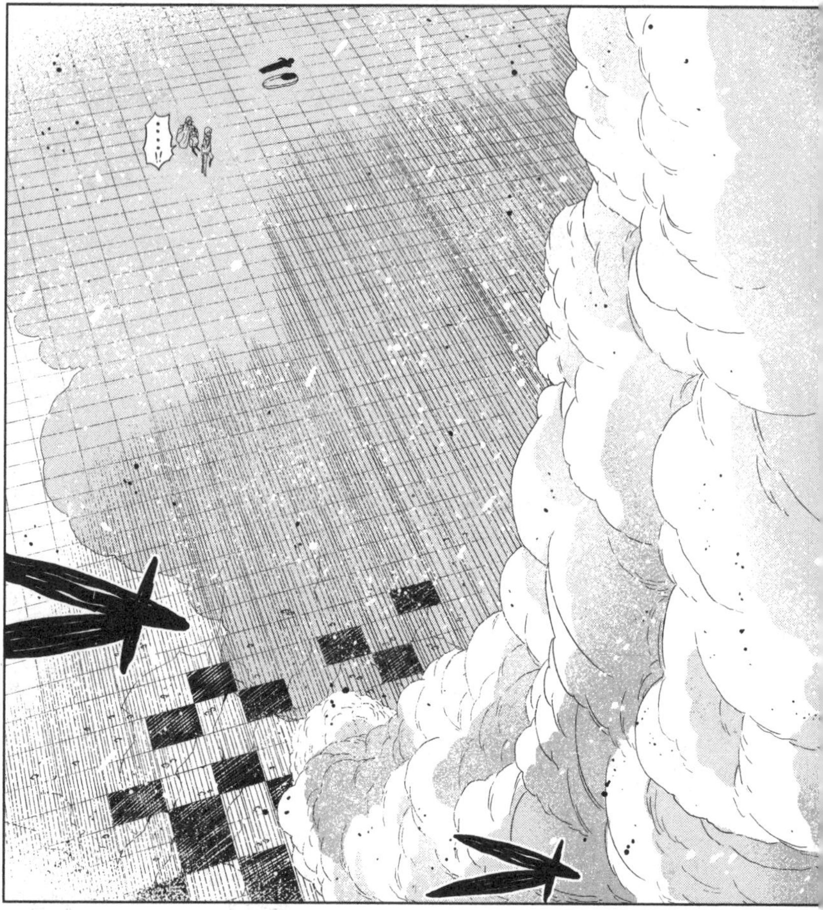
....!!
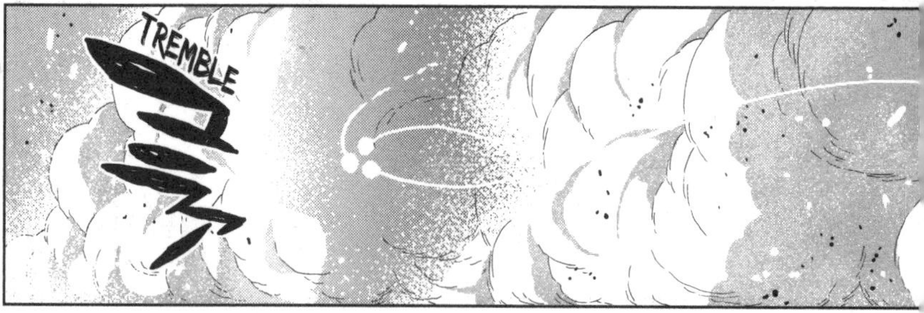
TREMBLE

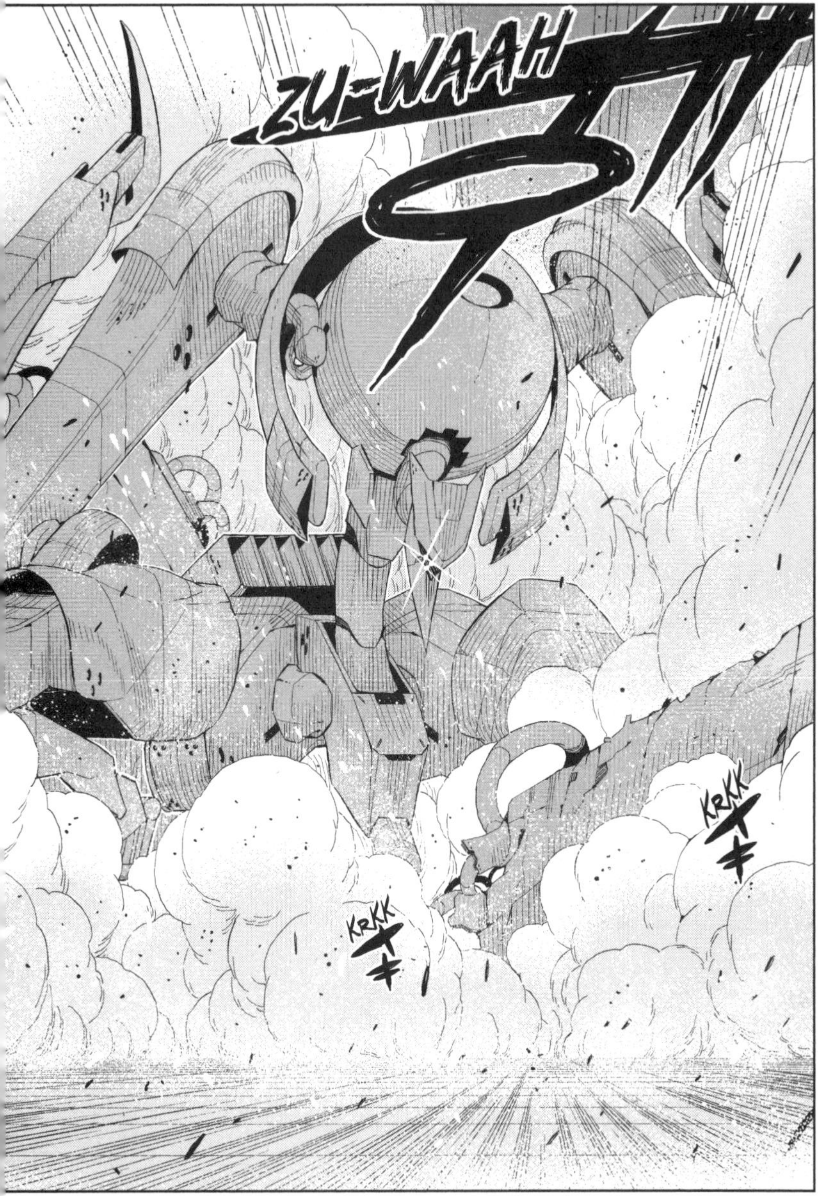
ZU-WAAH
KRKK
KRKK

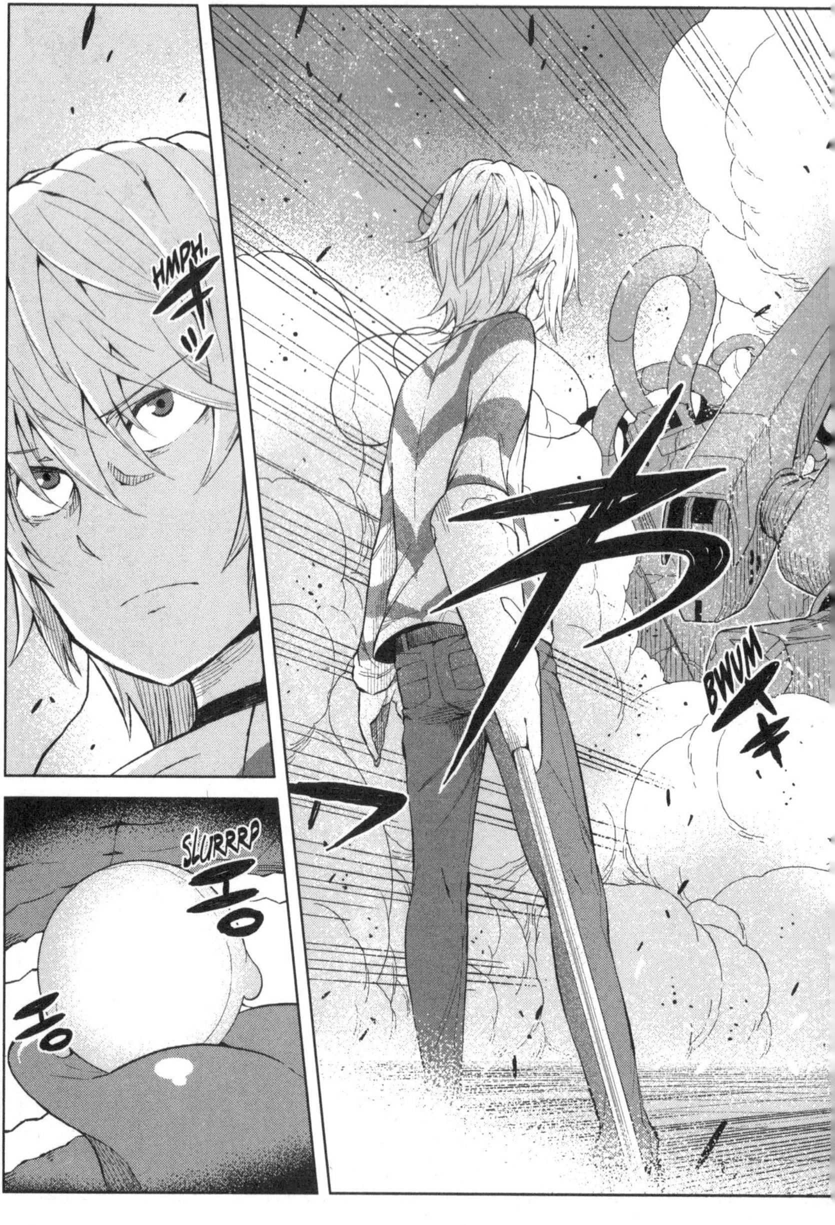
BWUM
HMPH.
SLURRRP

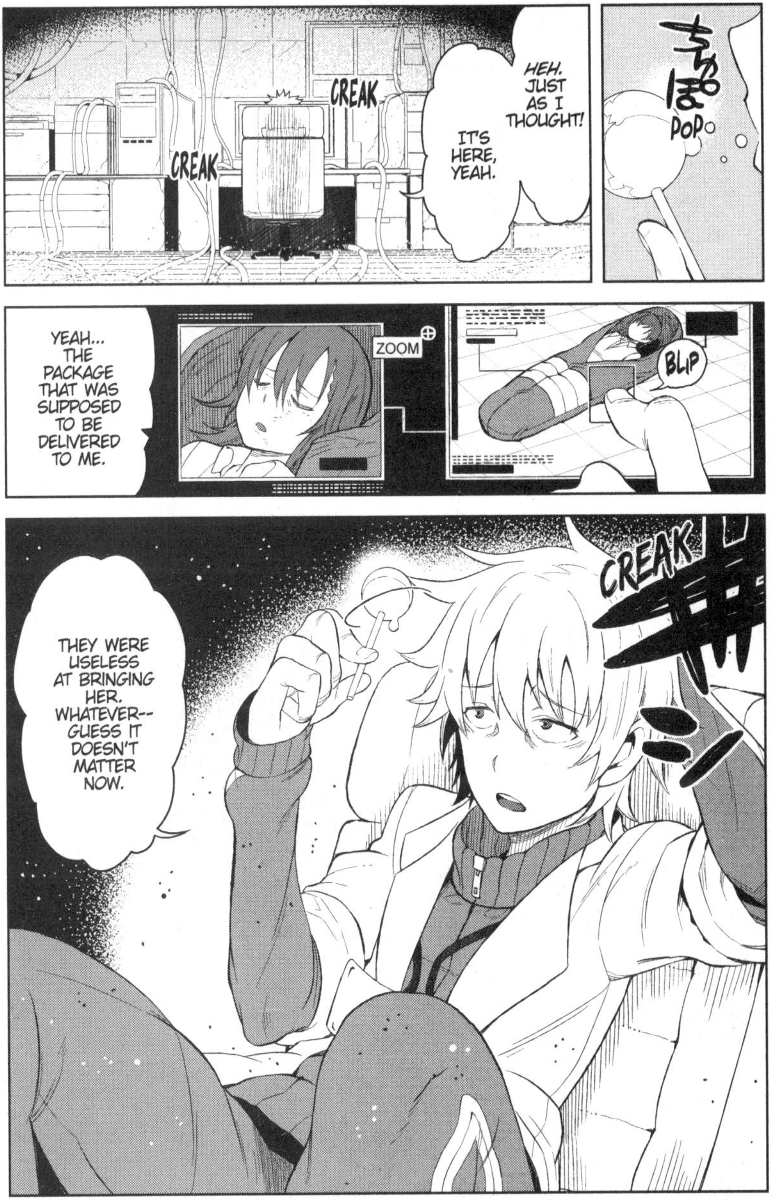
ちゅぽ
POP
HEH. JUST AS I THOUGHT!
IT'S HERE, YEAH.
CREAK
CREAK
BLIP
ZOOM
YEAH... THE PACKAGE THAT WAS SUPPOSED TO BE DELIVERED TO ME.
CREAK
THEY WERE USELESS AT BRINGING HER. WHATEVER-- GUESS IT DOESN'T MATTER NOW.

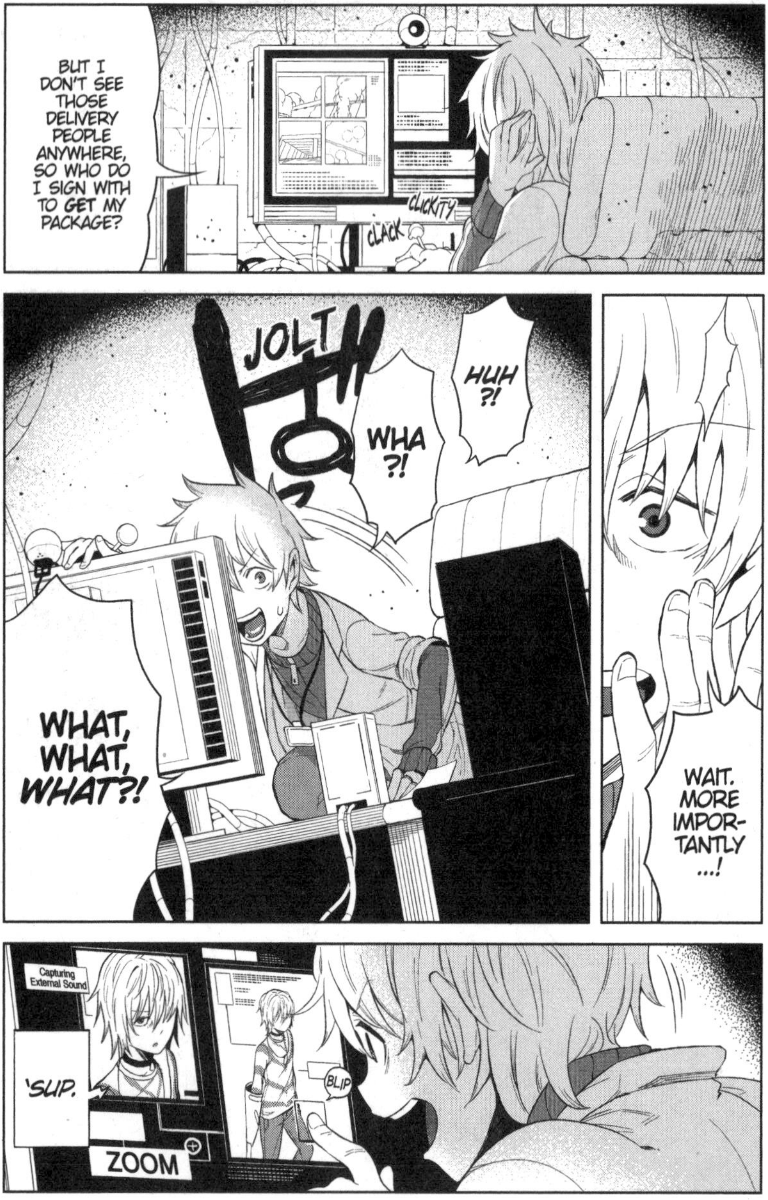
BUT I DON'T SEE THOSE DELIVERY PEOPLE ANYWHERE, SO WHO DO I SIGN WITH TO GET MY PACKAGE?
CLICKITY
CLACK
WAIT. MORE IMPOR-TANTLY ...!
HUH ?!
WHA ?!
JOLT
WHAT, WHAT, WHAT?!
BLIP
Capturing External Sound
'SUP.
ZOOM

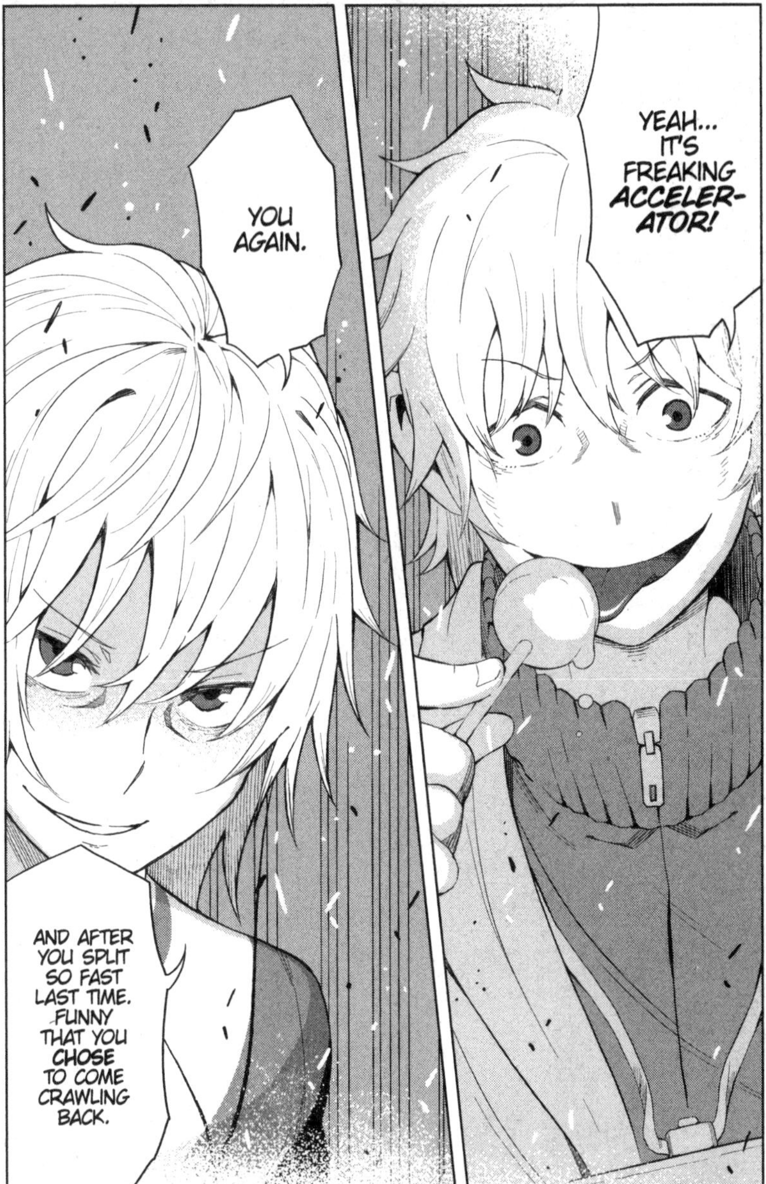
YEAH... IT'S FREAKING ACCELER-ATOR!
YOU AGAIN.
AND AFTER YOU SPLIT SO FAST LAST TIME. FUNNY THAT YOU CHOSE TO COME CRAWLING BACK.

To Be Continued...

a certain
SCIENTIFIC
ACCELERATOR

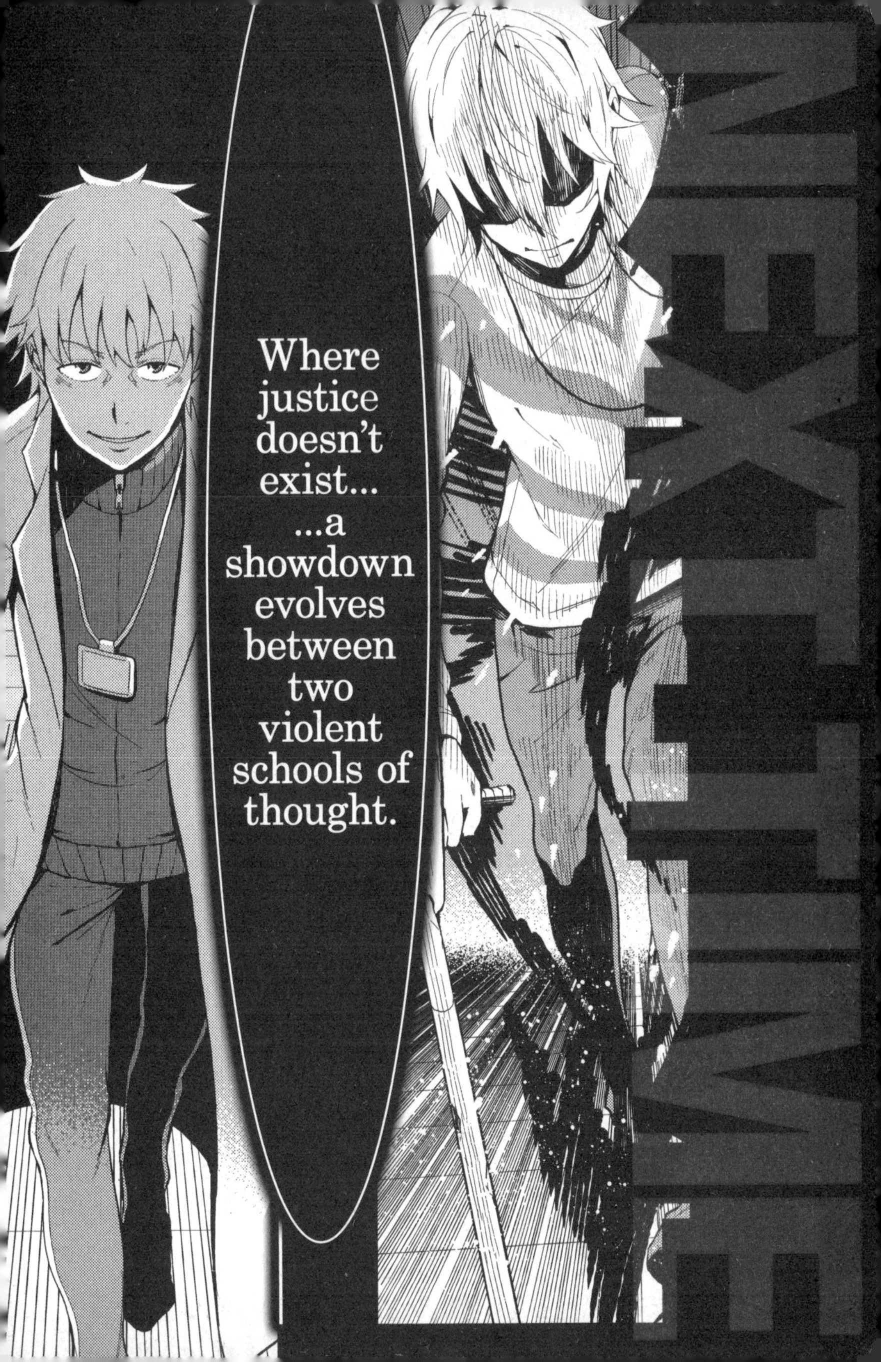
NEXT TIME
Where justice doesn't exist...
...a showdown evolves between two violent schools of thought.

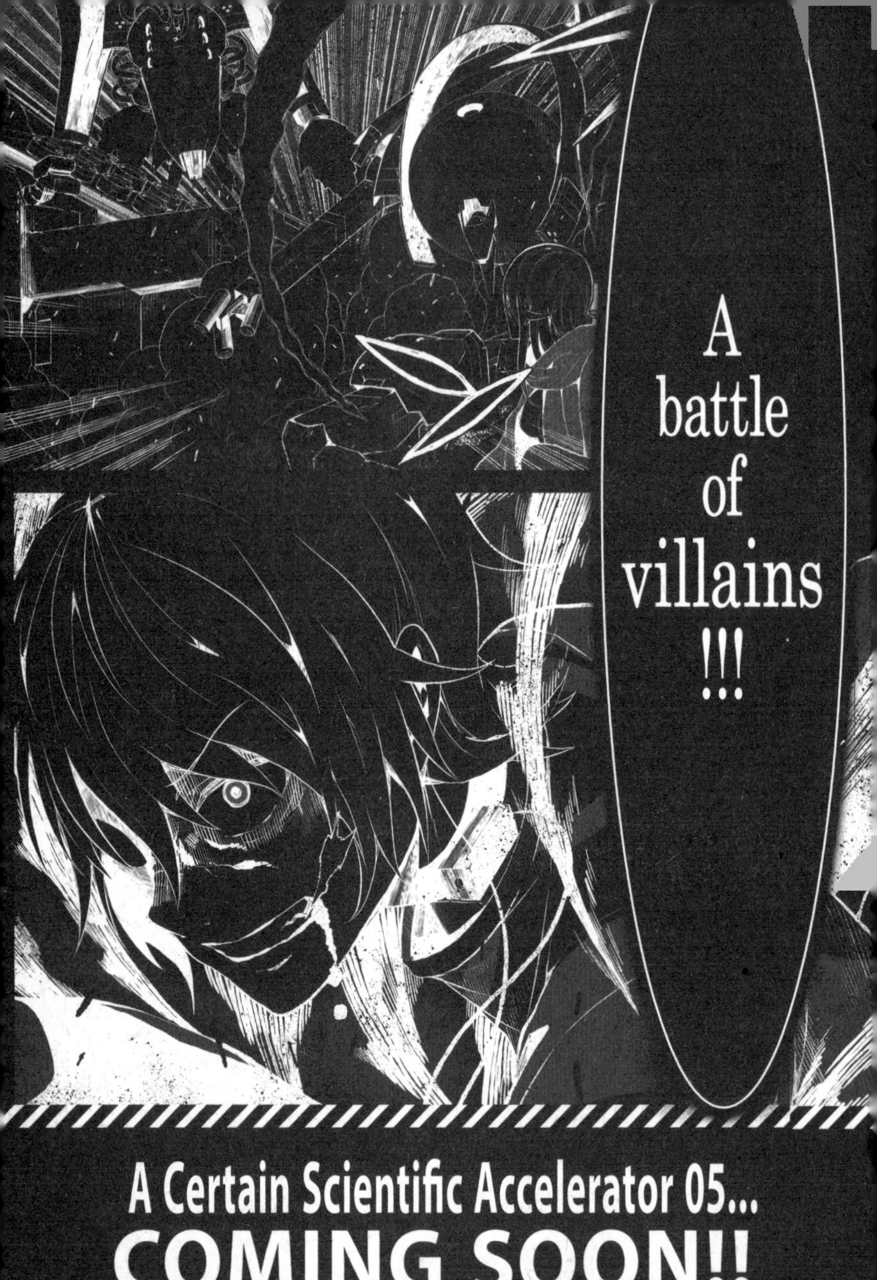
A battle of villains!!!

A Certain Scientific Accelerator 05...

COMING SOON!!

SEVEN SEAS ENTERTAINMENT PRESENTS

a certain SCIENTIFIC ACCELERATOR
volume 4

story by **KAZUMA KAMACHI** / art by **ARATA YAMAJI**

TRANSLATION
Nan Rymer

ADAPTATION
Maggie Danger

LETTERING
Roland Amago

LAYOUT
Bambi Eloriaga-Amago

COVER DESIGN
Nicky Lim

PROOFREADER
Shanti Whitesides
Janet Houck

PRODUCTION MANAGER
Lissa Pattillo

EDITOR-IN-CHIEF
Adam Arnold

PUBLISHER
Jason DeAngelis

A CERTAIN SCIENTIFIC ACCELERATOR VOL. 4

First published in Japan in 2015 by KADOKAWA CORPORATION, Tokyo.
English translation rights reserved by Seven Seas Entertainment, LLC.
under the license from KADOKAWA CORPORATION, Tokyo.

Seven Seas books may be purchased in bulk for promotional, educational, or business use. Please contact your local bookseller or the Macmillan Corporate and Premium Sales Department at 1-800-221-7945, extension 5442, or by e-mail at MacmillanSpecialMarkets@macmillan.com.

ISBN: 978-1-626923-37-9

Printed in Canada

First Printing: October 2016

10 9 8 7 6 5 4 3 2 1

FOLLOW US ONLINE: ***www.gomanga.com***

READING DIRECTIONS

This book reads from ***right to left***, Japanese style. If this is your first time reading manga, you start reading from the top right pan
take it from there. If you get
numbered diagram here. It ma
first, but you'll get the hang o

3
1
2
5
4
6
8
7

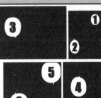

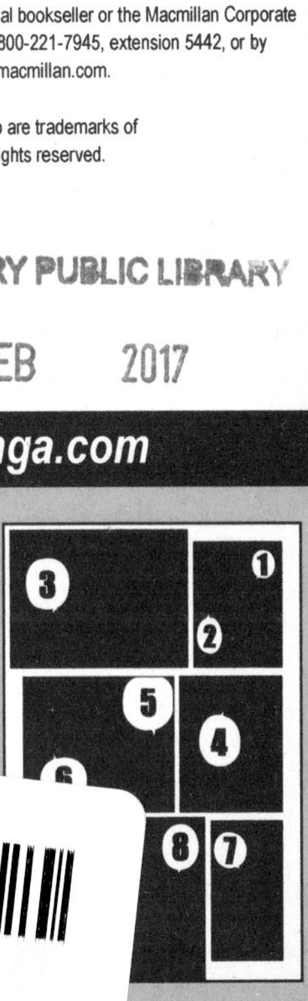